Roots of Nationhood

The Archaeology and History of Scotland

Edited by

Louisa Campbell
Dene Wright
Nicola A. Hall

Archaeopress Publishing Ltd

Summertown Pavilion
18-24 Middle Way
Summertown
Oxford OX2 7LG

www.archaeopress.com

ISBN 978-1-78491-982-5
ISBN 978-1-78491-983-2 (e-Pdf)

Printed in England by Oxuniprint, Oxford

This book is available direct from Archaeopress or from our website www.archaeopress.com

Contents

Introduction

Louisa Campbell and Dene Wright

As Scotland celebrated the Homecoming in 2009, we saw many claims made on Scotland's archaeology and history in support of discourses of national identity and distinctiveness. The failed referendum on independence on 18 September 2014, coinciding with another Homecoming, Year of Creative Scotland and Year of Natural Scotland combined with the hosting of major international sporting events, including the 20th Commonwealth Games, 40th Ryder Cup, and the Scottish Government's designation of 2017 as the Year of History, Heritage and Archaeology looked set to continue this trend. As did the deluge of political dialogue either supporting the SNP Government's drive for an independent Scotland by promoting a sense of Scottish national identity on the one hand, and unionist attempts to dampen a perceived swell of support for separatism on the other.

Such sentiments were roundly expected to cease at 7.00am on the morning of 19 September when the Prime Minister, David Cameron, delivered a now infamous speech outside 10 Downing Street after it became clear the 'Better Together' campaign had maintained the political status quo by a majority of 55%-45%. Perhaps unsurprisingly, the speech was not well received by pro-independence supporters in Scotland, many of whom immediately responded by formally joining the ranks of SNP membership and continue to confound most political commentators by successfully maintaining an independence movement that reinvigorated a latent grassroots-led campaign that appears unlikely to abate any time soon. Indeed, the First Minister of Scotland, Nicola Sturgeon, has recently made it clear that a second independence referendum was very much 'on the table' in order to protect Scotland's position within the European Union (EU) following an historic result on the so-called 'Brexit' referendum on 23 June 2016 in which the UK electorate voted by a small margin (52%-48%) to exit the EU. The political, economic and cultural ramifications of that result have yet to be fully revealed, but the overall result was very much at odds with the Scottish electorate who returned a resounding vote to remain in the EU (62%-38%), thus potentially sparking the break-up of both historic unions and signalling a growing divergence in the political leanings, sense of identity and nationhood between the Scottish electorate and other parts of the United Kingdom.

The political situation in the UK and other European nations is in a state of flux to the extent it is impossible here to provide a running commentary of the current state of government that appears to alter daily, the ramifications of which have yet to be felt. Indeed, the very concept of 'nationalism' is being manipulated by all sides with the governing class of larger constituent parts driving it as a vehicle to promote stability, strength and cohesive united identities while simultaneously deriding the 'nationalism' as identity of smaller constituent nations as a dirty word that spreads insularity, negativity and division.

Set against this political background, during the intervening years since the Scottish Archaeological Forum (SAF) first broached the subject of *Nationalism and Archaeology* (Atkinson *et al.* 1996) the debate has moved on apace, particularly within the context of a pro-independence party dominating the current political landscape. As discussed in Curtis' contribution to this volume, this situation is not unprecedented as there was significant movement in support of Scottish independence in 1911 which was interrupted by the First World War. It also finds a wider resonance outwith the UK. For example, regional elections in Catalan where the *Convergència i Unió* party, which advocates independence from Spain, gained power (though not the majority) to rule the autonomous Catalan government in 2012, culminating in a non-binding vote on Catalonian self-determination on 9 November 2014 and another on 1 October 2017 instigating a constitutional backlash from the Spanish Government through the Constitutional Court of Spain and the arrest of prominent leaders of the pro-independence movement. Thus, political, social and cultural conditions are ripe for an innovative and cross-disciplinary exploration of archaeology and history within this political milieu.

In a break away from the traditional mono-disciplinary scope of academic enquiry, this volume sets forth a challenge for practitioners within and outwith archaeology to develop multi-disciplinary approaches in the study of identity in general and aspects in the formation of national identity in particular. The entanglement of identity and nationhood is explored from the prehistory of northern Britain; the establishment of a proto-Scottish identity in the early Middle Ages; facets of Scottish identity at home and in the wider diaspora of Empire; and the more recent heralding of Scottish identity as a multi-ethnic construction. Set against the background of a groundswell change in the Scottish political landscape and the unprecedented, and largely unexpected, energised and proactive politicisation of the Scottish electorate in the lead up to and aftermath of the 2014 Independence Referendum, the volume is a timely and relevant contribution to discussions of national identities. By bringing together specialists covering a wide array of time periods and subject areas, we go beyond problematising the concept of identity. This is achieved by exploring the links of nationhood and Scottish identity in the early 20th and 21st Centuries in the ongoing quest for independence demonstrating the political manipulation of history, imagery and mythology entangled in political propaganda (Rowlands 1994; Meskell 2002).

The contributors to the volume seek to transcend previous approaches to this subject (e.g. Atkinson et al 1996) and transform discourse from the search for national identities to the dynamic processes of identity formation, negotiation and adaptation by exploring multi-disciplinary approaches to the study of identity. Some contributors explore material culture in its archaeological, historical and political contexts and its role in the formulation of identity. Collectively, the contributions highlight new ideas emerging from ongoing multi-disciplinary research on aspects of identity and nationhood and deliver a comparative approach, applying studies of identity to chronologically, materially and thematically disparate case studies.

Despite a growing literature on the subject of identity (e.g. Meskell and Preucel 2004; Schwartz et al 2011; Diaz-Andreu and Champion 2014, Pierce et al 2016), much of the research dealing with nationalism is cast within temporal and cultural epochs and generally restricted to academics working in the same discipline. This volume broadens academic enquiry by considering difference (Insoll 2007), crossing culturally constructed divisions of time and considering the fluidity and multifarious character of identities as well as the means by which they were made to appear fixed (Gardner 2011).

Themes and agendas

Since the prime function of SAF is to arrange events to promote the study of archaeology in Scotland, the editors took the opportunity to organise a very well attended symposium with the remit of sparking interdisciplinary academic discourse on the topic of archaeology, history, identity, politics and nationalism. We posed several questions and invited established academics to contribute a series of papers investigating how the issue of nationalism and identity are currently being explored. Topics put forward for discussion included: how have accounts of Scotland's past informed the ongoing political debate over devolution and independence? Does archaeology reveal the roots of nationhood or are other themes of diversity, discontinuity and far-flung connections and allegiances just as compelling? These developed into distinctive themes, explained below, which attracted the participation of eminent scholars as session chairs, namely Professors Julian Thomas from the University of Manchester, Siân Jones from the University of Stirling, Simon James, University of Leicester and Dauvit Broun, University of Glasgow.

The introductory paper is from Professor Ian Ralston, Abercromby Chair of Prehistoric Archaeology and Head of the School of History, Classics and Archaeology at the University of Edinburgh. Professor Ralston is an internationally renowned scholar who firmly sets the scene for an exciting, temporally and geographically diverse collection of papers, each of which takes a unique and innovative approach to the study of nationhood and identity in the past and present, including a codicil outlining developments since the 2014 Referendum on Scottish Independence. Each section thereafter explores these issues in a thematic manner drawing out the distinctive stands covered by each author's particular area of expertise. Wright sets the scene by exploring the earliest prehistory of northern Britain to trace the 'incipient seed' that distinguishes the inhabitants of this region from its closest neighbours as manifest in the archaeological record. As archaeologists we have to 'presence the past' to give meaning to the past. Political science provides insight into how politicians 'future the past' to claim authority and justify political agendas. Archaeology is entangled with and not immune from the political domain and as such must operate in and engage with changing political ideologies. Therefore, the concluding paper by Dr. Murray Stewart Leith, a leading specialist in the field of political science, provides a contemporary perspective to the topics covered in the volume.

The unprecedented recent success of a Scottish National Party elected into Government across the last 3 Scottish elections and installation of 56 Nationalist MPs out of 59 seats representing Scotland at Westminster cannot be dismissed as a political blip, despite a subsequent reduction in a snap election in 2017. But rather, it speaks to a groundswell movement, a seismic shifting of long-standing political affiliations by a Scottish electorate now awakened to the potential for independence within reach in a way that has not been conceivable since the passing of the Act of Union in 1707. As Leith demonstrates, the Scottish electorate has long been acknowledged as more politically engaged and mature than other constituent parts of the United Kingdom. The roots of this engagement are long-standing and first formally recorded through the Declaration of Arbroath, arguably the earliest document to express the idea of the nation state, which epitomises the Scottish tradition of drawing on history and myth to nurture a sense of national identity. Thus, Scotland serves as an exemplary model to investigate the roots of nationhood and this volume is published at a unique and opportune moment against a political milieu where Scottish history, heritage and archaeology is being actively appropriated to varying degrees by a political class across party divides at the level of local, national and UK government seeking to 'future the past'.

Despite the ambitious scale of these contributions, the book is structured by the reoccurrence of specific themes linking the various papers. Each represents a process by which the concepts of nationhood and/or identities are created, mediated or transformed across time and space, including Before Scotland: Cores, Peripheries and the Construction of Identities of Northern Britain; Origins of Alba and Scotland; and Forging Scotland's Identities at Home and Abroad.

Within these broad themes several emergent recurring commonalities can be highlighted. These include, but are not restricted to:

Place: going beyond archaeologies of landscape, place is explored as an integral component of the human experience. Whether we are discussing 'home' or 'abroad' (Nisbet) or 'core' and 'periphery' (Brophy, Campbell and Pierce), people establish roots and linkages to place (Broun) and these connections can be inclusive or exclusive, depending on the perspective of the observer.

Material culture: moving beyond visual observations, the material culture people use can evoke a range of social responses, all of which are culturally conditioned and situationally relevant (Knapp and van Dommelen 2010; Tilley 2011). We recognise that objects absorb meanings through use and they are central to the construction, reinforcement and transformation of identities (Campbell, MacSween and Wright).

Ideologies: a synthesis of the prehistory of northern Britain confirms that identity is forged as regionalities having moved away from the unsustainable concepts of dominant and enduring 'metropolitan' cores (Ralston). Regionalities are also evident in the Late Medieval period. For example, the significance of the First Estate in the almost exclusive patronage and appointment of Scots as clergy to maintain a sense of Gaeldom distinguishable from, although integral to, the wider Scottish identity (Thomas).

Engaging with Cultural Heritage: ranging from a qualitative study into the public presentation of archaeological sites (Timoney), to the presentation of artefacts at the Glasgow Exhibition of 1911 set within an underlying political discourse for Union (Curtis), i.e. British identity, to the appropriation of cultural heritage to advance the political agenda for an independent Scotland, i.e. Scottish identity (Leith).

Acknowledgements

The editors would like to express sincere thanks to Historic Environment Scotland and the Society of Antiquaries of Scotland for their support in exploring these concepts. We also extend our sincere thanks to Professors Siân Jones (University of Stirling), Dauvit Broun (University of Glasgow), Simon James (University of Leicester), and Julian Thomas (University of Manchester) for their contributions in chairing the workshop sessions that shaped the themes explored herein.

References

Atkinson, J., I Banks and J. O'Sullivan (eds) 1996. *Nationalism and Archaeology*, Glasgow: Cruithne Press.

Díaz-Andreu, M. and T. Champion (eds) 2014. *Nationalism and Archaeology in Europe*, London; Routledge.

Gardner, A. 2011. Paradox and praxis in the archaeology of identity. In L. Amundsen-Meyer, N. Engel and S. Pickering (eds.), *Identity Crisis: Archaeological Perspectives on Social Identity: Proceedings of the 42nd (2010) Annual Chacmool Archaeology Conference, University of Calgary, Calgary, Alberta*, 11–26. Calgary: Chacmool Archaeological Association.

Insoll, T. (ed.) 2007a. *The Archaeology of Identities: a Reader*. London: Routledge.

Meskell, L. and R.W. Preucel 2004. Identities. In L. Meskell and R. W. Preucel (eds.), *A Companion to Social Archaeology*, 121-34. Oxford: Blackwell Publishing.

Knapp, A.B. and P. van Dommelen 2010. Material connections: mobility, materiality and Mediterranean identities. In A. B. Knapp and P. van Dommelen (eds.), *Material Connections in the Ancient Mediterranean: Mobility, Materiality and Mediterranean Identities*, 1–18. London: Routledge.

Meskell, L. 2002. The intersection of identity and politics in archaeology. *Annual Review of Anthropology* 31: 279–301.

Pierce, E., A. Russell, A. Maldonado, and L. Campbell (eds) 2016. *Creating Material Worlds: The Uses of Identity in Archaeology*. Oxford: Oxbow Books.

Rowlands, M. 1994. The politics of identity in archaeology. In G. Bond and A. Gilliam (eds.), *Social Construction of the Past: Representation as Power*, 129–43. London: Routledge.

Schwartz, S.J., K. Luyckx and V. Vignoles (eds.) 2011. *Handbook of Identity Theory and Research*. New York: Springer.

Tilley, C. 2011. Materialising Identities: an introduction. *Journal of Material Culture 16(4)*: 347-57.

Contributor Affiliations

Dr Kenneth Brophy, Senior Lecturer, Archaeology, School of Humanities, University of Glasgow

Dr Dauvit Broun, Professor of Scottish History, History, School of Humanities, University of Glasgow

Dr Louisa Campbell, Lecturer in Archaeology, School of Humanities, University of Glasgow

Neil Curtis, Head of Museums, School of Biological Sciences, University of Aberdeen

Dr Murray Leith, Lecturer in Politics, School of Social Sciences, University of the West of Scotland

Dr Ann McSween, Head of Strategic Heritage Management, Historic Environment Scotland

Dr Stuart Nisbet, Honorary Research Associate, History, School of Humanities, University of Glasgow

Dr Elizabeth Pierce, Affiliate Researcher, University of Glasgow

Professor Ian Ralston - Abercromby Chair of Prehistoric Archaeology and Head of the School of History, Classics and Archaeology, University of Edinburgh

Dr Sarah Thomas, Lecturer in Medieval History, Department of History, University of Hull

Dr Steven Timoney, Lecturer in Archaeology, Perth College, University of the Highlands and Islands

Dr Dene Wright, Research Associate, University of Glasgow

Before Scotland: Cores, Peripheries and the Construction of Identities of Northern Britain

Reflections on the presentation of Scottish archaeology in British prehistories since Gordon Childe's *Prehistoric Communities* (1940)

Ian Ralston

Introduction

This paper was initially prepared as a keynote address to the *Roots of Nationhood* workshop that took place in the University of Glasgow just before St Andrew's Day 2009. Rather than revise it substantially in the light of subsequent developments, I have left it largely as a testament of one perspective on that particular time. In the autumn of that year, there was still the prospect of a referendum on independence (not abandoned until the following September and of course actually run in 2014) in the air, and a parliament at Holyrood that, at least intermittently, had Scotland's history as a subject for debate. There was then too still the admixture of cheering and wailing that had accompanied the 'Homecoming' events, then drawing to a close, and the foregrounding of the Scottish Diaspora. It seemed a fitting timing for a fresh consideration of the many issues wrapped up in the fundamentals of nationhood – a topic which the Scottish Archaeological Forum has previously tackled half a generation earlier (papers in Atkinson *et al.* 1996).

The view that I presented, however, was that of a prehistorian very conscious that, for the periods I standardly consider, the concept of nationhood is a chimera, that Scotland as an idea in the minds of men and women is something that then lay one or more millennia into the future. The political, cultural and other dimensions of the 'forging of the nation' as they are normally discussed in Scotland's case for the centuries after c. A.D. 1100 are thus off-limits to the prehistoric archaeologist. In terms even of somewhere perceptible graphically – in essence by the mapmaker's art – Scotland is a place with a pedigree less than five hundred years long, as Charles Withers has discussed (2000 and 2001). And yet, and yet: the idea of Scotland's remoter human past as something potent and significant in the making of the nation remains clear – I remember this, for instance, emerging from responses to a Council of Scottish Archaeology (now Archaeology Scotland) members' questionnaire in the late 1990s when I was its president. And the idea is there in the writings of Gordon Childe (1935, 1): '... Scotland in not an arbitrary political division but possesses ... a personality of its own'. This perspective encapsulates late nineteenth century French geographical thought – Paul Vidal de la Blanche (1845-1918) – transmitted northwards *via* Cyril Fox and twentieth century Archaeology's most potent depiction of Britain – Sir Cyril Fox's physical map of Britain (Map B) in the *Personality of Britain* (1932 opp. p. 26).

But even if the prehistoric periods in the area north of Cheviot are, in essence, an *antipasto* before the future main course of the emergence of the nation, to what extent does an understanding of Scotland's prehistory help or hinder a wider consideration of the roots of a future nationhood? I shall reflect on this, in part by considering aspects of the record and how it is constructed and presented to others; but initially by looking in outline at how Scottish prehistory has been treated in syntheses whose authors have considered the slightly wider canvas of British prehistory. I am conscious of Gordon Barclay's remarks (2001) about the dangers of internal comparisons within the British Isles, and the need to consider wider, seemingly 'peripheral', *comparanda*. For all the problems entailed, however, the British canvas seems a useful way of beginning to calibrate an external view of how Scotland's prehistory is perceived; and, however far devolution has advanced, it remains a key dimension, since, for instance, it is still at the British level that the parcelling out of much of the research money for our subject occurs; and such research of course underpins subsequent synthesis.

My immediate start point was a task I had in hand when the first announcement of this workshop appeared: that of editing, with John Hunter, the second edition of the *Archaeology of Britain*, a textbook that is not restricted to prehistory, as the addition of 'Joy Division' and 'Northern Soul Club' to its index makes plain (Hunter and Ralston 2009). This is a multi-authored work where the instructions to authors were to write at the British, and not simply the English (or indeed the Scottish), scale. In some chapters, inevitably, our colleagues were more successful at encapsulating the pan-British request than were others, for a diversity of reasons, including the unevenness of the relevant archaeological record and the level and nature of archaeological discussions – whether by region or type - of it. But this exercise – a snapshot of British archaeology towards the end of the first decade of this century – provided chronologically one of the book-ends for the time-span of British prehistoric studies (as represented by such syntheses) that I wished to consider.

Another important departure point was Gordon Barclay's 'Metropolitan and parochial' discourse in the *Proceedings of the Prehistoric Society* (2001), with its passionate advocacy of, I would submit, the inappropriateness of a tract of southern England as a kind of 'normal core' for prehistoric cultures against which other regions need to be measured. Barclay's 2001 piece, with other contributions he made around the same time, still represent the major individual effort to rebalance the presentation of British prehistory from a Scottish, indeed particularly lowland eastern Scottish, perspective - in his case as illustrated by the Neolithic (Ralston 2016).

Where to set the other chronological limit? For me, the obvious author to provide the baseline was Gordon Childe. The key reason is because he was the only author to write a British prehistory in the twentieth century who had already provided a substantial monograph on *The prehistory of Scotland* (1935); Robert Munro's treatment of this subject appeared in 1899, and thus marginally failed the chronological test, although his British prehistory was only published, posthumously, a quarter of a century later (1923). This particular aspect of Childe's work (and, of course, he presented another, distinctly more radical, synthesis of Scottish prehistory as the Rhind Lectures for 1944: Childe 1946) manifestly makes him significant for us north of Cheviot. More importantly, however, I have selected the first Abercromby Professor because the initial edition of Childe's British synthesis – *Prehistoric Communities of the British Isles* – which, a rare feature among British prehistories, includes Ireland - appeared only five years later, at a key time in the national story (1940). Childe thus provides us with both Scottish and British syntheses to compare. That *Prehistoric Communities* appeared in October 1940 retrospectively seems significant, although Childe (1940, v) was relatively disarming about this date in his preface:

> 'The first year of a great struggle, when all the original documents are packed away in cellars, is not altogether a favourable moment for the adventure of synthesis. The present author, who has contributed to the work of collection and construction only in a minor way and in a small corner, feels himself particularly ill-fitted to the task. Still someone must try it.'

By the small corner, we may assume he implies Scotland, where all his field projects (Ralston 2009, 73-5 fn 39 and Fig. 5) bar two (in northern Ireland), were conducted, even years later after his translation south to become Director of the Institute of Archaeology in London. Childe was almost fifty by the outbreak of the Second World War, and it is plain, for example from his correspondence with O. G. S. Crawford (see e.g. Hauser 2008, *passim*), that both men were acutely concerned at the outlook for them personally – aside from everything else – in the event of a German victory. But that view of the need to take stock of Britain's remoter human past in the face of impending doom permeates other syntheses of the time, including Grahame Clark's *Prehistoric England* also published that year by Batsford, with its particularly evocative dust-jacket illustration (by Brian Cook, later chairman of the company: Cook 2010) of quintessential southern English landscape behind a hillfort prominently in view. The same sentiment is most plain in the retrospectively-composed *Prelude*, written by Jacquetta Hawkes, to the 1958 impression of Jacquetta and Christopher Hawkes' *Prehistoric Britain*, a work also begun in 1940, albeit not published until 1944. That piece starts:

> 'I began upon the first edition of this book in 1940, when, if one listened to the intellect alone, a German victory seemed almost certain. I was in fact preparing to write about the deepest roots of a civilization whose topmost shoots were perhaps soon to be hacked off. Seeking a justification for this fiddle-playing, I was able to suggest that although my subject was remote in time, there was yet something topical in it. There was a sudden probability that the pattern of prehistoric events would be repeated, and that the repetition would be imposed on one's own life. As this book will show, prehistorians had spent much learning and ingenuity on

reconstructing thousand-year-old stories of continental invasions of Britain. In 1940 we awaited a practical demonstration in modern form' (Hawkes and Hawkes 1958, 11).

... and continues with further detailed reflections on the openness of south-eastern Britain to invasions through time, and the tendency as then perceived of the indigenous peoples to retreat westwards, as Jacquetta Hawkes herself did (to Dorset) in 1940.

My hypothesis, then, is that modern British prehistoric syntheses, and, within them, the fixing of the reading of the Scottish record, were built initially on perspectives made graphic in Fox's Map B (1932), a point Barclay has emphasized - and consolidated in the context of the perceived threat of military invasion in the initial stages of the Second World War. I also contend that, during the later 1940s, we can detect other intimations of the emergence and initial consolidation of a new and confident archaeology at the British scale, of which synthesis was, of course, but one strand. And Scotland and Scottish prehistoric material were at least to some extent intimately involved in this. Elsewhere, for example, I have drawn attention to volume 82 (for 1948) of the Society of Antiquaries of Scotland's *Proceedings* as representing a sea-change in outlook (Ralston 2005) in terms of some of its contained papers – Cairnpapple, Scotstarvit, Hownam Rings. That was too the year of publication of what would now be called a Research Agenda, by the fledgling Council for British Archaeology (n.d. but 1948). That document was also – seemingly unproblematically – both multi-period in its coverage (it ran from the Palaeolithic until the seventh century AD) and framed at the British scale; this was a confident experiment which has, to the limits of my knowledge, never been repeated. Childe and Stuart Piggott, his successor as Abercromby Professor, wrote much of what it had to say about Scotland.

Nowadays, in England at least, research agenda are regional; and on the Continent they may sometimes extend more than nominally beyond the nation-state – as for example in recent Franco-German (and Swiss) work on First Iron Age princely seats. Within Britain, only in Scotland (in the important ScARF initiative completed in 2012 and considered further below) and Wales (IFA Wales / Cymru 2008), has a state-wide approach to the laborious compilation of research agenda survived unquestioned, although ScARF has served as a platform for further growth and more recent years have seen efforts being devoted to the development of regional research agenda within Scotland, in Argyll for example.

British prehistories considered

How many syntheses of prehistoric Britain have appeared within the three quarters of a century since 1940? I estimate perhaps twice as many as I am going to mention, even in passing, here. I have identified what I consider the major or significant volumes, many, of course, not strictly academic texts but intended also for the general reader.

To keep the topic manageable, I have also almost completely ignored single-period surveys and also geographically-wider studies which have sought to place British evidence within its European context.

The first series within my self-imposed timeframe (Childe 1940; Hawkes 1945; Hawkes and Hawkes 1944; Winbolt 1943) are the products, both literally and metaphorically, of wartime. They replaced accounts that were by then distinctly dated in feel, such as Robert Munro's *Prehistoric Britain* (1923). Shared characteristics of the Forties volumes include the fact that two at least were avowedly intended for a general readership in the new, popular paperbacks being published by Allen Lane – *haute vulgarisation* at its best; and that the principal ones were re-issued, sometimes revised, after the war was over, in the case of the survey by the two Hawkeses, until the end of the 1950s – contemporary with the last reprints of Fox's *Personality of Britain*.

In some of these, the dominance of English, normally southern English, material and perspectives, is very plain as, again, Gordon Barclay has already remarked (2001). Only Childe really escapes from the worst imbalances, which see the Hawkeses (1944, 265) apologetically begin their regional appendix on Scotland as follows:

> 'Lack of resources makes it impossible to treat Scotland even with the modest degree of detail which has been attempted for England and Wales'.

Whereas, writing his preface in Horsham and by then well into his seventies, Samuel Winbolt, excavator *inter alia* of the East Cliff villa (1924) at Folkestone, concluded (Feb. 1944 aged 76):

> 'what the spade finds e.g. in southern England must be interpreted in the light of discoveries made in Portugal or Denmark, in the Outer Hebrides and by the Rhine. ... I have not limited the title to England, but have included in the frame a fair proportion of items from Wales, Scotland and Ireland. Admittedly England, especially Southern England, contributes the lion's share of archaeological evidence, but the other three cannot be excluded.... On the whole England, especially the lowland portion including Wiltshire, has more prehistory than the rest of the British Isles.'

Directly after the war, there was only one new synthesis, that produced by Stuart Piggott, Childe's successor at Edinburgh University (Piggott 1949), as a direct replacement for Munro's contribution in the same Home University series (1923). Published three years after Piggott's move north (Ralston and Megaw 2004), a little Scottish data is indeed incorporated into this volume but, it has to be said, at almost every turn, the peripherality of the Scottish material in the author's perceptions is made plain, most notably in the descriptions of the Late Bronze Age metal-worker at Jarlshof:

'... the pathetic case of the Irish bronze-smith who set up his shop in the remote Shetlands after all local markets had been closed to his products.' (Piggott 1949, 176).

Surprisingly, there was thereafter no further attempt to compile a British prehistory for a quarter of a century, and this at a time when archaeology was rapidly developing - on TV (e.g. the first sustained presentation of British archaeology by Brian Hope-Taylor (1965 – Anglia Television's *Who were the British?*), in the universities and in the public eye more generally. Within Scotland there were successive landmark volumes such as *The Problem of the Picts* (Wainwright 1955) as well as Piggott's extended essay on *Scotland before History* (1958a) and the first multi-authored overview, also edited by Piggott as *The Prehistoric Peoples of Scotland,* in 1962. In retrospect, this last contribution looks a rather strange and detached book, written by eminent specialists in their periods but sometimes with what seems to have been little more than a passing familiarity with Scottish data and Scottish circumstances. This was thus a curious endeavour, but significant in its heralding of multi-authored treatments, by the incorporation of new distribution maps, notably those prepared by Piggott's students and, in Richard Atkinson's treatment of the Neolithic, by the first stirrings of the recognition of a non-stone-built Neolithic record.

For Britain, I think we have to wait for the mid-1970s for a new landmark. This too was a multi-authored treatment, and the first consciously to see itself as the product of changing configurations in archaeological understanding and interpretation. With its editor fresh from Orcadian fieldwork at Maes Howe and Brogar, the synthesis masterminded by Colin Renfrew, then professor at Southampton, certainly intermittently includes Scottish material in all chapters, albeit the degree of integration is variable, probably being fullest in Colin Burgess's chapter on the Bronze Age and, for the Neolithic, split between the first national synthesis (by Isobel Smith) on the period since Piggott's major overview (1954), but with the Scottish funerary monuments corralled into a separate chapter by Audrey Henshall, contributed shortly after the second of her magisterial tomes on these sites had appeared. Henshall's two-volume corpus (1963 / 1972) remains one of the great individual achievements of Scottish archaeology and it seems to me regrettable that the opportunity was not taken here to meld its results into wider Neolithic perspectives.

The following quinquennium was productive; no fewer than five significant overviews, four of them single-authored, appeared. These coincide at the Scottish scale with the establishment for the first time of the teaching of Scottish archaeology (including its prehistory) in all four ancient Scottish Universities, most notably through the development of the Department at the University of Glasgow and Leslie Alcock's arrival as the first Dalrymple Professor. But, beyond the established Edinburgh department, there were also James Kenworthy and David Longley at St Andrews and myself at Aberdeen. These green shoots however were not to survive 1980s UGC-inspired rationalisations, and it is salutary to think that, despite the massive increases in archaeology across the UK tertiary education system since that time, Scottish archaeology across the now-further-extended Scottish university system has taken until very recently approximately to recover the position it held c. 1980. The reason to highlight – Glasgow apart - this rather faltering story is to contrast it with developments elsewhere, for in the remainder of mainland Britain at least, even if there was to be the occasional casualty such as Lancaster, Archaeology as a discipline, and with it British archaeology, grew apace. Some of the new overviews that accompanied this phase are avowedly introductory (e.g. Forde-Johnston (1976) and Branigan (1976) but even in these, and more than was the case in some earlier works, there are deliberate efforts to depict some Scottish material for its similarities to that recovered elsewhere rather than to focus exclusively on its differences: and so in Iron Age terms, Scottish hillforts – for which wider comparisons and contrasts can more readily be drawn - get as much prominence as brochs. Both these volumes, like that of Childe (1940), paid lip service to the wider context of 'the British Isles' albeit the coverage of Ireland is, with rare exceptions, vestigial; and indeed, despite the remark above, Scotland is included primarily – as so often - for its remarkable and distinctive stone-built monuments.

More experimental books marked the end of that decade. Paul Ashbee's 'social-archaeological narrative' from 1978 is a very different perspective, its author much more willing to meld historical testimony and archaeological evidence than has recently been fashionable. At times his overview tends towards a more romantic reading of the record. But it is, for much of its course, an avowedly British perspective.

Thereafter we come to the first of Richard Bradley's three British syntheses (Bradley 1978). This, and the second which followed six years later, are noteworthy for their thematic approaches, focused respectively on settlement and social relations. These different accounts, in my view, make Bradley considerably the most significant of British prehistory's recent synthesisers, and not least for the evolution in his perspectives and geographical reach over the thirty years since 1978.

The end of the decade was marked by the appearance of the second multi-authored British prehistory, edited from the Leicester Department, but including a number of authors who had trained, or been on the staff, at Edinburgh (Megaw and Simpson 1979). Indeed the preface defines the volume as encapsulating an approach labelled by Vincent Megaw and the late Derek Simpson as that of 'The Edinburgh School', characterised as marked by a blending of the practical and the theoretical and attributed to an inheritance from Richard Atkinson and Stuart Piggott, and so referring specifically to the period when both Megaw and Simpson were Edinburgh students in the 1950s. But this is a term which has never enjoyed wide currency and, on its second outing, as used by Dennis Harding in the preface to his Iron Age study (Harding 2004, xiv), it means something entirely different. What that designation has certainly never implied is the advocacy of a perspective rooted in the varied landscapes and archaeological remains of Scotland. Compared with the Renfrew edited compilation of 1974, however, Scottish material is more evenly distributed through the chapters of the Megaw-Simpson edited volume (1979).

The 1980s saw a second synthesis by Richard Bradley, marking the shift in his interests from settlement, economy and landscape to social considerations (1984). But this, perhaps inevitably because of the differential development of social interpretations at that time in British archaeology, is the most 'southerly' of his overviews. The middle of the decade was marked too by an important exhibition at the British Museum, organized by Ian Longworth and focused on progress in the knowledge and interpretations of pre-Medieval Britain over the forty years that had then passed since the end of the Second World War. Its main legacies were a brief popular account (Longworth 1985) and an edited book (Longworth and Cherry 1986). While northern British material was included in the displays in the museum itself, the accompanying books are much more avowedly southern in content and outlook, albeit curiously more so for the post-Roman world in which exclusively English material was considered. Shortly thereafter, there emerged the last single-authored multi-period British archaeology for almost twenty years (Darvill 1987). This represents a bold effort to cover the country in a wide-ranging synthesis, albeit it is plain that the author's account is fullest for the south of the country. A new edition has since appeared in which, alongside the introduction of fundamentally new kinds of data, notably those furnished by DNA, a distinctly more complex reading of the evidence is apparent (Darvill 2010).

By the late 1980s, however, the principal effort in terms of British synthesis seemed to be evolving in the direction of single-author period or regional reviews. In Scottish terms, heralded by the Ritchies' important contribution to Thames and Hudson's *Ancient Peoples and Places* series (1981), the 1990s were marked by the production, supported by Historic Scotland, of a number of period and regional syntheses – and not just of prehistory of the country - in both the Batsford co-editions (e.g. Wickham-Jones 1994; Turner, 1998) and in the Canongate series (e.g. Barclay 1998; Hingley 1998), as well as a multi-authored overview that juxtaposed environmental and archaeological perspectives (Edwards and Ralston 1997). This was a decade without parallel in the twentieth century in terms of the production of overviews of the Scottish archaeological record. It may be questioned whether it is purely coincidence that the emergence of synthetic literature on Scotland's prehistory and its archaeology more generally coincides, as it had c. 1960, with an apparent hiatus in the writing of British-scale overviews; or indeed whether what Joyce McMillan (2016) has termed 'the herculean efforts of Scottish writers … back in the 1980s to reinvent Scotland as a nation…' and the changing tempo of Scottish politics in the 1990s may also have been significant factors.

In 2009, it was premature to consider in detail the most recent British syntheses (e.g. Pryor 2003; Bradley 2007), except to show how far the genre has further mutated. Both these volumes also include a consideration of Irish evidence. More generally, it would now be much harder to pass off a 'southern' prehistory as adequate or significant for the entire islands of Britain. At least part of the rebalancing between the first and second editions of the *Archaeology of Britain* has been between north and south (Hunter and Ralston 2009 cf. 1999), although in terms of overall chapters this is more the case for post-Roman rather than pre-Roman Britain. It is not fair to include the studies edited by Joshua Pollard here (2008), for although entitled *Prehistoric Britain*, the focus therein is on innovations in theory and practice and there is no pretence at a synthetic overview, balanced geographically.

Bradley's (2007) maps of places and regions that accompany his main chapters, for example his Figure 3.1, with its early Bronze Age Britain and Ireland broken down into 26 unbounded areas, highlight the key change in these newer studies. This much looser cartographic framework shows how far we have travelled from Fox's Map B (1932), and perhaps from the concepts of the metropolitan and the peripheral to which Gordon Barclay introduced us. It makes hugely more challenging the tasks of meshing together these distinctive patterns of evidence; it makes more difficult the sifting to select which to prioritise to receive such research moneys as are available. If we manage to avoid a beauty contest simply amongst the most famous sites for such resources, I believe this leaves new scope to construct rich and variegated British and Scottish prehistories.

Looking forward 1: 2010

This section presents some of the issues that seemed to me significant as I wrote up this essay for submission in the wake of the workshop. At the editors' recommendation, and in light of the near-seismic shifts in Scottish politics since that time – including the independence referendum of September 18th 2014 - I have added a codicil.

As post-imperial Britain develops devolved political structures apace, how is the treatment of its component archaeologies being affected? Is communication amongst archaeologists working specifically on Scottish archaeology helped or hindered by the diverse changes in funding, academic, and legislative arrangements that are underway? Do prospects now look better or worse for Scottish archaeology, whether as part of an 'Archaeology of Britain', or on its own? Can the 'metropolitan' and 'parochial' attitudes that have been identified be reconciled – within Scotland too? Or might the primary aim now be to write Scottish prehistory / archaeology in some way independent of that of Ireland or the rest of the UK?

There are, of course, a range of issues that could be considered here. These include elements to do with the intellectual frameworks of archaeological practice, as well as matters intimately related to the political cultures of Scotland and our neighbours. This has never been more apparent in Scotland at least than it is now.

With our parliamentarians established in our not-so-shiny Catalan-designed Parliament, and the Museum of Scotland only a few years old, this is an opportune moment to take stock. Cultural policy and cultural matters (of which archaeology is a part) in Britain are now devolved issues. And we can widen matters to include Irish archaeologists who form a further identifiable community outwith the British state. Smaller areas, with their own rules and institutions – the Channel Islands and the Isle of Man - further complicate the pattern. One must immediately concede that, cutting directly across the advantage of having English as the *lingua franca* (now a trait shared more widely in archaeological writing within Europe), is this mosaic of polities within which archaeology is conducted.

Given what is happening politically within the United Kingdom, the diversity in the ways the archaeological record is managed, preserved, presented, studied and explained already present is set further to increase; and, since greater variation is likely, what are the likely consequences for opportunities to consider the archaeology of these off-shore islands as a group in times to come? In explicitly acknowledging the interplay between archaeology and politics, it seems that the prognosis for the short-to medium term must point strongly towards increasing diversity. The new political hierarchies, it may be argued, already take different views on the place of archaeology, and cultural heritage issues in the wider sense, within their cultural policies, educational programmes and so on. Nor should it be assumed that these will necessarily be more or less favourable to archaeology, just different.

It would be wrong to suggest that the transition under way is a simple one from – in archaeological terms - a united kingdom to a disunited one. The cursory examination of earlier 'British prehistories' I carried out above patently demonstrates that. Further, some issues directly impinging on archaeology, from educational priorities through to the ownership of newly-discovered artefacts, have retained differing emphases in some instances stretching back to the times before (in the Anglo-Scottish case) the union of parliaments three centuries ago. The ownership of small finds in Scotland has long been much less complex to determine than in England, at least until recent legislation there (Treasure Act 1996, as amended). Even now, there remain fundamental differences in how material is treated that have much wider ramifications. The reporting of finds is a key dimension of this, for far more new material is coming to light through the Portable Antiquities Scheme in England than Scottish procedures appear to generate, even allowing for a range of other variations, from soil characteristics to population densities, between the countries.

To set alongside these differences, too, are numbers of inherited (in some instances deep-seated) perceptions in the archaeological community about the character of the archaeological record within Britain itself. It is certainly possible to argue that what is seen as significant in the archaeology of the country has largely been dominated by southern perceptions, unsurprisingly given that areas from Yorkshire south, and more particularly Wessex and the catchment of the River Thames, have been the sectors with the most intensive research histories over the long term. They are also where many of the significant archaeological posts and agencies are based.

Less this appears just the complaint of a Scot with a chip on his shoulder, I offer two comments. Firstly, parts of Scotland, notably the Orkney Islands, effectively form for some prehistoric periods an extension of this core, as others have argued; and the archaeology of some areas within England – Cumbria is a clear case – suffer from equivalent, if not worse, neglect and peripheralisation than much of Scotland does. Perhaps the easiest way to illustrate this point is the British Museum volume *Archaeology in Britain since 1945: new directions.* The accompanying maps of key sites make this plain: after a chapter on British prehistory (even mentioning sites in the Republic of Ireland), the focus narrows significantly for Roman Britain, and then Anglo-Saxon England. By then, the remainder of Britain is not even peripheralised; it is simply omitted.

Such attitudes have been critically examined by Gordon Barclay (2001). The substance of his argument draws on the presence in the core areas mentioned above of iconic monuments and landscapes, which have long attracted archaeological attention. For later prehistory, one might set major hillforts and the most spectacular of the brochs alongside the great chambered tombs and stone circles of the Neolithic. But one of his key premises seems irrefutable. It is simply unsafe to assume, as tends to have been done, that remarkable archaeological survival in the present correlates with a particular, elevated significance for a given area in the past. Further, it is no longer justifiable to try to make the archaeological records of other regions, near or far, conform to patterns detectable in these well-studied areas, nor to assume that such apparent 'cores' necessarily have an unbroken record of cultural centrality. And, equally, it is time finally to dispose of ideas of the dominance of a particular, archetypal landscape – that of the 'Lowland zone' as designated by Sir Cyril Fox (1932). This blunt explanatory tool has long outlived its usefulness, as data on the productivity, weaknesses and opportunities of the mosaic of landscapes that make up Britain have multiplied. So older perspectives – such as those of Stuart Piggott (1958b) who saw Iron Age northern Britain as essentially a pastoral zone – in contrast, it has to be said, to his predecessor Gordon Childe's view (1946, 81-4), and in the teeth of a mass of evidence to the contrary – have crumbled. Any new writing has to be much more sympathetic to the textures of regional variation; and overviews perhaps need to be constructed more from the bottom up, rather than forcing a prevailing view, however robust it is for the region for which it was devised, more widely. Barclay and Irish colleagues have, for example, suggested the model of a mobile cattle-herding Neolithic favoured for southern Britain seems inappropriate to both Ireland and eastern Scotland (Barclay 2003).

Within the United Kingdom, in archaeology as in other matters, England is numerically the dominant partner. Scotland's population is just over 5 million and, even with net inward migration, is set at best to increase gently; England holds some fifty millions. England, thus, has approximately 84% of the total UK population (a proportion that is rising) and, given that much government spending is driven by such statistics, as for other reasons, this preponderance is, and will remain, significant.

What are the consequences of this state of affairs? Being a small country next to a much bigger neighbour, according to the Scottish political commentator, Ludovic Kennedy (1995), is like being in bed with an elephant. The idea originally came from a speech by Pierre Trudeau, sometime Prime Minister of Canada, and made in Washington, about Canada's bigger neighbour. In sum: the elephant will often hardly notice you are there, but it is impossible for you to ignore the elephant. It is a condition certainly applicable to the consideration of our archaeology. Being ignored is one matter. In the wake of devolution, however, the game has changed, or, since we are talking about British muddle here, some of the rules of the game have changed. As well as the difference in size already noted, and the opportunities and threats this presents, there are also now potentially likely to be greater differences in the directions of archaeological policies, and research priorities, between the constituent parts of the United Kingdom. In part this is unproblematic, even beneficial, but there are issues given that substantial proportions of research funding are decided and allocated at one end of the UK, or indeed now, at the European level (European Research Council funding).

In these still-early days following the first substantial round of devolution, the impression is that there are powerful pressures acting in opposite directions. In terms of research funding for example, staff of all UK universities must seek research moneys from the same key UK sources – principally the government-funded Research Councils, including that for the Arts and Humanities. A key driver here, reasonably enough, was the desire by the universities of Wales, Scotland and Northern Ireland not to be excluded from access to resources for 'big science' by the new political arrangements. In 2010, there remained doubts as to whether a single Arts and Humanities Research Council can successfully mesh with different political and cultural agendas in the constituent parts of the UK.

But, there are also pressures – some almost accidental – in the opposite direction. In the debate leading up to the creation of the first National Parks in Scotland, it was clear that, for many, just about any model for their structure was acceptable, except that long-adopted and refined on the other side of Hadrian's Wall. Contrastingly, a by-product of recent legislation, the *Dealing in Cultural Objects (Offences) Act of 2003*, brought in by Westminster with the laudable aim of making the international traffic in illegal antiquities more difficult, is to make it administratively complicated for archaeologists from England or Wales working in Scotland to take their finds over the border to study. Without appropriate authorisation, such finds are 'tainted' goods under the terms of the legislation, rendering the academic leader of the project liable to a possible penalty. This shows too, the messiness of our current situation: things that need tidied up by the Scottish legislature in the wake of this Act have never moved up the political agenda here.

What is already clear is that the occupants of the bed are moving around, and the elephant's opportunities hardly to notice who else is between the sheets are perhaps decreasing. There were and are signs of new shared archaeological communities – I am thinking of the emerging collaboration between the surviving Royal Commissions in Wales and Scotland for example, or the beginnings, coming geographically from both sides of the water, of a more sustained archaeological interest in what was once called the 'Irish Sea province' between Ireland and western Britain. Taking a slightly wider perspective, we have noted the important influence of Irish thought on the character of the Neolithic in the British Isles, producing in recent years a counterweight to previously dominant models. A later prehistoric equivalent would be Colin Haselgrove's (2001) definition for that period of 'central Britain', stretching north from the English midlands and encompassing both the Welsh Marches and part of southern and eastern Scotland north to Aberdeen – his Zone B on the accompanying map (Haselgrove 2001, Figure 3.1).

Overall, taking the appearance and scope of successive undergraduate textbooks on the archaeology of Britain as an indication, I see reason to be optimistic for Scottish archaeology. These are, of course, a very crude guide, but I would certainly argue that books such as Tim Darvill's *Prehistoric Britain*, from the late 1980s and now updated (2010), or the *Archaeology of Britain* which I helped edit in the following decade (Hunter and Ralston 1999 / 2009), managed rather better than most of their predecessors to demonstrate something of the diversity of the archaeological records apparent from region to region across Britain than is true of at least some earlier attempts. It has, even at this level, become much harder simply either to generalise without qualification from the 'metropolitan' areas, or to shunt off evidence from one part of Britain into a chapter separate from the mainstream.

If the political and administrative frameworks in which archaeology is conducted do evolve increasingly differently within Britain in response to political translations of different local needs and local ambitions, as seems likely, that is as it should be. And that may heighten awareness of, and respect for, difference and variability in archaeological cultures and traditions within Britain and within Scotland. That cannot be a bad thing. And it should, and must, provide a renewed impetus for the study of the past communities of Scotland, by archaeologists as by others. And, if there is any merit in the sub-Braudelian analysis offered above on the different production cycles of Scottish and British prehistories, we should now be entering a new 'Scottish phase'.

Looking forward 2: a 2016 codicil

Have we entered the new Scottish phase which I postulated above? Seen purely in terms of multi-period overviews of the country's archaeological past, which is the yardstick around which this contribution was constructed, the answer has to be no. There is a multitude of reasons as to why this might be the case, and only a few can be sketched here.

The Scottish National Party has been in power at Holyrood first as the single biggest party and subsequently, since 2011, with an overall majority throughout the period since the 'Roots of Nationhood' workshop. In 2013, the Scottish Government published *Scotland's future: your guide to an independent Scotland* in preparation for the referendum that was held in September of the following year. Overall, the document had relatively little to say about the historic environment, although it calculated that that environment was worth £2.3 billion to the economy (Scottish Government 2013, 313). It offered assurance that '… culture and heritage will continue to be valued in and of itself (sic) as the heart, soul and essence of a flourishing Scotland…' (Scottish Government 2013, 534). The 'Better together' campaign against independence none the less won the vote by some ten percentage points. It would be fair to say that in contrast to the heated debates within some sectors of the arts community, summarized for example by Gallagher (2016, Chapter 6), such matters did not in my judgement impact directly on the activities, or perhaps significantly on the attitudes, of the archaeologists of Scotland.

Rather I consider that the reduction in Scotland-level archaeological synthesis in recent years can be attributed to rather more domestic concerns, each of which has deflected endeavour elsewhere. In the universities, the pressures to produce what is judged as high-grade research for the Research Excellence Framework probably mitigated against the production of outputs that risk being construed as 'regional overviews'; other factors, including increasing internationalization of student bodies and staffing concerns may too have played a role in shifting the focus from local archaeology. Within Government, the priority – if long-drawn-out - task of merging Historic Scotland and the Royal Commission on the Ancient and Historical Monuments of Scotland has undoubtedly deflected endeavour (the two main series of synthesis produce half a generation ago were both led from within the Inspectorate of Ancient Monuments, by David Breeze and Gordon Barclay respectively). Set alongside this momentous change, now achieved, there have of course been other initiatives culminating in publications such as *Our place in time; the historic environment strategy for Scotland* (Historic Scotland 2014) and *Scotland's Archaeology Strategy*, the latter emanating from the Scottish Strategic Archaeology Committee (2015), itself established in 2013. Such policy-oriented and strategic overviews plainly have a significant role and conform to wider governmental objectives but their compilation deflects the efforts of an archaeological community which remains relatively small-scale, perhaps to the detriment of the kinds of endeavour I have highlighted.

Contrastingly, over the period since this piece was originally composed, there has been one productive collective outcome which represents a significant new departure in scale and ambition – the *Scottish Archaeological Research Framework*, funded by Historic Scotland, and run through the Society of Antiquaries of Scotland under the chairmanship of Roger Mercer (ScARF 2012). This was designed to 'establish a datum of achievement in 2012 and attempt to sketch out the research questions that are visible now as we approach the next five years' (Mercer 2012), a task involving many hands in much effort and in which its several period-based and other panels undoubtedly succeeded. Part overview, part data-dump, part manifesto and indeed part synthesis, its various chapters undoubtedly provide the frameworks for those seeking specific new research objectives, but also furnish in a unique manner the building blocks required for the next generation of synthesis. And in this way, the 'Scottish phase' alluded to above, may well – after a delay - now be in the offing.

Acknowledgements

I am very grateful to Richard Bradley, Tim Darvill and Roger Mercer for helpful comments on a preliminary draft of the 2010 paper, but they of course bear no responsibility for the use I have made of their observations. In updating this text, I have benefitted from useful observations from Stephen Driscoll.

Bibliography

Ashbee, P. 1978. *The ancient British: a social-archaeological narrative.* Norwich: Geo-Abstracts Ltd.

Atkinson, J.A., I. Banks and J. O'Sullivan 1996. (eds) *Nationalism and archaeology.* Glasgow: Cruithne Press.

Atkinson, R.J.C. 1962. Fishermen and farmers, in S. Piggott (ed.) *The prehistoric peoples of Scotland*, 1-38. London: Routledge & Kegan Paul.

Barclay, G.J. 1998. *Farmers, temples and tombs. Scotland in the Neolithic and Early Bronze Age.* Edinburgh: Canongate with Historic Scotland.

Barclay, G.J. 2001. 'Metropolitan' and 'parochial' / 'core' and 'periphery': a historiography of the Neolithic of Scotland, *Proceedings of the Prehistoric Society* 67, 1-18.

Bradley, R.J. 1978. *The prehistoric settlement of Britain.* London: Routledge & Kegan Paul.

Bradley, R.J. 1984. *The social foundations of prehistoric Britain.* London: Longman.

Bradley, R.J. 2007. *The prehistory of Britain and Ireland.* Cambridge: Cambridge University Press.

Branigan, K. 1976. *Prehistoric Britain: an illustrated survey.* Buckinghamshire: Spur Books.

Childe, V.G. 1935. *The Prehistory of Scotland.* London: Kegan Paul, Trench, Trubner & Co.

Childe, V.G. 1940. *Prehistoric communities of the British Isles.* London and Edinburgh: Chambers. (2 edn. 1947).

Childe, V.G. 1946. *Scotland before the Scots* (being the Rhind lectures for 1944). London: Methuen.

Clark, J.G.D. 1940. *Prehistoric England.* London: Batsford.

Cook, B. 2010. *Brian Cook's landscapes of Britain.* London: Batsford.

Council for British Archaeology (n.d. but 1948) *A survey and policy of field research in the archaeology of Great Britain. I Prehistoric and Early Historic ages to the seventh century A.D.* London: Council for British Archaeology.

Darvill, T. 1987. *Prehistoric Britain.* London: Batsford.

Darvill, T. 2010. *Prehistoric Britain.* London: Routledge. (2nd edn.).

Edwards, K.J. and I.B.M. Ralston (eds) 1997. *Scotland: environment and archaeology 8000 BC - AD 1000.* New York and Chichester: John Wiley and Son.

Forde-Johnston, J. 1976. *Prehistoric Britain and Ireland.* London: J. M. Dent.

Fox, C. 1932. *The personality of Britain. Its influence on inhabitant and invader in prehistoric and early historic times.* Cardiff: National Museum of Wales.

Gallagher, T. 2016. (foreword by A. Darling). *Scotland now: a warning to the world.* Edinburgh: Scotview Publications.

Harding, D.W. 2004. *The Iron Age in northern Britain. Celts and Romans, natives and invaders.* London: Routledge.

Haselgrove, C.C. 2001. Iron Age Britain and its European setting, in J. R. Collis (ed.) *Society and settlement in Iron Age Europe* (Actes XXVIII Coll. Assoc franç Etude Ages Fer: Winchester 1994), 37-72, Sheffield: J. R. Collis Publications.

Hauser, K. 2008. *Bloody Old Britain. O. G. S. Crawford and the archaeology of modern Britain.* London: Granta Books.

Hawkes, J. 1945. *Early Britain.* London: Collins.

Hawkes, J. and C.F.C. Hawkes 1944 / 1947. *Prehistoric Britain.* Harmondsworth: Penguin, then London: Chatto & Windus.

Hawkes, J. and C.F.C. Hawkes 1958. *Prehistoric Britain.* Rev edn. Harmondsworth: Pelican (with Prelude by Jacquetta Hawkes, 11-12).

Henshall, A.S. 1963. *The chambered tombs of Scotland.* Vol. 1. Edinburgh: Edinburgh University Press.

Henshall, A.S. 1972. *The chambered tombs of Scotland.* Vol. 2. Edinburgh: Edinburgh University Press.

Hingley, R. 1998. *Settlement and sacrifice. The later prehistoric people of Scotland.* Edinburgh: Canongate with Historic Scotland.

Historic Scotland 2014. *Our place in time: the Historic Environment Strategy for Scotland.* Accessible from http://www.gov.scot/Publications/2014/03/8522. Last accessed 13th March 2016.

Hope-Taylor, B.K. 1965. *Who were the British?* Norwich: Anglia Television 1965 (six programmes produced and directed by Forbes Taylor).

Hunter, J.R. and I.B.M. Ralston (eds) 1999. *The archaeology of Britain: an introduction from the Upper Palaeolithic to the Industrial Revolution.* London: Routledge.

Hunter, J.R. and I.B.M. Ralston (eds) 2009. *The archaeology of Britain: an introduction from Earliest Times to the Twenty-First Century.* Abingdon: Routledge.

IFA Wales / Cymru 2008. (Institute of Field Archaeologists Wales / Cymru Group) *Introducing a research framework for the archaeology of Wales.* Cardiff: CADW.

Kennedy, L. 1995. *In bed with an elephant. A journey through Scotland's past and present.* London: Bantam Press.

Longworth, I. 1985. *Prehistoric Britain*. London: British Museum.

Longworth, I. and J. Cherry (eds) 1986. *Archaeology in Britain since 1945*. London: British Museum.

McMillan, J. 2016. 'Scottish perspective - Targeting the vulnerable isn't funny', *The Scotsman*, 18th March 2016.

Megaw, J.V.S. and D. D. A. Simpson (eds) 1979. *Introduction to British prehistory from the arrival of Homo sapiens to the Claudian invasion*. Leicester: Leicester University Press.

Mercer, R. 2012. Chairman's introduction. http://www.scottishheritagehub.com/content/chairmans-introduction Last consulted 13th March 2016.

Munro, R. 1899. *Prehistoric Scotland and its place in European civilisation being a general introduction to the County Histories of Scotland*. Edinburgh and London: William Blackwood.

Munro, R. 1923. *Prehistoric Britain*. London: Williams & Norgate.

Piggott, S. 1949. *British prehistory*. London: Oxford University Press.

Piggott, S. 1954. *The Neolithic cultures of the British Isles*. Cambridge: Cambridge University Press.

Piggott, S. (illus. K. Henderson) 1958a. *Scotland before history*. London and Edinburgh: Nelson.

Piggott, S. 1958b. Native economies and the Roman occupation of north Britain, in I. A. Richmond (ed.) *Roman and native in north Britain*, 1-27. Edinburgh: Nelson.

Piggott, S. (ed.) 1962. *The prehistoric peoples of Scotland*. London: Routledge & Kegan Paul.

Pollard, J. (ed.) 2008. *Prehistoric Britain*. Oxford: Blackwell (Blackwell Studies in Global Archaeology eds. Meskell, L. and Joyce, R. A.)

Pryor, F.M. 2003 *Britain BC: life in Britain and Ireland before the Romans*. London: Harper Collins.

Ralston, I.B.M. 2005. Scottish roundhouses: the early chapters, *Scottish Archaeol Journ* 25.1, 1-26.

Ralston, I.B.M. 2009. Gordon Childe and Scottish archaeology: the Edinburgh Years 1927-1946, *European Journal of Archaeology* 12 (1-3), 47-90.

Ralston, I.B.M. 2016. Gordon Barclay: a career in the Scottish Neolithic, in K. Brophy, G. MacGregor and I. Ralston (eds) *The Neolithic of mainland Scotland*, 3-20. Edinburgh: Edinburgh University Press.

Ralston, I.B.M. and J.V.S. Megaw 2004. Beyond barbarian Europe: Stuart Piggott 1910-1996: an appreciation, in I. A. G. Shepherd and G. J. Barclay (eds), *Scotland in ancient Europe: the Neolithic and Bronze Age of Scotland,* 13-27. Edinburgh: Society of Antiquaries of Scotland.

Renfrew, C. (ed.) 1974. *British prehistory; a new outline*. London: Duckworth.

Ritchie, J.N.G. and A. Ritchie 1981. *Scotland: archaeology and early history*. London: Thames & Hudson.

ScARF (= Scottish Archaeological Research Framework) 2012. *The Scottish Archaeological Research Framework website.* http://www.scottishheritagehub.com/ last consulted 13th March 2016.

Scottish Archaeological Strategy Committee 2015. *Scotland's Archaeology Strategy.* Last accessed on 13th March 2016 at http://archaeologystrategy.scot/files/2015/08/ScotlandsArchaeologyStrategy.pdf

Scottish Government 2013. *Scotland's future. Your guide to an independent Scotland.* Edinburgh: Scottish Government. Also accessible online from http://www.

scotreferendum.com/reports/scotlands-future-your-guide-to-an-independent-scotland/ Last accessed 13th March 2016.

Turner, V. 1998. *Ancient Shetland*. London: Batsford / Historic Scotland.

Wainwright, F.T. (ed.) 1955. *The problem of the Picts*. Edinburgh: Nelson.

Winbolt, S.E. 1943. *Britain B.C.* London: Penguin Books.

Wickham-Jones, C.R. 1994. *Scotland's first settlers*. London: Batsford / Historic Scotland.

Withers, C.W.J. 2000. 'Knowing one's limits.' The geographical making of Scotland, *The Edinburgh Review* 103, 35-42.

Withers, C.W.J. 2001. *Geography, science and national identity: Scotland since 1520.* Cambridge: Cambridge University Press.

Setting the Scene: aspects of the Earliest Prehistory of Northern Britain

Dene Wright

Introduction

It is unsustainable to suggest that the roots of nationhood and Scottish identity are evident in the earliest prehistory of Northern Britain. However, it provides the incipient seed to the rhizome that follows. What follows is a brief exploration of this seed by tracing aspects of the earliest prehistory from the lithic assemblages as the dominant form of material culture available to us from the hunter-gatherers of the Late Upper Palaeolithic and Mesolithic periods. Is it possible to distinguish the archaeology of Northern Britain from our nearest neighbours?

Late Upper Palaeolithic

In the last decade or so there has been an increasing awareness of the possibility of 'pioneer' incursions into Northern Britain by the hunter-gatherers of the Late Upper Palaeolithic. These groups followed the reindeer herds across the north-west European landmass of which Britain was a part (Ward and Saville 2010). The relative narrowness of the Norwegian sea-trench would not have impeded access to Northern Britain from what is now Norway (Ballin and Bjerck 2016, 12). Rozoy (1978) evocatively referred to the hunter-gatherers of the Late Upper Palaeolithic have as '*Les Derniers Chasseurs*'.

The basis for the generalised chronology of the Late Upper Palaeolithic of north-west Europe subdivides into three cultural phases, namely Late, Final and Terminal. Changes in certain type fossils found mark the distinctions within lithic assemblages augmented, where available, by radiocarbon dates (e.g. Fischer 1991 and others).

The earliest known archaeological evidence in Northern Britain is from Howburn Farm in South Lanarkshire. A typological analysis of a number of the lithic tool forms were recovered indicating events during the Hamburgian phase of the Late Upper Palaeolithic (13,000-12,000 BP/13,600-11,850 BC); coeval with the Creswellian in Southern Britain. In particular, these tool forms included tanged points, blade scrapers, and a 'zinken-like' piercer. There are also references to technological practice in the preparation of core platforms attributable to Hamburgian assemblages and the imported use of non-local flint and chert (after Ballin *et al.* 2010a). The site at Howburn Farm was a palimpsest with lithics typologically attributable to the Mesolithic and Neolithic periods (Ballin *et al.* 2018; Ballin *et al.* 2010a, 324). Lithics recovered from

Nethermills Farms, Aberdeenshire provide further evidence for Hamburgian events (cf. Ballin and Wickham-Jones 2017). Recent news reports indicate lithics from the Headland Archaeology excavations at Milltimber, Aberdeenshire revealed artefacts attributable from 13,000 BC to 10,000 BC (Scottish Government 2018). Publication of the excavations is tentatively due by the end of 2018 (Dingwall *et al.* In press).

There has been a reappraisal of the Mesolithic lithic assemblage from Kilmelfort Cave, Argyll (Coles 1983). It is suggested that in addition to Mesolithic artefacts there are curved-backed points that have broad common differences with the Federmesser tradition of the Final Late Upper Palaeolithic, and may be relatively dated by typology to the second half of the 12th millennium BP [11,850-11,400 BC] (Saville and Ballin 2009, 37). There are no radiocarbon dates for the Hamburgian events at Howburn Farm, Nethermills Farm, or the Federmesser events at Kilmelfort Cave. The relative proposed 'BP' dates offered by the authors have been calibrated to calendrical using OxCal 4.2 (Bronk-Ramsey 2009) expressed as the mean dates at 2σ. The Hamburgian and Federmesser cultural complexes fall within the climatic phase of the Late Glacial Interstadial, following the retreat of the Devensian ice sheet (after Clark *et al.* 2012).

Recent work on Islay recovered a lithic assemblage sealed by a layer of tephra underlying Mesolithic artefacts (cf. Mithen *et al.* 2015). A comparison of the tephra deposit to other comparable dated deposits indicated events at 10,240-10,000 BC (Mithen *et al.* 2015, 405). This would position the assemblage within the Ahrensburgian cultural tradition of the Terminal Late Upper Palaeolithic, and the climatic phase of the re-advance of the ice sheet during the Loch Lomond stadial (Clark *et al.* 2012; Mithen *et al.* 2015).

There is a preliminary report on the recovery of putative Late Upper Palaeolithic and Mesolithic lithics from excavations at South Cuidrach, Skye (Hardy *et al.* 2017).

The other possible evidence for the Ahrensburgian in Northern Britain are the stray finds of tanged points from Balevullin, Isle of Tiree and Shieldaig, Wester Ross (Saville and Ballin 2003). The recovery of a tanged artefact associated with Mesolithic lithic material, during excavations at Links House, Orkney (Woodward 2008), has been interpreted as a tanged projectile point with typological affinities to artefacts from the Early Mesolithic in Norway [9500-8000 BC] (Ballin and Bjerck 2016). An illustration of a tanged artefact from Millfield, Stronsay, Orkney (Livens 1956, Figure 1.1) indicates that it is typologically comparable to the artefact from Links House. A single edged point from the Ness of Brodgar, Orkney (Ballin and Bjerck 2016; Livens 1956, Figure 1.2) further strengthens the connection between Northern Britain and Scandinavia. This artefact has a typological affinity to artefacts from assemblages in the Early Mesolithic of Norway and the Ahrensburgian in Denmark. The absence of radiocarbon dates leaves open to further research whether the connections between Northern Britain and Scandinavia correspond to either the Early Mesolithic, or the Terminal Late Upper Palaeolithic and Early Mesolithic (after Ballin and Bjerck 2016).

Mesolithic

The onset of the Holocene at 10,000 BP/c.9600 BC marked the start of the Mesolithic period. This Boreal climatic phase is defined by rapid increases in mean temperatures rising as much as 1ºC per decade (Ballantyne 2004).

The earliest known date for the Mesolithic in Northern Britain is from the coastal site at Cramond, near Edinburgh [8630-8290 BC (9250 ± 60 BP; OxA-10180)] (Ashmore 2004, 99; Lawson 2001). There is an early inland date from Daer Reservoir 1, Daer Valley, South Lanarkshire [8550-7950 BC (9075 ± 80 BP; AA-30354)] (Ashmore 2004, 100; Ward 1998). Issues with this date have been noted (Edwards *et al.* 2004), although the probability is that the event dated was pre-8000 BC. This, albeit limited evidence, is particularly important as it arguably heralds what may be the first known innovative practice in Northern Britain. Arguably, it contradicts the usual default position of cultural changes spreading from Southern to Northern Britain. One of the issues highlighted by Gordon Barclay (2001) in a paper on Neolithic Scotland (see Brophy and Ralston this volume). The lithic assemblages from Cramond and Daer Reservoir 1 include narrow blade microliths which is approximately 400 years before their first appearance in the lithic assemblages of Southern Britain (cf. Barton and Roberts 2004; David and Walker 2004; Reynier 2005; Saville 2008).

It is important at this point to take a step back to understand the chronology of the Mesolithic in Southern Britain. The change of assemblages dominated by broad blade microliths to narrow blade microliths, i.e. 'English model' determines the demarcation between the Early and Late Mesolithic. The three key type-sites in Southern Britain are Star Carr and Deepcar in Yorkshire, and Horsham and Horsham in Surrey (cf. Reynier 2005; Saville 2008 and others). The earliest date for assemblages dominated by narrow blade scalene triangle microliths is c.8000 BC (Conneller *et al.* 2016; Barton and Roberts 2004, 346; David and Walker 2004, 317; Saville 2008, 212). There are relatively few broad blade microliths recovered in Northern Britain compared to narrow blade microliths, generally assemblages dominated by the latter. Broad blade microliths have been found at a number of sites throughout Northern Britain (e.g. cf. Saville 2004, 2008; Saville *et al.* 2012 for a review of those sites), however, none of the other tool forms associated with broad blade microlith assemblages in Southern Britain (Barton and Roberts 2004; Reynier 2005) were present. Saville (2008, 211) has tentatively offered a date of c.8400 BC as the demarcation, based on the 'English model', although there are no radiocarbon dates to support this.

Another distinctive feature of Northern Britain when compared to Southern Britain is in the variation of raw materials used during the Mesolithic period. There are flint bearing tertiary Buchan Ridge gravels at the Den of Boddam, Aberdeenshire. Saville (2008a, 5) makes the point that the presence of flint must have known from the later millennia of the Mesolithic, although systematic utilisation and quarrying for flint did not occur until the Neolithic period. Unlike the flint rich terrestrial chalks in Southern Britain, flint as a Mesolithic raw material resource is largely restricted to beach pebble and fluvio-glacial resources (Finlayson 1990a, b; Wickham-Jones and Collins 1977). Flint pebbles eroding out of the offshore Cretaceous sediments around the coast of Northern Britain are deposited on many of its beaches (after Hall 1991). The only terrestrial location for these sediments is the southwest of Mull (Hall 1991; Wickham-Jones and Collins 1977). Finlayson (1990b, 44) summarised the situation 'while good nodular flint is rare, 'knappable' material is not.' For example, other raw materials used include radiolarian chert (Wright 2012), carboniferous chert (Davidson *et al.* 1949), quartz (Ballin 2008), quartzite (Wright 2012), chalcedony and agate (Coles 1971), siltstone (Saville *et al.* 2012), mudstones (Davidson *et al.* 1949; Saville *et al.* 2012), Rùm bloodstone (Clarke and Griffiths 1990), Skye tuff (Ballin *et al.* 2010b), andesite (McFadzean 1984), and Arran pitchstone (Affleck *et al.* 1988; Ballin 2009). The siliceous 'blue stone' recovered from three of the sites at Daer Reservoir, South Lanarkshire by Tam Ward and the Biggar Archaeology Group is currently unique and not known to be found at any other sites in either Northern, or Southern Britain.

Furthermore, the impact on the differential quality and character of available raw materials in Northern and Southern Britain, and its impact on stonecraft remains to be fully addressed. Such differences may provide evidence for nuances of variation in the micro-phenomena of the reduction of different materials demonstrating alternative working traditions (Finlay *et al.* 2003, 108; Warren 2001; Wickham-Jones and Hardy 2004). Arguably, the imposition of the 'English model' in Northern Britain remains contentious.

There is a continuity of technological practice as a macro-phenomenon across the greater part of the *longue durée* of the Mesolithic in Northern Britain (cf. Wright 2012, 2016). Despite this, there is increasing evidence for regionality (Finlay *et al.* 2003, 113) which is largely drawn from variations in raw materials within assemblages. For example, tracing the presence of Rùm bloodstone in lithic assemblages (Ballin 2018; Clarke and Griffiths 1990). Such an approach is not without pitfalls, one of which is that the distribution of sites may not indicate the diversity of the human experience in a region, but merely represents the geographic focus from the history of research and/or the survival of sites (Finlay *et al.* 2003, 105; Saville 1998; Wright 2012, 51-52). To avoid such problems, the region of West Central Northern Britain was defined by reference to watersheds (Wright 2012, 25-26). An approach used to give the region geographic integrity which may have been meaningful in the past (after Hughes 1991; Spikins 1999). The analysis of the lithic assemblages permits the researcher to make intra-site, inter-site and intra-regional scales of enquiry to build a regional profile. Unfortunately, the paucity of regional syntheses makes inter-regional comparanda difficult (cf. Wright 2012, 2016).

Concluding remarks

The destructive character of the Devensian glaciations ensures that that the time depth in the archaeology of Northern Britain is comparatively shallow at c.15000 years. For example, in Southern Britain the footprints and artefacts recorded at Happisburgh, Norfolk date to c.950,000-850,000 years ago (Ashton *et al.* 2014). The 'pioneer' incursions of the reindeer hunters of the Late Upper Palaeolithic into Northern Britain shows connections across the north-west European landmass in the millennia following the retreat of the ice sheets. It is when for Northern Britain space became place. It is in the Mesolithic where it is possible to see innovative practice, and distinguish Northern Britain from Southern Britain. The hunters-gatherers in Mesolithic Northern Britain may also be said to have been creating regional and intra-regional identities. Research in West Central Northern Britain indicates separate identities for those hunter-gathers whose lifeways were either predominantly coastal or inland (Wright 2012, 2016). A similar interpretation was offered by Fitch (2011) when researching submerged occupation events in Doggerland.

References

Ashton, N., S. G. Lewis, I. De Groote, S.M. Duffy, M. Bates, R. Bates, P. Hoare, M. Lewis, S.A. Parfitt, S. Peglar, C. Williams and C. Stringer. 2014. Hominin Footprints from Early Pleistocene Deposits at Happisburgh, UK. *PLoS ONE* 9(2): doi:10.1371/journal.pone.0088329.

Ballantyne, C.K. 2004. After the Ice: Paraglacial and Postglacial Evolution of the Physical Environment of Scotland. In A. Saville (ed.), *Mesolithic Scotland and Its Neighbours: The Early Holocene Prehistory of Scotland, its British and Irish Context and some Northern European Perspectives*: 27-43. Edinburgh: Society of Antiquaries of Scotland.

Ballin, T.B. 2008. *Quartz Technology in Scottish Prehistory*. (http://www.sair.org.uk/sair26/): SAIR 26.

Ballin, T.B. 2009. *Archaeological Pitchstone in Northern Britain*. Oxford: Archaeopress.

Ballin, T.B. 2018. The procurement of Rhum bloodstone and the Rhum bloodstone exchange network – a social territory in the Scottish Inner Hebrides? *Archäologische Informationen* 41(Early View): http://www.dguf.de/fileadmin/AI/ArchInf-EV_Ballin.pdf.

Ballin, T.B. and H.B. Bjerck. 2016. Lost and found twice: Discussion of an early post-glacial single-edged tanged point from Brodgar on Orkney, Scotland. *Journal of Lithic Studies*, 3(1): doi:10.2218/jls.v2213i2211.1393.

Ballin, T.B., A. Saville, R. Tipping and T. Ward. 2010a. An Upper Palaeolithic Flint and Chert Assemblage from Howburn Farm, South Lanarkshire, Scotland. *Oxford Journal of Archaeology*, 29: 323-360.

Ballin, T.B., A. Saville, R. Tipping, T. Ward, R. Housley, L. Verrill, M. Bradley, C. Wilson, P. Lincoln and A. MacLeod. 2018. *Reindeer hunters at Howburn Farm, South Lanarkshire: A Late Hamburgian settlement in southern Scotland – its lithic artefacts and natural environment* Oxford: Archaeopress.

Ballin, T.B., R. White, P. Richardson and T. Neighbour. 2010b. An early Mesolithic stone tool assemblage from Clachan Harbour, Raasay, Scottish Hebrides. *Lithics: The Journal of the Lithic Studies Society*, 31: 94-104.

Barclay, G.J. 2001. 'Metropolitan' and 'parochial' / 'core' and 'periphery': a historiography of the Neolithic of Scotland. *Proceedings of the Prehistoric Society*, 67: 1-18.

Barton, R.N.E. and A.J. Roberts. 2004. The Mesolithic Period in England: Current Perspectives and New Research. In A. Saville (ed.), *Mesolithic Scotland and Its Neighbours: The Early Holocene Prehistory of Scotland, its British and Irish Context and some Northern European Perspectives*: 339-358. Edinburgh: Society of Antiquaries of Scotland.

Bronk-Ramsey, C. 2009. Bayesian analysis of radiocarbon dates. *Radiocarbon*, 51(1): 337-360.

Clark, D.C., A.L.C. Hughes, S.L. Greenwood, C. Jordan and H.P. Sejrup. 2012. Pattern and timing of retreat of the last British-Irish Ice Sheet. *Quaternary Science Reviews*, 44: 112-146.

Clarke, A. and D. Griffiths. 1990. The use of bloodstone as a raw material for flaked stone tools in the west of Scotland. In C.R. Wickham-Jones (ed.), *Rhum, Mesolithic and Later Sites at Kinloch: excavations 1984-86*: 149-156.

Coles, J.M. 1971. The early settlement of Scotland: excavations at Morton, Fife. *Proceedings of the Prehistoric Society*, 37(2): 284-366.

Coles, J.M. 1983. Excavations at Kilmelfort Cave, Argyll. *Proceedings of the Society of Antiquaries of Scotland*, 113: 11-21.

Conneller, C., A. Bayliss, N. Milner and B. Taylor. 2016. The resettlement of the British landscape: towards a chronology of lithic assemblage types. *Internet Archaeology* (42).

David, A. and E. Walker. 2004. Wales during the Mesolithic period. In A. Saville (ed.), *Mesolithic Scotland and its Neighbours: the early holocene prehistory of Scotland, its British and Irish context, and some Northern European perspectives*: 299-338. Edinburgh: Society of Antiquaries of Scotland.

Davidson, J.M., J. Phemister and A.D. Lacaille. 1949. A Stone Age Site at Woodend Loch, near Coatbridge. *Proceedings of the Society of Antiquaries of Scotland*, 83: 77-98.

Dingwall, K., M. Ginnever, S. Spanou, R. Tipping and J. van Wessel. In press. *The Land Was Forever: 15000 Years in North-East Scotland: Excavations on the Aberdeen Western Peripheral Route/Balmedie-Tipperty*. Oxford: Oxbow.

Edwards, K.J., C.K. Ballantyne, R. Tipping and P. Ashmore. 2004. Conference Discussion Session: Sunday Morning, 7 September 1999. Scotland in the Early Holocene. In A. Saville (ed.), *Mesolithic Scotland and Its Neighbours: The Early Holocene Prehistory of Scotland, its British and Irish Context and some Northern European Perspectives*: 159-164. Edinburgh: Society of Antiquaries of Scotland.

Finlay, N., G. Warren and C.R. Wickham-Jones. 2003. The Mesolithic in Scotland: East meets West. *Scottish Archaeological Journal*, 24(2): 101-120.

Finlayson, B. 1990a. The function of microliths: evidence from Smittons and Starr, SW Scotland. *Mesolithic Miscellany*, 11(1): 2-6.

Finlayson, B. 1990b. Lithic exploitation during the Mesolithic in Scotland. *Scottish Archaeological Review*, 7: 41-57.

Fischer, A. 1991. Pioneers in deglaciated landscapes: the expansion and adaptation of Late Palaeolithic societies in southern Scandinavia. In N. Barton, A. J. Roberts, and D. A. Roe (eds), *The Late Glacial in north-west Europe: Human adaptation and environmental change at the end of the Pleistocene*: 100-121. London: Council for British Archaeology.

Fitch, S. 2011. The Mesolithic landscape of the southern North Sea. University of Birmingham, Unpublished PhD Thesis.

Hall, A.M. 1991. Pre-Quaternary landscape evolution in the Scottish Highlands. *Transactions of the Royal Society of Edinburgh*, 82: 1-26.

Hardy, K., M. Wildgoose and T.B. Ballin. 2017. South Cuidrach - Early People of Skye. *Discovery and Excavation in Scotland*, 18: 128.

Hughes, I. 1991. Solway and Clyde: Some Comments. *Scottish Archaeological Review*, 8: 33-34.

Lawson, J. 2001. Cramond, Edinburgh [radiocarbon dates]. *Discovery and Excavation in Scotland*: 124.

Livens, R.G. 1956. Three tanged points from Scotland. *Proceedings of the Society of Antiquaries of Scotland*, 89: 438-443.

Mithen, S.J., K. Wicks, A. Pirie, F. Riede, C. Lane, R. Banerjea, V. Cullen, M. Gittins and N. Pankhurst. 2015. A Lateglacial archaeological site in the far north-west of Europe at Rubha Port an t-Seilich, Isle of Islay, western Scotland: Ahrensburgian-style artefacts, absolute dating and geoarchaeology. *Journal of Quaternary Science*, 30(5): 396-416.

Reynier, M. 2005. *Early Mesolithic Britain: Origins, development and directions*. Oxford: Archaeopress.

Rozoy, J.G. 1978. *Les Derniers Chasseurs: L'Epipaleolithique En France Et En Belgique: Essai De Synthese*. Charleville: Societe Archaeologique Champenoise.

Saville, A. 1998. Studying the Mesolithic Period in Scotland: A Bibliographic Gazetteer. In N. Ashton, F. Healy, and P. Pettitt (eds), *Stone Age Archaeology: Essays in honour of John Wymer*: 211-224. Oxford: Oxbow.

Saville, A. 2004. The Material Culture of Mesolithic Scotland. In A. Saville (ed.), *Mesolithic Scotland and Its Neighbours: The Early Holocene Prehistory of Scotland, its British and Irish Context and some Northern European Perspectives*: 185-220. Edinburgh: Society of Antiquaries of Scotland.

Saville, A. 2008. The Beginning of the Later Mesolithic in Scotland. In Z. Sulgostowska, and A.J. Tomaszewski (eds), *Man - Millennia - Environment: Studies in Honour of Romuald Schild*: 207-213. Warsaw: Institute of Archaeology and Ethnology; Polish Academy of Sciences.

Saville, A. and T.B. Ballin. 2003. An Ahrensbergian-type tanged point from Shieldaig, Wester Ross, Scotland and its implications. *Oxford Journal of Archaeology*, 22(2): 115-131.

Saville, A. and T.B. Ballin. 2009. Upper Palaeolithic evidence from Kilmelfort Cave, Argyll: a re-evaluation of the lithic assemblage. *Proceedings of the Society of Antiquaries of Scotland*, 139: 9-46.

Saville, A., K. Hardy, R. Miket and T.B. Ballin. 2012. *An Corran, Staffin, Skye: A Rockshelter with Mesolithic and Later Occupation*. SAIR 51: (http://www.sair.org.uk/sair51/).

Scottish Government 2018. Archaeologists unearth amazing finds on Aberdeen bypass. Last Viewed 9th July 2018, <https://news.gov.scot/news/archaeologists-unearth-amazing-finds-on-aberdeen-bypass>.

Spikins, P. 1999. *Mesolithic Northern England. Environment, population and settlement.* Oxford: Archaeopress.

Ward, T. 1998. Cornhill; Weston Farm; Daer Reservoir (Sites 1 and 2). *Discovery and Excavation in Scotland*: 90, 128.

Ward, T. and A. Saville. 2010. Howburn Farm: excavating Scotland's first people. *Current Archaeology*, 243: 18-23.

Warren, G. 2001. Marking space? Stone tool deposition in Mesolithic and early Neolithic eastern Scotland. In M. Zvelebil, and K. Fewster (eds), *Ethnoarchaeology and Hunter Gatherers: pictures at an exhibition*: 91-100. Oxford: Archaeopress.

Wickham-Jones, C.R. and G.H. Collins. 1977. The sources of flint and chert in northern Britain. *Proceedings of the Society of Antiquaries of Scotland*, 109: 7-21.

Wickham-Jones, C.R. and K. Hardy. 2004. *Camais Daraich: a Mesolithic site at the Point of Sleat, Skye.* (http://www.sair.org.uk/sair12/): SAIR 12.

Woodward, N. 2008. Links House, Orkney (Stronsay parish), fieldwalking, geophysics and excavation. *Discovery and Excavation in Scotland*, 9: 137.

Wright, A.D. 2012. The Archaeology of Variation: a case study of repetition, difference and becoming in the Mesolithic of West Central Scotland. Unpublished PhD Thesis: University of Glasgow.

Wright, A.D. 2016. There is No Identity: Discerning the Indiscernible. In E. Pierce, A. Russell, A. Maldonado, and E. Campbell (eds), *Creating Material Worlds: The Uses of Identity in Archaeology*: 175-194. Oxford: Oxbow.

Scotland's Neolithic / Neolithic Scotland

Kenneth Brophy

'From the remains that have been found in these cairns or barrows, we know that these Neolithic men – men of the Late Stone Age – must have been of comparatively small stature ... and that their heads must have been long in proportion to their breadth, like the heads of Scotsmen of to-day' (MacKie 1930, 5)

'... the archaeological record of earlier periods should not normally contribute to the discussion of a nation's identity' (Sharples 1996, 79)

Preamble

It seems incongruous to discuss the Neolithic period in the context of a book on the topic of Scottish identity and nationalism, especially one in part inspired by the 'Homecoming' year of 2009. It barely needs re-stating that the modern country of Scotland as we understand it, both geographically and culturally, did not exist in the Neolithic (the period between 6000 and 4500 years ago). Therefore it seems difficult to see how this distant, ancient past, could contribute much, if anything, to a sense of Scottishness, or help us to understand what it is to be Scottish today. Yet this is not to say that the political borders of Scotland have not been used as boundaries for studies and syntheses. Nor, indeed, would it be fair to say that 'being Scottish' has not had some impact on the study of Neolithic sites and materials found in Scotland (see for instance Ralston, this volume). In this paper, then, I would like to reflect on the possible ways that the role the Neolithic of Scotland has had in defining our modern identity. I will also consider how contemporary identities impact on our attempts to make sense of the Neolithic. In particular, I will reflect on my own situation, as a Scot trying to make sense of Scotland in the Neolithic.

Part of the collective identity of Scots in my experience seems to me to revolve around what has been called 'inferiorism', in particular in relation to our status within the United Kingdom (or more precisely, our relationship with England). We seem to be concerned with how others view us, and this includes how others write about us, about our past and present. The columnist Ian Bell has written about what he called the 'secret history' of Scotland (*The Sunday Herald*, 15th November 2009). This article was prompted by reading two books by journalist-historian Dominic Sandbrook on a history of Britain in the 1960s, *Never had it so good* (2005) and *White Heat – a history of Britain in the Swinging Sixties* (2006). These volumes cover various momentous events in history and pop culture from that decade. However, Bell noted: '... in indices covering the best part of 1800 pages across two volumes no space has been found for a thing called Scotland'. Bell argued that these volumes sit within a tradition of histories of the United Kingdom in this respect. He asked, '...why a Union of nations can be such a boon when one nation winds up so poor – 'historically''? It is interesting that Bell accepts that even by noticing this at all – by searching out Scotland in the index rather like looking for a rude word in a dictionary – he is probably being 'parochial'.

This struck me as interesting because Neolithic studies of Scotland have been discussed in similar terms. For instance, Ian Kinnes (1985), then of the British Museum in London, was asked to write a review of the current state of knowledge of Scotland's Neolithic by the Society of Antiquaries of Scotland in the early 1980s. His review started with a very brief overview of Scottish Neolithic studies, which was rather damning in its own way. For instance he argued that there was a 'recurrent need to derive innovation from without and then to resort to the **parochial** for explanation and understanding' (Kinnes 1985, 15, my emphasis). More recently, in reviews by an 'insider' rather than an 'outsider', Gordon Barclay made arguments almost identical to Bell's in relation to the study of Scotland's Neolithic. In a series of important papers, Barclay (e.g. 2001a, 2004) argued that the study of the Neolithic of Scotland had suffered from being regarded as peripheral to the much more visible and better-understood Neolithic of southern England. He argued that a general, pervasive and deeply historically rooted use of the concept of Britishness when Englishness was what was really meant had bedevilled studies of Scotland's Neolithic (2001, 4-5), with many 20th century studies viewing Scotland as no more than an uninhabitable Highland scene from a shortbread tin. Indeed, when effort was applied to looking north, the focus was inevitably Orkney, a 'luminous centre' to rival Wessex, Stonehenge, Avebury and so on, and yet not in any way representative of Scotland in the Neolithic. For Barclay, the sense that Scotland's Neolithic was secondary to England's, derivative, even inferior, has only recently been shaken off. Yet the status of Scotland in prehistory is still not assured. Thomas (2010, 6) has recently noted that models suggesting material culture, or monument styles, originated in Scotland and spread southwards to England had not yet been widely accepted because they 'flowed in the wrong direction'.

The contemporary world matters when we study the Neolithic of Scotland, for both Scots and non-Scots. The arguments of both Bell and Barclay are relatively familiar refrains for many people from Scotland, perhaps more commonly played out in the world of sport than (pre)history. Scottish sportsmen suddenly become British when they become successful, while football hooligans in the 1980s and 1990s who following England were often portrayed as 'British' in media reports (or so it seemed to Scots). I myself experienced similar frustration on holiday abroad once when an English guide on a coach informed us that there was plenty of English alcohol on sale at the local airport including whisky! Such viewpoints and experiences, it could be argued, are part of the contemporary and complex Scottish psyche. We want to see some kind of Scottish identity reflected in academic, sporting and cultural contexts, but we also suspect that to want this is petty minded and parochial. These are complex issues, and suggest that our current preconceptions, beliefs, cultural affiliation and chips-on-shoulders probably have much more of an impact on the way that we study Scotland's Neolithic, than the ways that Scotland's Neolithic sites and monuments impact on contemporary Scottish identity. Within this category I would include the Homecoming in 2009. The 'Year of Homecoming' forced a lot of people in Scotland to become introspective, to think about what Scotland means to them, and generally this is no more stone circles and henges than it is kilts and bagpipes.

This paper will cover a loosely connected series of issues based around the study of the Neolithic of Scotland. These include the role of the current national borders in structuring studies of the Neolithic, as well as reflecting on being a Scot studying the Neolithic of Scotland. In other words, does the contemporary psyche of being a Scot (as perhaps exemplified by Barclay's approach) have an impact on the way we study the Neolithic, and indeed what impact – if any – does Scotland's Neolithic have on our contemporary national identity? Throughout this paper, it is important to remember that Scotland's Neolithic, and Neolithic Scotland, are two very different – modern – constructs. Yet the two concepts seem at times to become entangled.

On the edge

That most simple of devices, the map, has a lot to tell us about the perception, role and definition of Scotland in the Neolithic period (cf. Brophy 2009). Our underlying feelings of insignificance and sense of being peripheral could well be re-enforced, for instance, by looking at the treatment of Scotland in maps depicting all kinds of Neolithic data. Broad-brush maps depicting the spread of farming across Europe, for instance, commonplace throughout much of the 20th century, depicted (inevitably) Scotland as teetering on the very edge of the known world, almost disappearing over the edge of the page (Figure 1). Arrows, or isochrons (effectively time contours), suggest the inexorable movement of farming in an easterly and northerly direction, with Scotland receiving the civilising bounty of farming last, seemingly the last resort for farmers looking for virgin land. Such models are ingrained in the archaeological psyche to some extent, regardless of how we believe farming was transmitted. As Thomas (2010, 6) notes, 'we are always happier to accept a migration if it proceeds from southeast to northwest'. The same arguments – and similar maps – could be made in relation to megalithic tombs, beaker pottery (and the 'beaker folk') and even the Celts. One could argue that diffusionist archaeologies, underpinned by mass immigrations or invasions into the British Isles causing social, religious and economic change, implicitly depict Scotland as 'secondary'. In this European outpost, developments happened last, and not only that, more often than not came via England. Within this context, it is easy to see how developments in Scotland could come to be viewed as secondary, peripheral or even derivative (e.g. Piggott 1954). This is all the more pervasive when we reflect that such processes were seldom believed to be anything other than one-way.

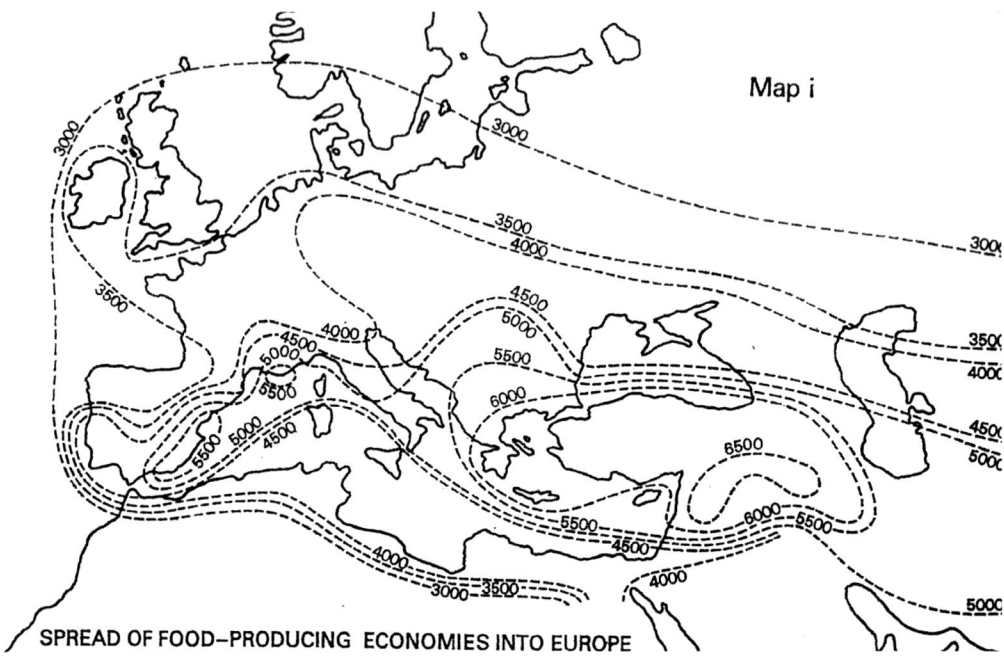

Map i

SPREAD OF FOOD–PRODUCING ECONOMIES INTO EUROPE

Figure 1. Childe's map showing the advance of 'food-producing economies' across Europe with Scotland at the edge of the Neolithic world (from Childe 1957, 29, map i)

The use of maps in this way continued even after models of diffusion were being broken down thanks to radiocarbon dating (cf. Renfrew 1973). This is evident when we look at maps such as those showing the distribution of causewayed enclosures in the British Isles produced in the 1970s and 1980s (Figure 2). These maps ignore Scotland because when the maps were produced it was thought there were no causewayed enclosures in Scotland (or indeed in northern Britain). This was a pragmatic decision by the mapmaker: some would believe that there is no need to map negative evidence. However Mercer's (1990) map (Figure 2b) does acknowledge that there was a causewayed enclosure in Ireland, Donegore. Yet this site is merely depicted by an arrow pointing off into the Irish Sea. These maps make the point rather forcibly that this is a (southern) English distribution of a southern English monument type, although this position has since been challenged (Sheridan 2001; Oswald *et al.* 2001; Barclay 2001b). I have argued elsewhere (Brophy 2004) that the initial identification of causewayed enclosures in the southern English chalklands left the indelible impression that these were primarily monuments of the southern English Neolithic (re-enforced by such maps). Furthermore, any sites found to the north, or in Ireland, would be viewed as later or secondary developments (and see Barclay 2001a for a similar broader argument). Yet radiocarbon dating suggests that one of the earliest causewayed enclosures in the British Isles was located in the Isle of Man (Billown, see Darvill 2001).

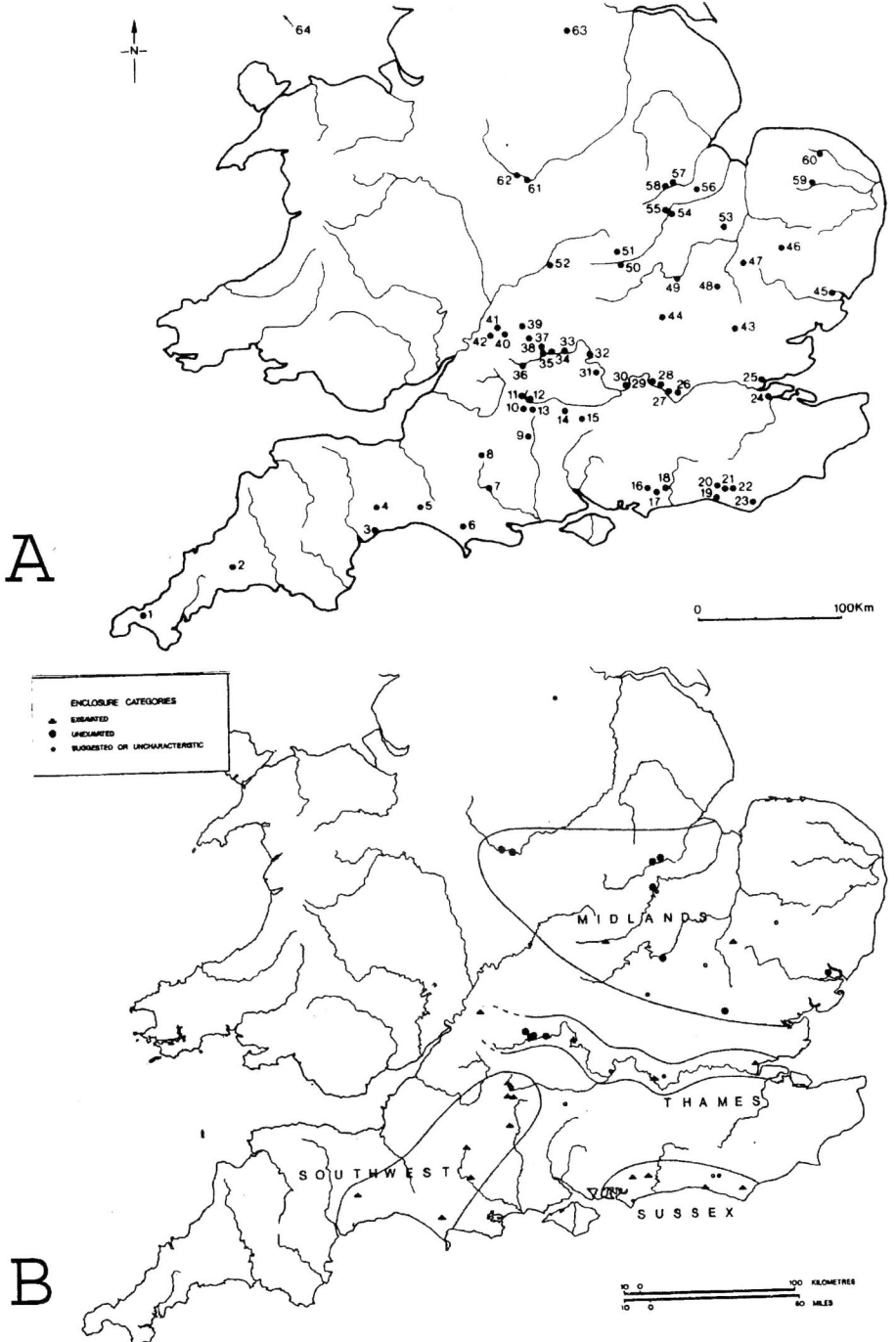

Figure 2. The distribution of known causewayed enclosures in the British Isles, with Scotland amputated, reflecting negative evidence at the time that these maps were produced (a from Mercer 1990, illus 1 and b from Palmer 1976, 172, fig 9)

In a mirror image of maps where Scotland has been amputated from the British mainland, Barclay (2001a) has acknowledged that he had been guilty in the past of producing maps that stopped at the Scottish border, and Figure 3 is one of the maps that he probably had in mind (from Barclay 2003). It depicts the distribution of henge monuments, cursus monuments, recumbent stone circles and Clava Cairns in Scotland (although when this was produced in the mid 1990s it was not known for sure that the Clava cairns and recumbent stone circles were Bronze Age). In its own right, such maps are hardly rabid statements of nationalism, but nonetheless the map has imposed on it an entirely arbitrary modern political boundary relative to the date it depicts. Some monument types depicted on this map are found in England, Wales and Ireland, transcending the mapped border. Yet other monument types depicted have what Sharples has termed 'distinctive Scottish characteristics' (1996, 81). The point here is that Neolithic (and Bronze Age) monument and material culture distributions can rarely be framed by national boundaries, and indeed there is probably a better argument to draw a boundary defining the northeast (Barclay 2003) or between eastern and western Scotland (Telford 2002) than across the Cheviots. It goes without saying that different ideas had different spheres of influence, some mutually exclusive, others overlapping, and these rarely respect our modern boundaries. Key to identity in the Neolithic was a sliding scale of traditions that spanned what we would call the local, regional, national and international although the true extent of the use of Grooved Ware and henges as opposed to carved stone balls and timber halls were almost certainly not apparent to people at that time. So while there were boundaries in the Neolithic, these were not the boundaries we now see on our maps, the boundaries we define ourselves by. Rather they were fluid, flexible, overlapping and porous – and almost certainly in places we would not expect.

The irrelevance of the modern political border of Scotland – and indeed the problematic nature of this boundary – is illustrated by a remarkable complex of cropmarks at Sprouston, near Kelso on the south banks of the River Tweed (Smith 1991). These cropmarks have revealed the location of an extensive Anglian settlement complex, complete with field systems and timber buildings. Adjacent to this complex is a rectilinear structure defined by pits and a ring ditch; these have been interpreted as a possible Neolithic timber hall similar to Balbridie, Aberdeenshire (Fairweather & Ralston 1993) and Bronze Age barrow. There is also a possible causewayed enclosure here on the bank of the Tweed, again, a cropmark. Only excavation could confirm those interpretations. The possible Neolithic timber hall sits within 5km of the border with England, located in modern Scotland by nothing more than modern political expediency. Thanks to this good fortune, however, this hall can safely be included in maps and lists that deal with the 'Neolithic timber halls of Scotland' (see Brophy 2007). Had it been built a short walk along the bank of the Tweed, however, it would instead in the literature have become a unique English example of this otherwise characteristically Scottish structure. Yet there is another way of looking at this site. Despite its superficial similarity to other early Neolithic timber halls (ibid.) this

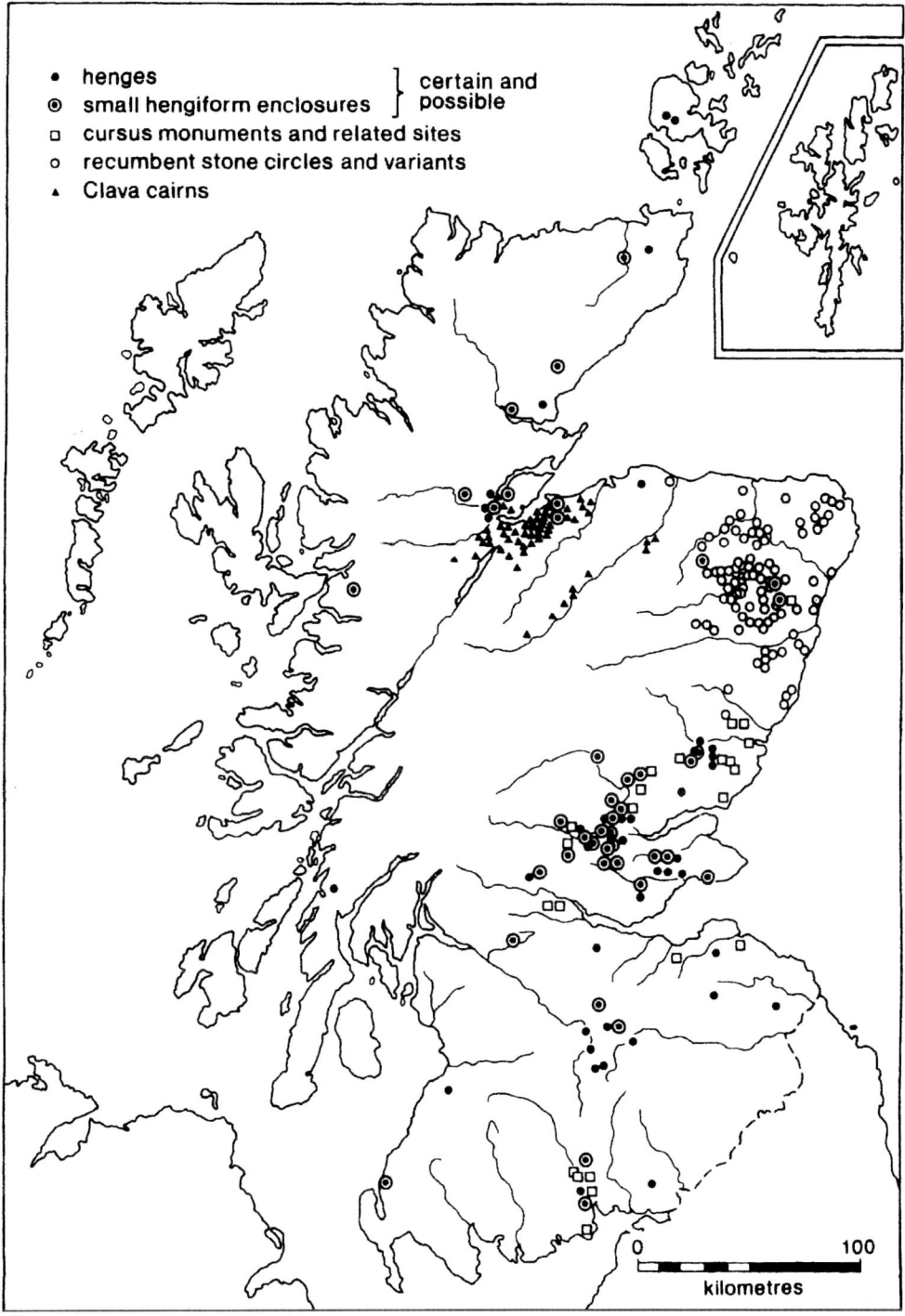

Figure 3. Barclay's map showing the distribution of various Neolithic (and Bronze Age) monument types only in Scotland (from Barclay 2003, 136, fig 8.2)

site could also be interpreted as an Anglian timber hall. Here, the location of the monument makes perfect sense in a wider, regional, tradition of such structures from Yeavering in Northumbria to Doon Hill B in East Lothian and political boundaries at that time (Figure 4). There are a whole series of serendipities here that make little sense in terms of the past, but make perfect sense in the terms set by our modern methods of depicting, and gathering, data. Ultimately, the boundedness of Scotland's Neolithic, where one site can be three miles away from dropping off a list of Scotland's timber halls, is a product of archaeological discourse as much as anything else. Every map can tell its own story.

The border between Scotland and England is a relatively easy one to traverse, marked at worst by the Tweed. But the border between Scotland and Ireland is

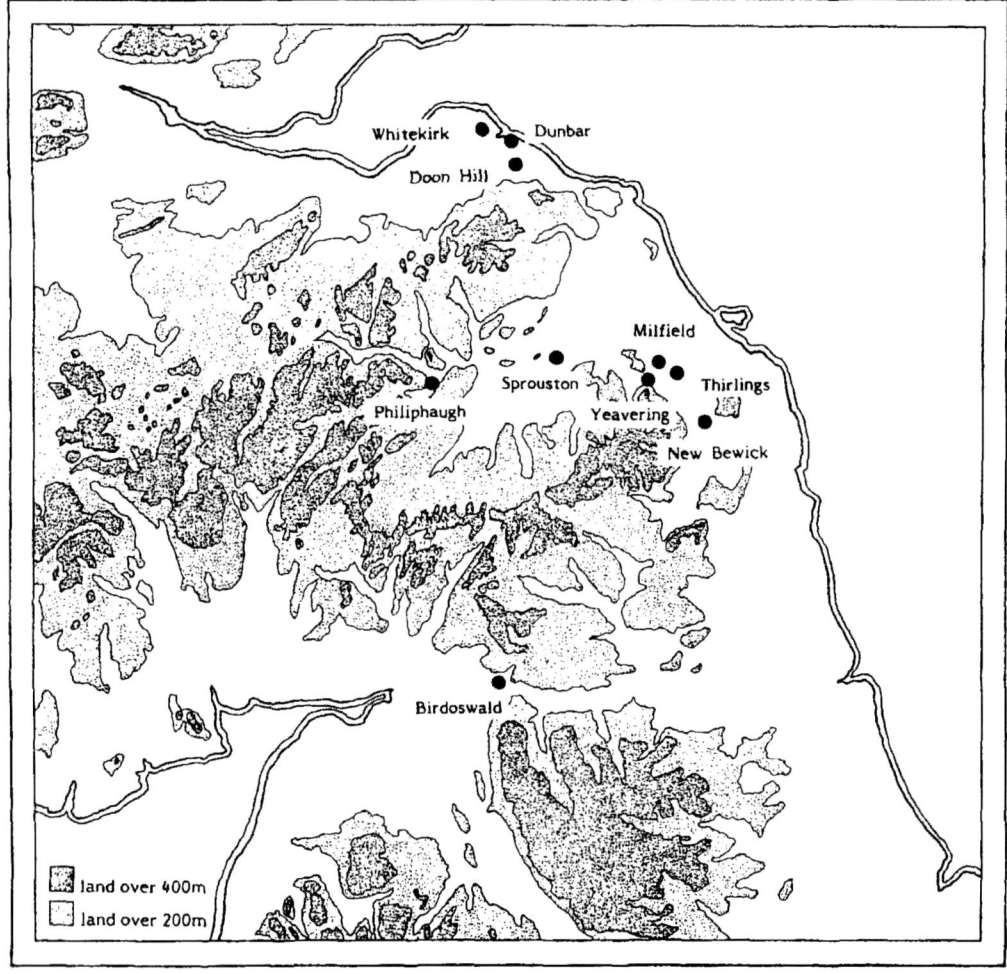

Figure 4. Map showing the location of Anglian sites and halls in SE Scotland / NE England, reflecting very different political 'borders' (Smith 1991)

more troublesome, with the Irish Sea having been viewed on and off (depending on prevailing fashions in Neolithic studies) as a barrier to connections between these two 'countries' in prehistory. Yet this prevaricating prehistoric narrative has run parallel with a more enduring and consistent sense that strong connections with Ireland have long been part of Scottish identity (see elsewhere in this volume). Despite the fact that Campbeltown is closer to Northern Ireland than Glasgow the Neolithic of Ireland, and the Neolithic of Scotland, are studied by different people in different ways. Our modern national boundaries do in a very real sense impact on the study of the prehistoric past, creating a gulf that is unlikely to reflect the reality some 5000 years ago. It is unclear why the Neolithic of the Kintyre peninsula, or chambered cairns in Wigtownshire, should not be considered in the same context as contemporary sites, monuments and material culture elsewhere in the 'Irish Sea Zone', other than modern political expediency. (This, in part, has been enshrined by each of the 'four nations' having their own government heritage agencies and national monuments records (Cummings 2009, 1)). A recent revival in interest in connections across the Irish Sea is a welcome development in the study of British and Irish prehistory (cf. Cooney 2000; Cummings & Fowler 2004; Cummings 2009). Material and social connections such as this have no modern political implications, and have nothing to do with modern national identities. Rather they reflect a pragmatic approach to studying the Neolithic of this area that suggests we should consider the context of Northern Ireland, or the Isle of Man, or Cumbria, when looking at southwest Scotland, not necessarily Perthshire and Aberdeenshire (or even worse, Orkney). Such cross-boundary, ex-Scotland connections – maintained no doubt by a lot more sea travel than had previously been imagined – hang together rather well (Figure 5).

I was recently gifted some old school history textbooks by a friend who has retired from teaching. Amongst these was a thin brown volume entitled *Prehistoric Britain* (Place 1959), part of the Then & There Series. The final image in the book is a map which shows sites of the 'Neolithic Age' in Britain (Figure 6) (strangely the only map in the book). The map stops abruptly half way up Scotland more or less across the Firth of Tay to Oban, and the bisected nation of Scotland is empty of Neolithic sites, save for the (wrongly spelled) Cairnpapple Hill henge (perhaps included because it had been excavated by that great proponent of the southern English Windmill Hill Culture, Stuart Piggott). Do maps like this matter? Am I annoyed at this map because I am a Scot and it suggests Scottish school kids were not being properly informed about the Neolithic of Scotland? Should it surprise me that the first words in such a book are: 'The winds blow strong across the uplands of Salisbury Plain' (ibid., 1)? Should I be annoyed that Childe once wrote that, 'Scotland cannot have been an inviting country for agricultural settlement' (Childe 1935)? Or is this parochialism once again? Suffice it to say that maps are powerful tools, drawing on the subconscious baggage of the map-maker and the map-reader. Our modern engagements with patterns of people, objects and materials from the Neolithic are ultimately mediated through grid references, council areas and countries, as well as north, south, east and west.

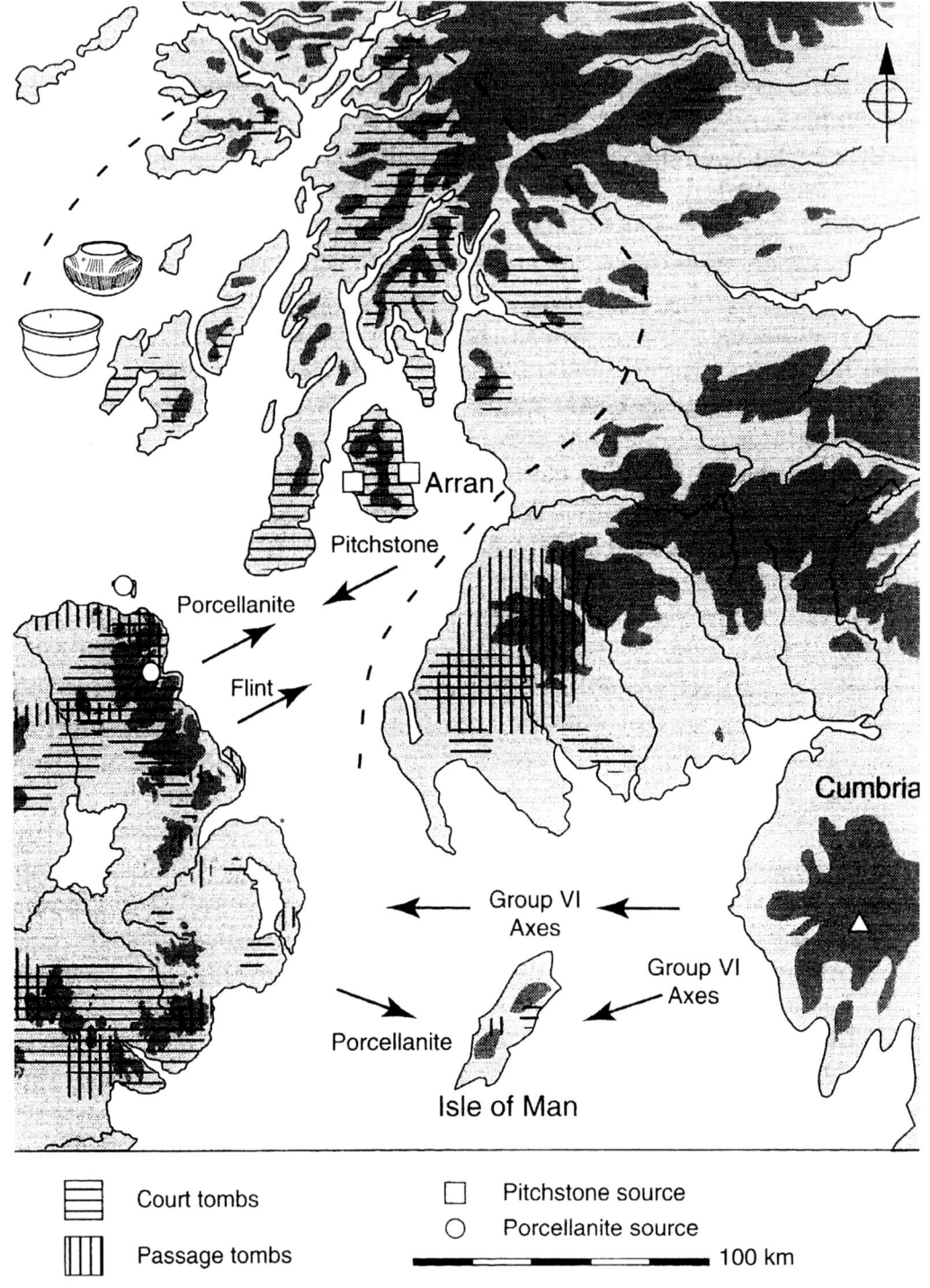

Figure 5. The Irish Sea Zone, with comings, goings and connections indicated
(from Cooney 2000, 226, fig 7.3)

Figure 6. Map showing sites of the 'Neolithic Age' in Britain (from Place 1959) complete with Wessex doodles by an unknown pupil!

Yet what do maps matter for those who transcend national boundaries, the comings and goings that have defined Scotland even before it was Scotland, and the diasporas celebrated in the Year of the Homecoming?

Going over the edge

The mechanisms by which people crossed the Irish Sea in the Neolithic period are unclear, but small wooden vessels and a good knowledge of the best time to make the short journeys involved would likely have been central to these comings and goings. Of course there were no passport controls, no border guards, no customs or duty free. The act of crossing the sea in the Neolithic was probably fraught with danger, and people and materials associated with such journeys may have been afforded special status. The modern Scottish identity is also concerned with the emotional power of sea journeys, in particular those leaving Scotland, as celebrated in the Year of the Homecoming. A key theme of the 'Homecoming' was to connect with Scotland's Diaspora: there are people with connections to Scotland all over the world and this connectedness transcends national boundaries. If the modern Scottish identity is dominated by people leaving Scotland, models of Neolithic Scotland have largely been defined by people *arriving*, and bringing new objects, ideas and ways of life with them. We are all familiar with the diffusionist ideas of culture-historians when the building blocks of Neolithic life in Scotland were viewed as being brought in from outsiders, one-by-one, often from continental Europe (cf. Childe 1935, 1957; Piggott 1954). These migrations acted as an explanation for changes in economy, monumentality and material culture. Thus maps were produced, like Figure 1, with Scotland on the edge of the world.

Such grand narrative diffusionist models have, of course, fallen from favour, and current trends across Neolithic studies are more sympathetic to a patchwork of comings and goings, where social and cultural change results from dynamic processes involved in both indigenous development and the occasional external nudge (cf. Whittle et. al. 2011). Certainly, arguments are still being made for people coming into Scotland as stimuli for something 'new'. It has been suggested that the timber hall at Balbridie was a continental style longhouse (Fairweather and Ralston 1993), perhaps built by settlers who had sailed up the River Dee (Ashmore 1996). More recently, Alison Sheridan (2000, 2003) has argued that an unusual pottery vessel, found within an unusual tomb at Achnacreeabeg, Argyll, is indicative of connections with Brittany around or before 4000BC, perhaps even evidence for the presence of a group of Brittonic farmer settlers. The very nature of the start of the Neolithic period in Scotland is complex and arguments could be made for both limited arrivals of new people, but also for an indigenous take-up of new food sources and material culture being used elsewhere (in England or Ireland). There has also been a noticeable trend recently suggesting that some significant aspects of Neolithic monumentality, material culture and social change may have originated in Scotland. For instance, although cursus monuments were initially identified in southern England (on the Wessex chalklands) it seems likely that the earliest cursus monuments in the British Isles are found in mainland Scotland (Thomas 2006; Brophy 2012), with this 'idea' gradually moving southwards into England and Wales. A similar southwards movement also seems to characterise the spread of Grooved Ware (in this case originating in Orkney) and perhaps some of the other changes associated with this pot style (the so-called Grooved Ware complex, see Thomas 2010).

Such comings and goings, with ideas, objects and probably small groups of people (or individuals) moving across and around the British Isles in a variety of different directions, suggests a dynamic social situation that had nothing to do with England and Scotland, north and south. One does not have to have 'diffusionist tendencies' to realise that people in Scotland had wide and varied connections, in the shape of the movement of ideas and exotic objects such as Alpine jadeite axes. The domestication of animals was not a notion dreamt up from nowhere by an isolated hunter-gatherer Highlander. Nor does one have to be a Scottish nationalist to propose that certain innovations within the Neolithic period occurred north of the border, although this is hardly a source of nationalistic pride in the same league as, for instance, Irn Bru, John Logie Baird or Sean Connery. The definition of 'Neolithic Scotland' in this respect blurs the value of such ideas and establishes a whole range of alternative myths and orthodoxies (as is also evidence for Neolithic Ireland). And, of course, the flow of ideas, culture and people in and out, comings and goings, porous boundaries and complex identities are all aspects of the historic and modern identity of Scotland.

The Year of Homecoming caused a lot of such soul-searching about the nature of being Scottish for those still living in Scotland, as well as warming the hearts of those living elsewhere who have tartan blood running in their veins. Amidst the imagery used to promote the Homecoming, there was little role (perhaps unsurprisingly) for prehistory, especially when considered in relation to the Highland Clearances and subsequent emigrations. This paper opened with an important comment by Niall Sharples regarding the lack of appropriateness of using the archaeological records of periods to help define national identity (Sharples 1996, 79) and of course this includes the Neolithic period. This is not to say that prehistory has not been used in some cases to do so, although this is generally problematic and often sinister (cf. Atkinson et al 1996), as attested to by activities associated with archaeologists working under the banner of German National Socialism (Arnold 1990). In a more contemporary twist on much the same thing, The British National Party makes a great deal of its claim to the rights of 'indigenous Britons', a notion with no basis in reality whatsoever. The mission statement of the BNP includes the banal (and inaccurate) comment that, 'We enthuse with pride at the marvels of architecture and engineering that have been completed on these islands since the construction of the great megaliths 7,000 years ago'. Matthew Stout (1996) has written about Emyr Esten Evans' 'Ulster exceptionalism', an attempt to demonstrate that megalithic tombs in Northern Island were different from those elsewhere on that island, with obvious political motivations. Yet such agendas are doomed to failure. The people who lived in 'what is now Scotland' (as Barclay (2001a, 1) has put it) 5000 years ago were not Scottish, not did they have any sense of – or identity associated with – the political unit we recognise as Scotland. In the Neolithic period there was no Scotland, no Ireland, no Britain, no Germany, and no national boundaries or identities.

In this respect it is little wonder that the Homecoming engaged only superficially with the Neolithic period as indicative of Scottish identify. Yet there were engagements, and the most high profile of these was the depiction of a stone circle on a bank note. A new set of bank notes were produced by the Clydesdale Bank as part of the Year of the Homecoming, and on the back of each note was a depiction of one of Scotland's World Heritage Sites (WHS). And so the Ring of Brodgar, Neolithic henge and stone circle, and part of the Heart of Neolithic Orkney WHS, can be found on the £100 bank note (although I suspect not too many of these will turn up in the average wallet). Alex Salmond, First Minister, noted that, 'The new [banknote] designs showcase our unrivalled landmarks and landscapes as well as the contributions of some of Scotland's greatest minds' (The Herald, 14th January 2009). The bank itself stated that the 'new banknote family showcases the best of Scotland – its people and its heritage (Clydesdale Bank 2009). Yet how representative is Brodgar and the Orcadian Neolithic? Barclay (2001a) has argued persuasively that there has been an unhealthy bias towards Orkney within Scottish (and British) Neolithic studies. The banknote (as well as WHS status) re-enforced this pre-eminent location, and iconic status of these monuments, although they are for the most part atypical and non-representative of the Neolithic of the rest of Scotland. Nor can we with any conviction attribute them to the brightest and best minds available around 2700BC. Yet perhaps Brodgar does reflect something of the essence of Neolithic Scotland within the modern Scottish psyche: rugged, arable, romantic, Highland (although Orkney is hardly Highland in character in reality). Perhaps also this is how some of the Scottish Diaspora imagine Scotland: pre-industrial, mysterious and endearingly ancient.

One final event seems to have been inspired by a combination of the Neolithic, and the Homecoming – the 'Sconestone'. This bizarre object was created from a piece of grey 'Wonderstone' by Warren McLeod (a Canadian whose parents are Scottish) and was inspired by his interest in Neolithic carved stone balls (or orbs as he describes them) (Sconestone 2009a). In a stramash of Scottishness one could hardly make up, this stone was launched upon the public by Alex Salmond at a Runrig concert in August 2009, before it commenced upon a journey, being passed from one 'keeper' to another to promote a 'spirit of kindness'. This fist-sized spherical lump of stone (Figure 7) was conceived as a mishmash of 'Scottish' associations, with McLeod describing the spiral design in the raised areas of the stone as 'Celtic' (ibid.). The very name of this object is redolent of the Stone of Destiny. The First Minister was happy to associate this project, and object, with the Homecoming and noted at its launch that

Figure 7. The Sconestone

this 'initiative can help inspire many people around the globe, while also highlighting Scotland's ancient heritage and close ties with Canada and other nations of the world' (Sconestone 2009b). Again, this contemporary sense of Neolithic Scotland, of our shared 'heritage', is woolly and non-representative.

Conclusion

In this paper I have tried to reflect a series of entanglements between the ideas of Neolithic Scotland, and Scotland's Neolithic. I have suggested that our maps, and political boundaries, have at times acted as a constraint upon understanding fully the nature of Neolithic traditions and cultural change across the British Isles. It is also clear that the expanse of land we now call Scotland was inhabited in the Neolithic period by people fully engaged and in communication with neighbours across both land and sea. These people were innovators, and adopters, with a series of inter-connected and overlapping aspects to their identity. However, none of these identities involved being Scottish. David Clark (1996, 67) has noted, in the Neolithic 'the concept of a Scottish nation as we now understand it [was] meaningless'. There is nothing inherent within the Neolithic that led to Scotland as it is today. But nonetheless, it is possible to argue that Scottish identity could be shaped by how we understand our prehistoric past today. It is also probably the case our narrative of that past – in terms of boundaries, movement and a whole range of interpretations of Neolithic life – are to some extent entangled with who we are as archaeologists and people.

Within this context it would be remiss (and indeed very un-Scottish of me) not to express the role Scots, and theories developed using Scottish material, have had on Neolithic studies in general. The value of the archaeological record in Scotland has long been recognised, and in particular theoretical developments have been pioneered using this material, in stark contrast to any lingering feelings of parochialism . Childe wrote (1935, preface), 'Scotland should be able to afford data for the solution of several most fascinating problems in British, and indeed in European prehistory'. Childe himself built on one of the earliest chambered tomb typologies anywhere in Europe advanced by Joseph Anderson in an Edinburgh Rhind Lecture in the 1880s (Anderson 1886) and based on sites in Caithness. New theoretical models developed in the 1970s included Renfrew's (1973) analysis of the 'social context' of chambered cairns on Arran and Rousay. This ground-breaking theoretical work was placed within the context of an internationally important book, *Before civilisation* (ibid.). Such studies were at the forefront of Processual thinking. Since then, Neolithic studies in Scotland have been characterised by innovative post-processual and interpretive approaches. Phenomenology, hermeneutics, metaphor, biography, sensory archaeology and aspects of landscape archaeology have been employed, and in some cases, developed, in Scotland. This includes important and ground-breaking research such as Watson's study of the use of sound in chambered cairns (Watson & Keating 1999), Jones's (2002) analysis of the differing composition of Grooved Ware at houses in Barnhouse Neolithic settlement, Richard's (1991, 2005) work on Orcadian settlements, henges and standing stone quarries, Cummings's (2009) phenomenological fieldwork at chambered tombs in the southwest and so on. None of this research could be described as derivative or parochial, and speaks of an academic dynamism that mirrors the fluidity, the comings and goings, of Neolithic society in and beyond Scotland. (Incidentally, Anderson is the only Scottish archaeologist listed in this paragraph.)

As for the traces of Neolithic Scotland that survive today, there is no doubt that these can contribute to 'Scotland the brand', and offer great potential for tourist numbers and income. Yet Neolithic monuments have become entangled in not just how we market Scotland, but also in how we define what it is to be Scottish. They have become in some ways enmeshed with notions of identity in modern Scotland, amongst archaeologists and tourists, historians and members of the Diaspora. During the Homecoming year the First Minister endorsed and supported the use of Neolithic imagery in various ways. Yet we must be careful to fully recognise the difference between the Neolithic of Scotland, and the Scottish Neolithic. Otherwise we run the risk of drawing on, promoting, and even believing in a Scotland that never was from a time when there never was a Scotland.

Acknowledgements

In part this paper was inspired by the kind gift of some old school books from Andy Grinly so my thanks to him. I would also like to thanks the organisers of the original conference, Dene Wright, Nicki Hall and Louisa Campbell, for inviting me to speak and also for their patience in awaiting my contribution to this volume and editorial feedback they subsequently provided. Gordon Barclay, Gabriel Cooney, Roger Mercer and Rog Palmer kindly allowed me to reproduce illustrations, and figure 4 is reproduced courtesy of the Society of Antiquaries of Scotland. The photograph of the Sconestone was very kindly provided by its maker, Warren MacLeod, and reproduced with his permission. Finally, I am indebted to Jan Brophy for her careful reading of this paper before its completion.

Bibliography

Anderson, J. 1886. *Scotland in pagan times: the Bronze and Stone Ages*, Edinburgh: David Douglas.

Arnold, B. 1990. The past as propaganda: totalitarian archaeology in Nazi Germany, *Antiquity*, 64, 464–78.

Ashmore, P. 1996. *Neolithic and Bronze Age Scotland*, London: Historic Scotland/Batsford.

Atkinson, J., I. Banks. and J. O'Sullivan (eds) 1996. *Nationalism and archaeology*, Glasgow: Cruithne Press.

Arnold, B. 1990. The past as propaganda: totalitarian archaeology in Nazi Germany, *Antiquity*, 64, 464–78.

Barclay, G.J. 2001a. 'Metropolitan' and 'Parochial' / 'Core' and 'Periphery': a historiography of the prehistory of Scotland, *Proceedings of the Prehistoric Society*, 67, 1–18.

Barclay, G.J. 2001b. Neolithic enclosures in Scotland, in T. Darvill and J. Thomas (eds), *Neolithic Enclosures in Atlantic Northwest Europe*, 144–154. Oxford: Oxbow Books.

Barclay, G.J. 2003. The Neolithic, in K.J. Edwards and I.B.M. Ralston (eds) *Scotland after the Ice Age. Environment, archaeology and history, 8000BC - AD1000*, 127–149. Edinburgh: Edinburgh University Press.

Barclay, G.J. 2004. 'Four Nations Prehistory': cores and archetypes in the writing of prehistory, in H. Brocklehurst and R. Phillips (eds), *History, Nationhood and the question of Britain*, 151–9. London: Palgrave MacMillan.

Brophy K. 2004. The Searchers: the quest for causewayed enclosures in the Irish Sea area, in V. Cummings and C. Fowler (eds), *The Neolithic of the Irish Sea: materiality and traditions of practice*, 37–45. Oxford: Oxbow.

Brophy, K. 2007. From big houses to cult houses: early Neolithic timber halls in Scotland, *Proceedings of the Prehistoric Society*, 73, 75–96.

Brophy, K. 2009. The map trap: the depiction of regional geographies of the Neolithic, in K. Brophy and G.J. Barclay (eds), *Defining a regional Neolithic: the evidence from Britain and Ireland*, 5–25. Oxford: Oxbow.

Brophy, K. 2012. *Reading between the lines: the Neolithic cursus monuments of Scotland*, Stroud: Amberley.

Brophy, K. Forthcoming, From hard to soft: theory and Neolithic studies in Scotland, *Scottish Archaeological Journal*.

Childe, V.G. 1935. *The prehistory of Scotland*, London: Kegan Paul, Trench and Trubner.

Childe, V.G. 1957. *The dawn of European civilisation* (5th edition), London: Paladin.

Clarke, D.V. 1996. Presenting a national perspective of prehistory and early history in the Museum of Scotland, in J. Atkinson, I. Banks and J. O'Sullivan (eds), *Nationalism and archaeology*, 67–76. Glasgow: Cruithne Press.

Clydesdale Bank 2009. Clydesdale Bank to launch new banknote family. Press release dated 14/01/2009. http://www.cbonline.co.uk/media/news-releases/2009/clydesdale-bank-to-launch-new-banknote-family. Last viewed 15th January 2012.

Cooney, C. 2000. *Landscapes of Neolithic Ireland*, London: Routledge.

Cummings, V. 2009. *A view from the west. The Neolithic of the Irish Sea Zone*. Oxford: Oxbow.

Cummings, V. and C. Fowler (eds) 2004. *The Neolithic of the Irish Sea. Materiality and traditions of practice*, Oxford: Oxbow.

Darvill, T. 2001. Neolithic enclosures in the Isle of Man, in T. Darvill and J. Thomas (eds), *Neolithic enclosures in Atlantic Northwest Europe*, 155–70. Oxford: Oxbow.

Fairweather, A. and I.B.M. Ralston 1993. The Neolithic timber hall at Balbridie, Grampian Region, Scotland: the building, the date, the plant macrofossils, *Antiquity*, 67, 313–23.

Jones, A. 2002. *Archaeological Theory and Scientific Practice*, Cambridge: Cambridge University Press.

Kinnes, I. 1985. Circumstance not context: the Neolithic of Scotland as seen from the outside, *Proceedings of the Society of Antiquaries of Scotland*, 115, 115–157.

MacKie, R.L. 1930. *A short history of Scotland*, Edinburgh: Oliver & Boyd.

Mercer, R.J.C. 1990. *Causewayed enclosures*, Prices Risborough: Shire.

Oswald, A., C. Dyer and M. Barber 2001. *The creation of monuments: Neolithic causewayed enclosures in the British Isles*, Swindon: English Heritage.

Palmer, R. 1976. Interrupted ditch enclosures in Britain, *Proceedings of the Prehistoric Society*, 42, 161–186.

Piggott, S. 1954. *The Neolithic cultures of the British Isles*, Cambridge: Cambridge University Press.

Place, R. 1959. *Prehistoric Britain*, London: Longman.

Renfrew, C. 1973. *Before civilization. The radiocarbon revolution and prehistoric Europe*, London: Cape.

Richards, C. 1991. Skara Brae: revisiting a Neolithic village in Orkney, in W.S. Hanson and E.A. Slater (eds), *Scottish Archaeology: new perceptions*, 24–43. Aberdeen: Aberdeen University Press.

Richards, C. 2005. *Dwelling amongst the monuments. The Neolithic village of Barnhouse, Maeshowe passage grave and surrounding monuments at Stenness*, Orkney, Cambridge: McDonald Institute.

Sandbrook, D. 2005. *Never had it so good: a history of Britain from Suez to the Beatles*, London: Little, Brown.

Sandbrook, D. 2006. *White Heat - a history of Britain in the Swinging Sixties*, London: Little, Brown.

Sconestone 2009a. What is the Sconestone? www.sconestone.com/WhatistheSconestone.aspx. Last viewed 15th January 2012.

Sconestone 2009b. Sconestone.com has successful launch with Runrig at Scone Palace. Press release dated 30th August 2009. Available from www.sconestone.com

Sharples, N. 1996. Nationalism or internationalism: the problematic Scottish experience', in J. Atkinson, I. Banks, and J. O'Sullivan (eds), *Nationalism and archaeology*, 77–88. Glasgow: Cruithne Press.

Sheridan, A. 2000. Achnacreebeag and its French connections: vive the Auld Alliance, in J.C. Henderson (ed.), *The prehistory and early History of Atlantic Europe*, 1–15. Oxford: BAR.

Sheridan, A. 2001. Donegore Hill and other Irish Neolithic enclosures: a view from the outside, in T. Darvill and J. Thomas (eds), *Neolithic enclosures in Atlantic Northwest Europe*, 171-89. Oxford: Oxbow.

Sheridan, A. 2003. French connections I: spreading the *marmites* thinly, in I. Armit, E. Murphy, E. Nelis and D. Simpson (eds), *Neolithic settlement in Ireland and Western Britain*, 3-17. Oxford: Oxbow.

Smith, I. M. 1991. Sprouston, Roxburghshire: an early Anglian centre of the eastern Tweed Basin, *Proceedings of the Society of Antiquaries of Scotland*, 121, 261– 94.

Stout, M. 1996. Emyr Estyn Evans and Northern Ireland: the archaeology and geography of a new state', in J. Atkinson, I. Banks and J. O'Sullivan (eds), *Nationalism and archaeology*, 111-127. Glasgow: Cruithne Press.

Telford, D. 2002. The Mesolithic inheritance: contrasting Neolithic monumentality in eastern and western Scotland, *Proceedings of the Prehistoric Society*, 68, 289–315.

Thomas, J. 2006. On the origins and development of cursus monument in Britain, *Proceedings of the Prehistoric Society*, 72, 229–41.

Thomas, J. 2010. The return of the Rinyo-Clacton folk? The cultural significance of the Grooved Ware complex in Later Neolithic Britain, *Cambridge Archaeological Journal*, 20.1, 1–15.

Watson, A. and D. Keating 1999. Architecture and sound: an acoustic analysis of megalithic monuments in prehistoric Britain, *Antiquity*, 73, 325–36.

Whittle, A., F. Healy and A. Bayliss 2011. *Gathering time: dating the early Neolithic enclosures of southern Britain and Ireland*, Oxford: Oxbow Books.

Regional and local identities in the later Neolithic of Scotland as reflected in the ceramic record

Ann MacSween

'...art evolves, like science, in a cumulative manner – but only for a while, and within limits, until all that can be done has been done along that particular line; at the great turning points, however, which initiate a new departure along a new line, we find bisociations in the grand style – cross-fertilization between different periods, cultures, and provinces of knowledge' Koestler (1964).

Introduction

This paper considers whether regional and local identities in the later Neolithic of Scotland can be traced in the ceramic record, using one type of pottery, Grooved Ware, as a case study. Some of the narratives that have developed to interpret the distribution of Grooved Ware in the farming communities of the later Neolithic of Scotland, for a millennium from around 3100 BC to 2200 BC, are also reviewed.

Grooved Ware was the first flat-based pottery in Great Britain and Ireland and its introduction followed a period of about a thousand years when round-based vessels were used (Gibson 2002, 83-4; Brindley 1999, 23; Sheridan 1995, 15). The typical Grooved Ware forms are bucket or barrel-shaped vessels, and more tub-shaped, 'open' vessels, designed to be stable on flat surfaces (Gibson 2002, 84). As its name suggests, incised grooves are a common decorative feature of Grooved Ware although applied cordons and impressed decoration are also part of the decorative repertoire (Figure 1). Grooved Ware is found in most parts of Great Britain and Ireland, in varying quantities, but not on the European Mainland. In Scotland it is recovered from house sites and ritual sites such as stone circles and henges, but not from the primary phases of chambered tombs.

The use of pottery to define regional and local identities

In commenting on the use of pottery to indicate local and regional identities, Gibson (2002, 25) has noted, 'This is not a new idea: pottery was one of the major artefact types used in Gordon Childe's concept of culture. As pottery changes over time and in parallel with other artefact types, so may it change regionally. These regional differences may indicate territorial identity and suggest the existence of cultural or even tribal systems'.

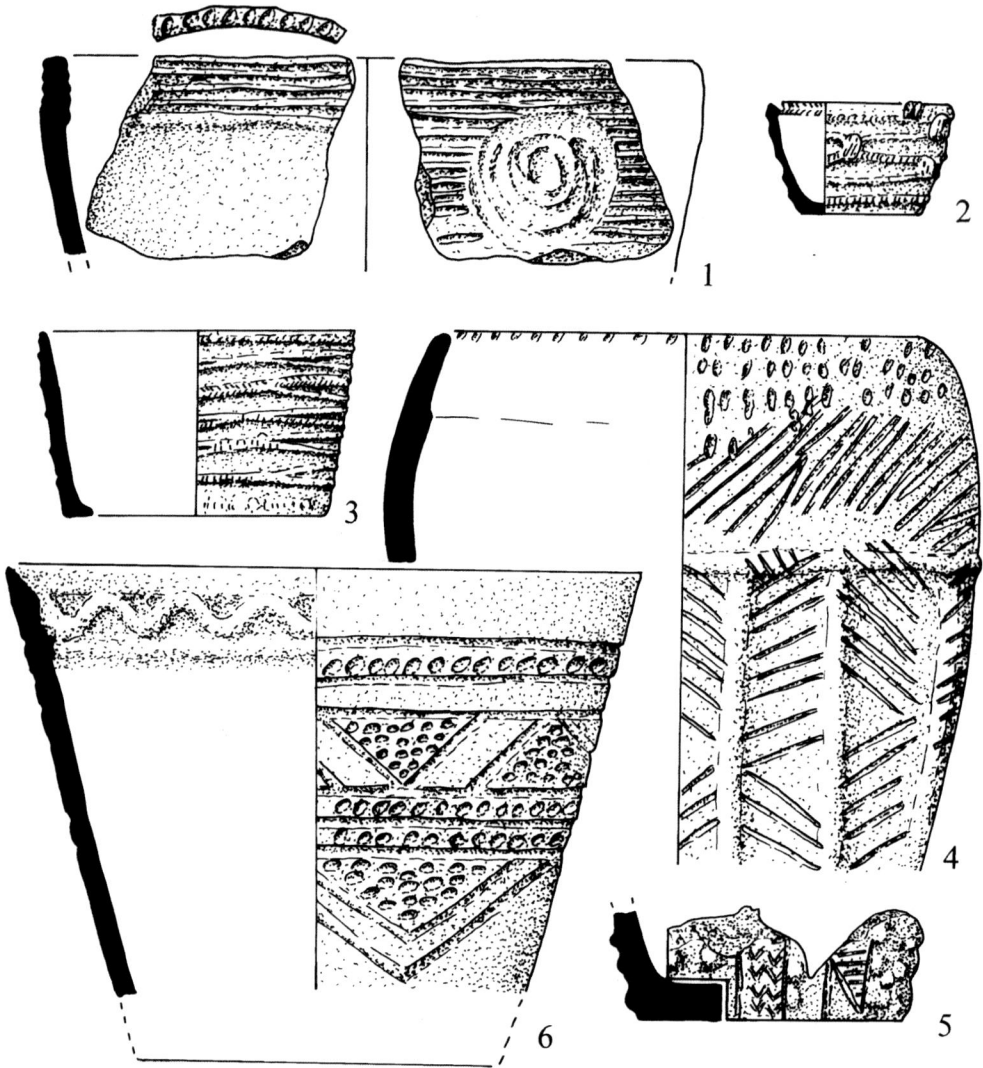

Figure 1. Grooved Ware from Britain and Ireland, (Gibson 2002 (illus 40)). 1. Durrington Walls, Wiltshire;
2. Woodlands, Wiltshire; 3. Balfarg, Fife; 4. Durrington Walls, Wiltshire; 5. Skara Brae, Orkney;
6. Clacton, Essex; 7. Newgrange, Co Meath; 8. Knowth, Co Meath

There are a number of reasons why pottery might be a useful indicator of regional and local identity in the Neolithic population of Scotland. Firstly, pottery is a common find from excavations of Neolithic sites. As the environmental conditions on the majority of sites are not favourable for the preservation of organic artefacts, pottery and stone tools represent the surviving material culture on many sites. Secondly, the manufacture of pottery is not restricted by the availability of materials. Most areas will have clays suitable for potting and material suitable for use as temper and studies of prehistoric pottery have shown that clays and temper were often collected locally (e.g. MacSween 2007A, 216-7). Thirdly, while not wishing to diminish the inherent challenges in making even a competent simple vessel, it is likely that the equipment and skills necessary for hand-building a pot would have been available to most communities. Fourthly, and importantly, pottery can be relatively easily adapted by its makers to take in changes in vessel shape and decoration, so the decision to adopt new fashions or to retain the existing shape and decoration will probably relate to some extent at least, to a deliberate choice by a potter or community (Rice 1984, 246-7). For these reasons, at the simplest level of interpretation, pottery can give an indication of the distribution of groups that made similar decisions in their choice of one aspect of their material culture, either through what they manufactured, or what they chose to acquire.

The Study of Grooved Ware

The choice of decoration

The elements and motifs that were combined to produce decorative patterns on Grooved Ware vessels have been studied in some detail (e.g. Wainwright and Longworth 1971a). They include horizontal parallel lines of twisted cord impressions and parallel incised lines on the inside of the rim, occasional use of grooved spirals and concentric circles, applied cordons (both plain and decorated), zoned decoration with combinations of chevrons, lozenges and triangles and the infilling of these with incised lines and dots, vertical panels separated with grooved lines or cordons, and impressed decoration. Many suggestions have been put forward to explain the patterns found on Grooved Ware. Lekky Shepherd's analysis of the motifs on the pottery from Skara Brae, Orkney (Shepherd 2000, 149), for example, includes the interpretation of some of the bands of decoration as representing hills (triangles) with the interface between land and sea represented by horizontal lines. She has also noted that some of the motifs have direct comparisons in nature, for example, the lozenge based decoration has parallels with the natural cleavage of the sandstone beds which outcrop around the Orkney Islands (ibid., 151).

A previous study of the Grooved Ware assemblages from Scotland (MacSween 1995), considered vessel shape, motifs and area of decoration, the portion of the vessel decorated, and the method of decoration. The available data suggested a common tradition indicated by the presence of a few vessel types in all areas of the country, with the remaining types perhaps indicating local variation. Bucket-shaped vessels with straight or inverted rims, decorated with incised multiple lines often forming vertical or horizontal zones of chevrons or lozenges are, for example, found throughout Scotland. So too are small squat vessels with applied cordon decoration arranged in linked horizontal bands or in elongated chevron patterns on smaller pots, covering much of the body, or a similar effect achieved by false relief rather than cordons (ibid.,

Figure 2. Tomb slab from Pierowall, Westray, Orkney. (Shepherd 2000)

42). Thus Grooved Ware can perhaps be thought of as having an overall 'syntax', evidenced in the repeated incidence of grooved chevron patterns, with possible indications of regional 'dialects', represented by geographically restricted decorative preferences. In addition, some of the motifs found on the pottery are repeated on a range of other media including burial chambers and portable stone objects, for example, the spiral motif found on the tomb slab from Pierowall, Westray in Orkney (Figure 2) (Shepherd 2000, 144, Figure 12.9), or the lozenge and triangle decoration found on a three-spiked stone object from Skara Brae (ibid., Figure 12.13j). This recurrence of motifs on architectural components and artefacts indicates that the motifs combined to form the patterns had a symbolic significance and would have held a meaning understood by those making and using the vessels.

This recurrence of decorative forms suggests an element of common identity or 'connectedness' from the north of Britain to the south. Cleal (1995, 1), for example, has noted that complex decorative motifs including spirals and applied lattices, have been found at opposite ends of the country, such as at Radley, in Oxfordshire and Pool on Sanday, Orkney (Figure 3).

Grooved Ware narratives

As with many areas of archaeological research, the way that Grooved Ware has been studied has influenced the narratives that have developed since it was first identified. In particular, the focus of the early identification and

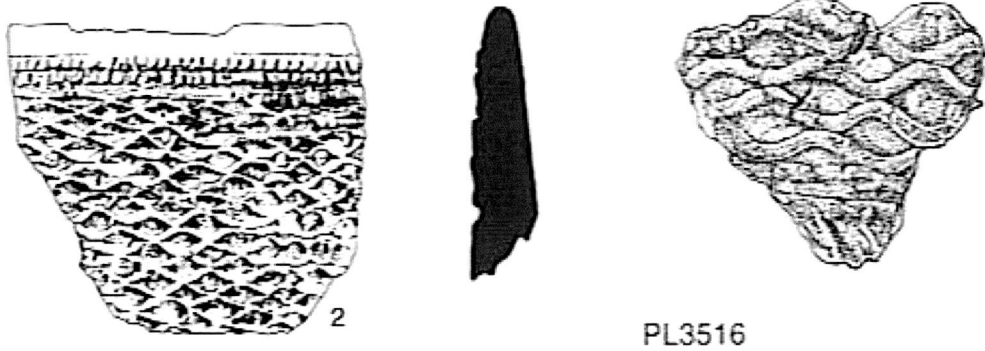

Figure 3. Pottery from Radley, Oxfordshire and Pool, Sanday, Orkney (Cleal XXXX, Hunter 2007)

study of Grooved Ware in the south of England led to the development of narratives which presupposed an origin and spread from south to north.

Grooved Ware was first defined by Stuart Piggott in 1936 in a review of the pottery from the Essex coast at Clacton (Warren *et al.* 1936). In his *The Neolithic Cultures of the British Isles* (1954) he defined Grooved Ware as a 'Secondary Neolithic Culture'. Smith (1956) split southern British Grooved Ware into three sub-styles – Clacton, Woodlands and Woodhenge. Grooved Ware was reassessed in the publication of the excavations at Durrington Walls in 1971, when Wainwright and Longworth defined four sub-styles of Grooved Ware – Woodland, Clacton, Durrington Walls and Rinyo. Smith (1974, 119) concluded that it was not possible to isolate a developmental sequence for Grooved Ware, nor were formative influences for any recognised class of pottery identifiable. Wainwright and Longworth's (1971a) four sub-styles have been reassessed by Paul Garwood (1999) who has suggested that Woodlands and Clacton may, in fact, be one sub-style and that most assemblages, at least in England, can be characterised as either Clacton-Woodlands, or Durrington Walls.

The Clacton-Woodlands sub-style is characterised by open tub-shaped forms, with zig-zag cordons arranged in chevron patterns and applied mesh being typical motifs (Garwood 1999, 157) and the Durrington Walls sub-style by bucket or barrel-shaped vessels, often decorated with raised vertical ribs with patterns between (ibid). Rinyo is characterised by a variety of decorative rims forms, including scalloped rims, and the use of plastic decoration including applied dots (Wainwright and Longworth 1971, 242-3).

This use of site names to describe pottery types, while a helpful shorthand, has a number of drawbacks. As well as implying origins and movement it also, even subconsciously connects the pottery to the character of activities being carried out at the type site. In the case of Grooved Ware, the two main pottery sub-styles, Woodlands and Durrington Walls, took their names from sites in the south of England, pits in the case of Woodlands, and a henge in the case of Durrington Walls, both in Wiltshire. As Kinnes (1985, 15) noted in his review of research on the Scottish Neolithic:

'It seems that Scottish prehistory depends upon a persistent sense of the marginal: geographically, culturally and economically. Perceptions are coloured by a recurrent need to derive innovation from without and then to resort to the parochial for explanation and understanding.'

He noted (ibid., 21-22) that while the potential for regional analysis of Grooved Ware existed, the low number of assemblages and the 'looseness of definitions' made this challenging and he called for more detailed study and classification. By 1999, enough new material had been published to allow Cleal (1999, 4-5), in her introduction to *Grooved Ware in Britain and Ireland*, to observe that some of the features which had been attributed to the three southern sub-styles owed more to a northern contribution than had previously been acknowledged. She noted that '...it is perhaps the 'northern-ness' of much, perhaps all, Grooved Ware that I am attempting to stress here and to point out that some of the features which we have recognised in the past as part of the well-defined southern three sub-styles are much more related to the less well defined (in the [Wainwright and Longworth] 1971 volume) Rinyo Grooved Ware than might appear....'.

Clarke (2004, 46) called for a greater range of narratives, more restricted than those dealing with regions, in particular narratives about local areas and individual sites, which would look to explain patterns in one region without requiring comparison with other regions. He noted that, for example, the artefact assemblages associated with Grooved Ware which developed in Orkney are not mirrored anywhere else in Britain (ibid., 52) and emphasised the need for multiple narratives to describe the differing uses of Grooved Ware throughout Britain.

Identification of regional groupings in Scotland

While the usefulness and relevance of the sub-styles to the Scottish material has been questioned (MacSween 1995), it became apparent with an increase in the assemblages available for study (MacSween 2007, 371) that much of the Scottish pottery, especially along the east coast, can be attributed to one of the two main sub-styles, either Clacton-Woodlands, such as the assemblage from Balfarg Riding School, Fife (Barclay and Russell-White 1993), or Durrington Walls, such as the assemblage from Littleour, Perthshire (Barclay and Maxwell, 1998). Not all assemblages, however, easily fit one of the sub-styles and suggestions of regional preferences can be detected. For example, tapered rims decorated with small incisions across the lip; incisions forming patterns with parallel horizontal lines and chevrons; the use of impressions to infill; and the occasional use of rim scalloping are found in the south-west of Scotland. These features are, for example, present on assemblages associated with the timber circle of Site 11, Machrie Moor, Arran (Haggarty 1992,85) and from Townhead, Bute as well as Knappers Farm, Dunbartonshire (Mackay 1950; Ritchie & Adamson 1981).

Thomas (1999, 114) questioned what the sub-styles represent and suggested that, rather than representing distinct ethnic or social groups, it is possible that the pottery with different sub-styles was used in different ways. He noted, for example, that roughly a quarter of Grooved Ware assemblages from the south of Britain combine elements of more than one sub-style. Some of Scotland's Grooved Ware assemblages, such as Balfarg, fit neatly into one sub-style, while others, including the assemblage from Raigmore near Inverness (Simpson 1996), are less easy to define in this way. In progressing our understanding of Grooved Ware substyles, we have to find some way of describing and accounting for assemblages which don't fit into one of the main sub-styles.

Interpretation

Distribution maps

When prehistorians move from site-based interpretations to look more widely at questions such as local and regional identities, the narratives that are constructed are often based on assessing patterns in the distribution of artefact and monument types across the country. The use of distribution maps to chart the extent of a certain material type is common. Brophy (2009, 7), in his recent paper *The map trap: the depiction of regional geographies of the Neolithic* delivered this health warning on use of this staple of many generations of prehistorians:

> 'It is precisely because we view distribution maps as reliable and inherently meaningful that they can be weak and biased methods of depicting patterns in the past.'

This certainly holds true for Grooved Ware. Figure 4 shows the distribution of Grooved Ware finds in Scotland as known in 1999. The distribution indicates that Grooved Ware is concentrated in the south and east of the country. An analysis of the focus of developer funded archaeology between 1990 and 2003 (Phillips and Bradley 2004) demonstrated that this too is concentrated in the south and east. It is likely, therefore, that the lack of Grooved Ware in the north-west of Scotland is at least in part due to the fact that relatively little developer-funded excavation has been carried out in that area.

Too much reliance on distribution maps can lead to the construction of overcomplicated explanations for artefact distributions. Cowie and MacSween (1999), for example, concluded that while very little Grooved Ware had been recovered in the north of Scotland, a few stray finds and reasonably diagnostic lithic material indicated that this might reflect the absence of excavation. In Grampian, however, where much more excavation had been undertaken, they argued that the absence of Grooved Ware was likely to be 'real' and suggested that the use of other media, such as carved stone balls, to carry symbols, negated the need for Grooved Ware. They also highlighted the virtual absence of henge monuments in north-east Scotland as another indication of regional distinctiveness.

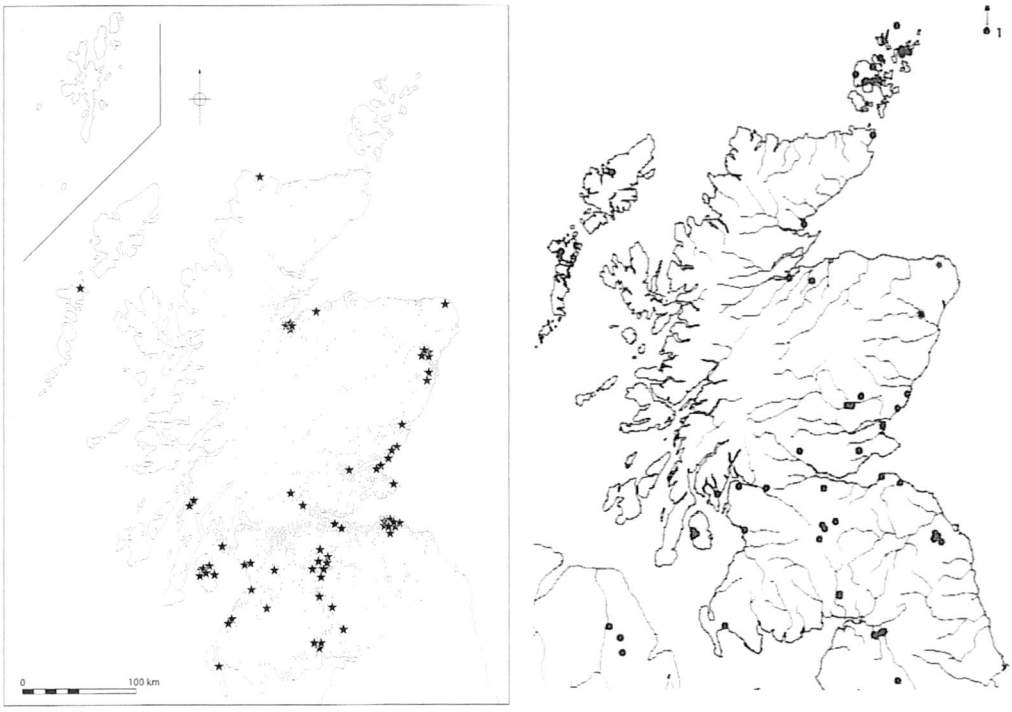

Figure 4. Distributions of developer-funded excavation 1990-2003 (Philips and Bradley 2004)
and Grooved Ware pottery (to be updated)

Recently, however, during excavations carried out at a cropmark site at Kintore, near Aberdeen, in advance of housing development, Clacton-Woodlands style Grooved Ware was recovered from three pits (Cook and Dunbar 2008, 181; MacSween 2008). Some aspects of the deposition indicated the special selection of sherds, a trait that has been noted from excavations the length of the country (Thomas 1999, 65). A further find of a single sherd of Grooved Ware was made around the same time, at Fordafourie, in the north-east extent of Aberdeenshire (Murray 2004). These finds have rendered the 'no grooved ware from the North-East' theory obsolete and there is now no region in Scotland where we can say that Grooved Ware is definitely absent.

The explanation for the distribution of Grooved Ware is not due solely to the increase in the amount of developer funded excavation. Previously, excavation of Neolithic sites in the North-East tended to concentrate on burial rather than domestic archaeology and this may be another reason for the lack of recovery of Grooved Ware in that area. This was also noted by Barclay (2004, 39) in reference to the distribution of known Neolithic sites in the lowlands of Scotland. In particular, he suggested that some sites excavated prior to development may not have been natural targets for research as they would not ordinarily have been found through terrestrial or aerial survey (Barclay 2004, 39).

As well as difficulties in interpreting the evidence 'gaps', a second major problem with distribution maps is that the distribution of find spots on a map does not account for the fact that, especially with a long-lived ceramic tradition such as Grooved Ware which was in use for over a thousand years, the distribution will not represent communities which were all in existence and making Grooved Ware at the same time. As Brophy (2009, 20) has observed, '...the points that we depict on maps have no temporal depth. They are situated in map space. Map space is both timeless and infinite...'.

Barclay (2009, 2) has argued that the key to interpreting distribution maps is to reach a more detailed understanding of the data, rather than relying on gross patterns. He has observed, 'as we learn more about the Neolithic, the use of broad-brush explanations becomes less sustainable...it has been strongly argued that material must be placed in its regional context before broader parallels are sought or a 'national' picture drawn' (Barclay 2009, 2). He counters this by proposing that, in looking in more detail at the deeper cultural influences, we must be careful not to replace 'national' prehistories with micro-regional approaches that underplay the very real shared traditions and complex relationships between regions.

Regional differences

There are, as yet, few regions in Scotland where the amount of material recovered is sufficient to warrant the kind of approach proposed by Barclay. One of those regions is Orkney, where there have been a number of large research excavations over the past 30 years, including Links of Noltland, Barnhouse, Pool and Skara Brae, and we are now reaching the point where there is enough material to make a micro-regional approach worthwhile. In Orkney, the tendency to rebuild over existing house sites (Hunter 2007, 6) produced long-lived sites with stratified sequences of pottery. For these sites, we can begin to look at how their pottery assemblages changed over time.

The recent publication of two Orcadian settlement sites excavated in the 1980s, Pool on the island of Sanday, excavated by John Hunter (Hunter 2007), and Barnhouse, on Orkney Mainland, excavated by Colin Richards (Richards 2005), has provided the opportunity to look in detail at two well contextualised Grooved Ware assemblages from the same region. The assemblages are large, Pool having over 10,000 sherds and Barnhouse having over 6,000 sherds. At both sites the excavations uncovered a number of houses which had been occupied over several centuries from around 3,100 to 2,900 BC (Ashmore 2005, 387). In terms of their usefulness for furthering our understanding of Grooved Ware, the excavations at Pool provided a well-stratified sequence and the chance to look in detail at how a Neolithic pottery assemblage changed over time (Hunter and MacSween 1991), while the large-scale excavations at Barnhouse provided an opportunity to assess how use of the pottery varied across the settlement.

Pool

The Grooved Ware from Pool derived from a series of rubbish tips which built up around structural features, forming a low mound. Three main phases of Neolithic pottery were identified. At the base of the mound (Phase 1), identified in just a small part of the excavated area, the assemblage was characterised by sandy fabrics. Although badly fragmented, some of the sherds could be classified as round-based Unstan Ware bowls. Phase 2 was split into three sub-phases. In phase 2.1, 37 vessels were identified, one of which was decorated with incised lines, though the pottery was too fragmented for vessel forms to be identified. In phase 2.2, 210 vessels were identified, and again only one was decorated. Much of the pottery was shell-tempered, and baggy vessels with small flat bases were identified as well as a number of vessels with straighter sides. By phase 2.3, decoration was being added to vessels otherwise similar in terms of fabric and vessel shape, the decorative elements including curved lines, chervons and dots. Clarke (2004, 51) was critical of the idea that Unstan Ware 'evolved' into Grooved Ware. 'Evolution' was not, however, suggested in the interpretation of the assemblage as the type of change observed at Pool was not a continuous linear process. What the Pool sequence indicates is, between Phases 1 and 2, a change in the shape of the vessels, with the fabric remaining the same, and then the form and fabric remaining the same with decoration being added, demonstrating a gradual change where the addition of a new decorative element to an established tradition of pottery manufacture was seen as important (Figure 5).

In the next settlement phase at Pool, Phase 3, which followed a break in occupation, the character of the assemblage had changed in terms of fabric, decoration and vessel shape. Flat-based, bucket-shaped vessels dominate and there are a variety of rim types, including scalloped and notched. The assemblage is mainly rock-tempered and decorated with applied motifs. Decoration is predominantly restricted to a band around the upper part of the vessel, often filled with incised or applied lines, but sometimes more complicated decorative forms such as trellis decoration or fish-scales is included.

This is important for the status of the 'Rinyo' sub-style, characterised by Wainwright and Longworth (1971a, 1971b) by its applied cordons and pellets and cordons with impressed dot decoration. Where Orcadian Grooved Ware has been recovered from vertical sequences in Orkney, such as at Pool, Skara Brae and Rinyo, the use of plastic decoration usually follows after the use of incised decoration and it is possible that the Rinyo sub-style was a local development from the earlier incised Grooved Ware.

Barnhouse

At Barnhouse the excavations uncovered a sequence of house construction around an open central area (Richards 2005, 29). In analysing the Barnhouse assemblage,

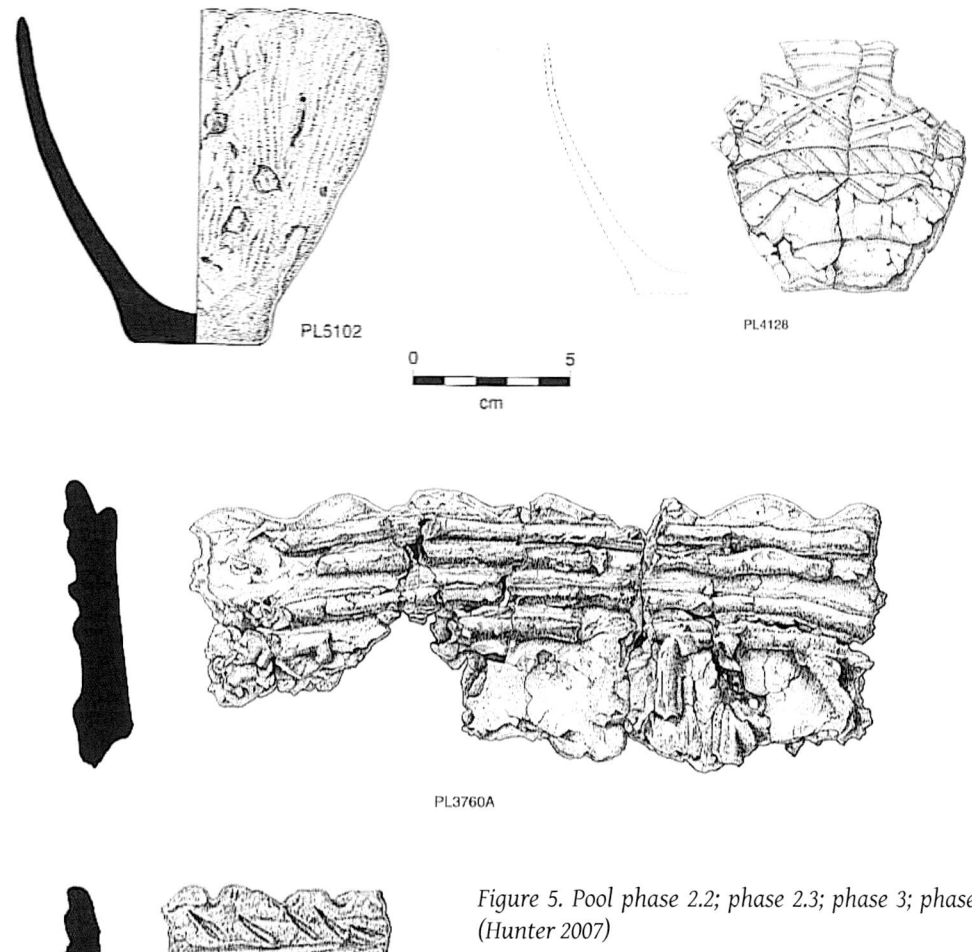

PL5102

PL4128

PL3760A

PL6327B

Figure 5. Pool phase 2.2; phase 2.3; phase 3; phase 3 (Hunter 2007)

Jones (2005, 281) noted that the houses around the central area contained shell temper while those around the periphery had either shell or rock temper, and suggested that the shell-tempered pottery was made communally in the central area (ibid., 282). He also suggested that the rock-tempered pottery may have been made by individual households and that each house had its own particular recipe. Some decorative schemes were used throughout the village, while others were specific to individual households. It appears that at Barnhouse fabric and decoration were used both to express shared identity but also to emphasise differences between the users of different pottery forms and perhaps also the functions of the buildings where they were used.

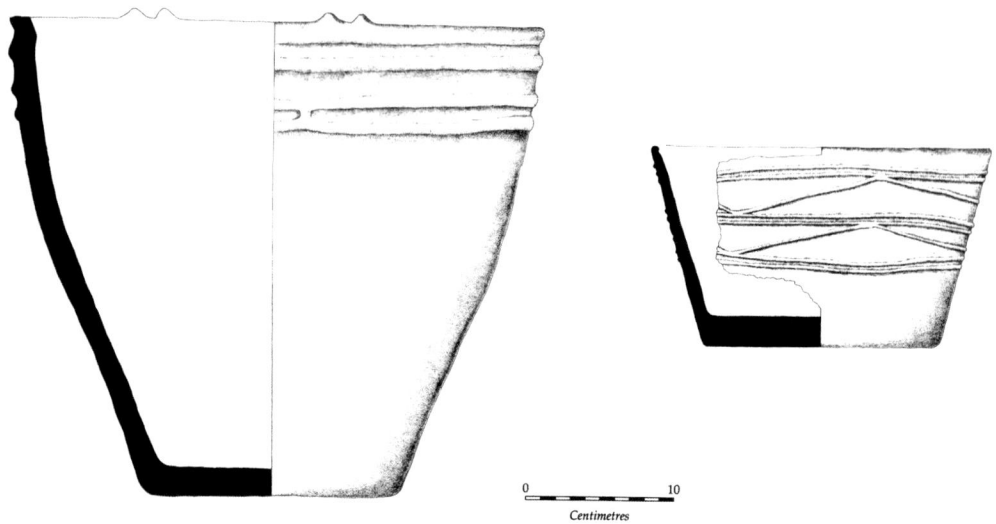

0   10
Centimetres

Figure 6. Pottery from Barnhouse (Richards 2005)

The Barnhouse study highlights an observation often made in relation to Grooved Ware which is that individual communities used Grooved Ware in different ways (Cleal 1999). Different vessel shape or decoration could, for example, be related to the function of the vessels, or the status of the user. The indications from published excavations of Orcadian sites is that there was a considerable amount of variation in the combinations of vessel shape, fabric, and decorative choices even within a small area, but also some close parallels between assemblages. The applied decorated assemblage from Pool, for example, has close parallels with the Links of Noltland assemblage (Sheridan 1999, 123), whereas some elements of the Barnhouse assemblage, such as the pottery from House 6 with its tub-shaped vessels and wavy lines in false relief (Richards 2005, 101, Figure 4.61) is more similar to 'classic' Woodlands-Clacton forms (Figure 6).

Dating

Analysis of the C14 dates for the Grooved Ware from the south and east of Scotland (MacSween 2007) adopted the approach taken by Garwood (1999) in his analysis of the English Grooved Ware dates which was to include only dates derived from charcoal from short-lived species from the same context as the pottery. Analysis of the Scottish Grooved Ware dates from mainland Scotland show one early date of 3,340-3,020 BC for pottery from a pit at Milton of Leys near Inverness (Conolly and MacSween 1999), a batch of dates centred at around the turn of the millennium, namely Kintore in Aberdeenshire (Cook and Dunbar 2008), Balfarg Riding School in Fife (Barclay and Russell-White 1993), Beckton Farm (Pollard 1997) and Hillend (Armit et al 1994) in the South-West, and a slightly later batch comprising dates from Kintore, Littleour (Barclay and Maxwell 1998), Balfarg Riding School (Mercer 1981) and Beckton Farm.

Ashmore (Ashmore and MacSween 1998, 145), in considering the available dates from Orkney concluded that Barnhouse and Skara Brae were probably settled from around 3,100 BC, from which it could be implied that the earliest Grooved Ware in Scotland is from the north of the country. A recent analysis of the available dates from Orkney using Bayesian modelling concluded that the use of Grooved Ware in Orkney probably preceded c3100BC but by how much is difficult to assess (Schulting at al 2010, 38). The date from Milton of Leys near Inverness hints that we can expect similarly early dates from the northern mainland. At the other end of the date range, most of the available Grooved Ware dates precede the generally accepted date of around 2,500BC for the beginning of Beaker use in Britain (MacSween 2007).

The emerging narrative

Barclay (2009, 2) has suggested that we look carefully at the available data and understand the regional patterns in detail before using them as the basis for broad-brush explanations, and Clarke (2004, 46) has issued similar warnings about 'pick and mix' archaeology. The provision of wider frameworks is, however, also important, to provide a national, regional and local context for the interpretation of new material, for example for the small numbers of sherds from watching briefs and evaluations. For Grooved Ware use in Scotland, the national picture for Grooved Ware could perhaps be summarised as follows (Figure 7):

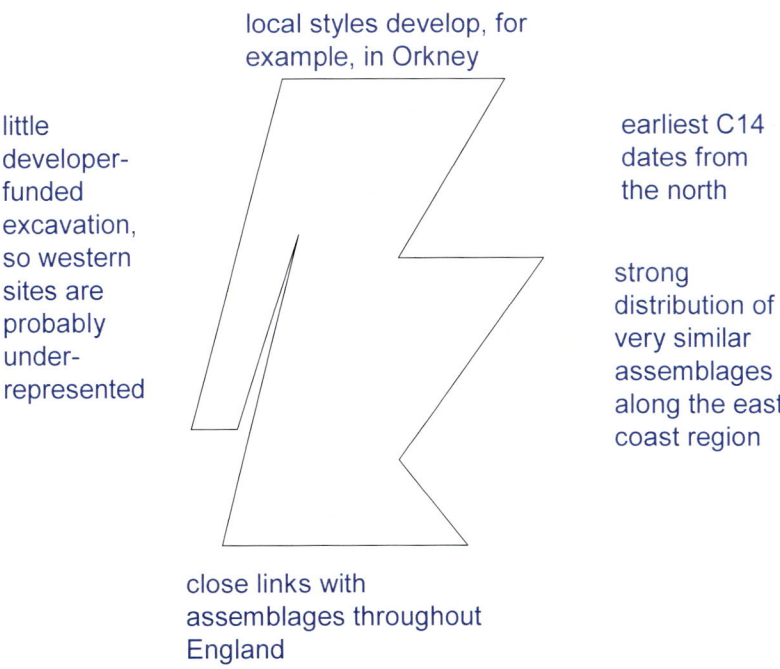

local styles develop, for example, in Orkney

little developer-funded excavation, so western sites are probably under-represented

earliest C14 dates from the north

strong distribution of very similar assemblages along the east coast region

close links with assemblages throughout England

Figure 7. Grooved Ware themes and issues

In the later Neolithic, apparently in all parts of Britain and Ireland, a new style of pottery known as Grooved Ware and characterised by a variety of well-defined decorative forms, has been recognised. The similarities in this material is most obvious along the east coast where open tub-shaped forms decorated by zig-zag cordons arranged in chevron patterns dominate, although bucket-shaped vessels with decoration arranged vertically are also common. Along the west coast of Scotland, there are similarities in the preference for vessel styles between that area and the east coast of Ireland. Assemblages which include a wider range of motifs and patterning may represent the development of regional styles, indicating local expression and preference within the confines of a commonly understood range of motifs.

In addition to domestic sites, Grooved Ware has been found in chambered tombs, although not in a primary context. It has also been found at henges and stone circles, but associated with different points in their development and, therefore, not necessarily linked to the spread of those types of site. The number of these associations is, at least in part, a result of research projects focussing on monumental sites. In areas with a high level of developer funded archaeology there has been a substantial increase in the number of sites containing Grooved Ware, particularly associated with possible domestic contexts. Conversely, where there has been little developer funded archaeology, for example, in the western highlands and islands, Grooved Ware is probably under-represented. A typical context for this pottery is in pits and the deposition within these sometimes indicates the special selection of sherds. The dates for the north of the country are so far the earliest; however, there are relatively few dates and more dates for pottery in primary contexts will be important in advancing our understanding of Grooved Ware use in Great Britain and Ireland.

The question of identity

To return to the question of whether regional and local identities can be recognised within the Neolithic of Scotland from the ceramic record, it seems that, while Grooved Ware was used over much of Britain, regional preferences varied greatly and within regions individual communities using Grooved Ware had their own strong site-based identities, within a wider regional framework. Through detailed work on some large assemblages, including Barnhouse (Jones 2005), we are beginning to understand how complex these relationships were. How Grooved Ware came to be used across the country in a relatively short time is a more complex question and one which needs to be considered in the context of both finds and monuments (Brophy 2006).

This process is beginning. Sheridan (2004, 32), for example, has highlighted the scatter of Grooved Ware finds and of circles of timber and stone along the western fringe of Scotland from Lewis to Arran and has suggested that the spread of both occurred around 3000 BC. She concludes that 'the use of Grooved Ware and of 'open air' ceremonial structures is likely to have resulted from links with Orkney....[and this] offers a simple and plausible explanation for the observed changes in Ireland' (Sheridan 2004, 32). The ongoing excavations at the extensive complex of buildings at Ness of Brodgar, Orkney, are providing further evidence for the importance of this area as a focus for ceremony in the late Neolithic (Card 2011).

Thomas (2009) has suggested that Grooved Ware and its associated domestic architecture, originating in the north of Scotland, was used to establish an imagined community through the practices in which artefacts and architecture were made, used, consumed and ultimately remembered. The result was that commonalities with people living far away and continuities with past generations were seen as important and in this way the Grooved Ware community extended across space and time (Thomas 2009, 12).

As yet, there is no evidence from the analysis of pottery fabrics which indicates the long-distance movement of Grooved Ware vessels. It seems more likely that Grooved Ware use spread because someone in a community had either seen or used Grooved Ware and decided to encourage their social group to use it, or by the movement of individuals or communities that used Grooved Ware, '...networks involving movements of ideas, objects and people, of exchange and obligation' Brophy (2006, 38). Thomas (1999, 117) has noted that while Grooved Ware was one of the most formal 'material languages' of prehistoric Britain, the way in which it was used lay in the 'objectification of difference' and that is, perhaps, what makes it so difficult to categorise through studying its stylistic variation, context and distribution. At any one time, ideas were being exchanged, absorbed and translated. Local communities being introduced to Grooved Ware could choose to ignore it, adopt it, or modify it.

What is striking is that, even with all the opportunity for change over the time that Grooved Ware was in use, the common elements of its decorative repertoire were maintained throughout. As indicated above, the use of these elements on other media indicates a symbolic significance and strengthens the argument for a shared identity of its users. Given the variation in the way it was used, it can be suggested that, if its use represents a shared identity, this was perhaps similar to the way in which identity is shared through language - understood by all its users at a basic level, its regional diversity acknowledged widely, but its dialects only properly understood and appreciated locally.

Dedication

This paper is dedicated to the memory of Jenny Shiels, colleague, friend and fellow pottery enthusiast.

Acknowledgements

I would like to thank the conference organisers for inviting me to contribute and Louisa Campbell for being an extremely patient editor. The paper includes material delivered at a session on Grooved Ware organised by Ian Heath at the Theoretical Archaeology Group conference in Southampton in December 2008. Both that session and the Nationalism and Identity Conference provided an impetus for me to update my knowledge of Grooved Ware from Scotland, and think some more about its interpretation. Thanks also to those who discussed elements of this en route especially Jim Killgore, Anne Crone, Aonghus MacKechnie, Alison Sheridan...

Bibliography

Armit, I, T. Cowie and I. Ralston 1994. Excavation of pits containing Grooved Ware at Hillend, Clydesdale District, Strathclyde Region, *Proceedings of the Society of Antiquaries of Scotland* 124, 113-27.

Ashmore, P. 2005. Dating Barnhouse, in C. Richards *Dwelling among the monuments: the Neolithic Village of Barnhouse, Maeshowe Passage Grave and Surrounding Monuments at Stenness, Orkney.* 385-88. (McDonald Institute Monographs) Cambridge: McDonald Institute for Archaeological Research.

Ashmore, P.J. and A. MacSween 1998. Radiocarbon dates for settlements, tombs and settlement sites with Grooved Ware in Scotland, in A. Gibson and D. D. A. Simpson (eds) *Prehistoric Ritual and Religion*, 139-47. Stroud: Sutton.

Barclay, G. 2009. Introduction: a regional agenda? in K. Brophy and G. Barclay (eds) *Defining a Regional Neolithic: The Evidence from Britain and Ireland*, 1-4. Oxford: Oxbow Books.

Barclay, J.G. 2004. '...Scotland cannot have been an inviting country for agricultural settlement': a history of the Neolithic of Scotland, in I. A. Shepherd and G. J. Barclay (eds) *Scotland in Ancient Europe: The Neolithic and Early Bronze Age of Scotland in their European Context*, 31-44. Edinburgh: Society of Antiquaries of Scotland.

Barclay, J.G. and G.S. Maxwell 1998. *The Cleaven Dyke and Littleour: Monuments in the Neolithic of Tayside.* Edinburgh. Society of Antiquaries of Scotland Monograph 13.

Barclay, J.G. and C.J. Russell-White 1993. Excavations in the ceremonial complex of the fourth to second millennium BC at Balfarg/Balbirnie, Glenrothes, Fife, *Proceedings of the Society of Antiquaries of Scotland* 123, 43-210.

Brindley, A. 1999a. Irish Grooved Ware, in R. Cleal and A. MacSween (eds) *Grooved Ware in Britain and Ireland*, 23-34. Oxford: Oxbow Books, Neolithic Studies Group Seminar Papers 3.

Brophy, K. 2009. The map trap: the depiction of regional geographies of the Neolithic, in K. Brophy and G. Barclay (eds) *Defining a Regional Neolithic: The Evidence from Britain and Ireland*, 5-25. Oxford: Oxbow Books.

Brophy, K. 2006. Rethinking Scotland's Neolithic, *Proceedings of the Society of Antiquaries of Scotland* 136, 7-46.

Card, N. 2011. 'Ness of Brodgar', *Discovery and Excavation in Scotland* New Series Vol 11 (2010), 129-30.

Clarke, D.V. 2004. The construction of narratives for Neolithic Scotland, in I. A. Shepherd and G. J. Barclay (eds) *Scotland in Ancient Europe: The Neolithic and Early Bronze Age of Scotland in their European Context*, 45-53. Edinburgh: Society of Antiquaries of Scotland.

Cleal, R. 1999. Introduction: The What, Where, When and Why of Grooved Ware, in R. Cleal and A. MacSween (eds) *Grooved Ware in Britain and Ireland*, 1-8. Oxford: Oxbow Books, Neolithic Studies Group Seminar Papers 3.

Cleal, R. and A. MacSween (eds) 1999. *Grooved Ware in Britain and Ireland*. Oxford: Oxbow Books, Neolithic Studies Group Seminar Papers 3.

Conolly, R. and A. MacSween (eds) 2003. A possible Neolithic settlement at Milton of Leys, Inverness, *Proceedings of the Society of Antiquaries of Scotland* 133, 35-46.

Cook, M. and L. Dunbar 2008. *Rituals, Roundhouses and Romans: Excavations at Kintore, Aberdeenshire, 2000-2006: Volume 1 Forest Road*. Edinburgh: Scottish Trust for Archaeological Research, Monograph 8.

Cowie, T.G. and A. MacSween 1999. Grooved Ware from Scotland: a review, in R. Cleal and A. MacSween (eds) 1999. *Grooved Ware in Britain and Ireland*, 48-56. Oxford: Oxbow Books, Neolithic Studies Group Seminar Papers 3.

Garwood, P. 1999. Grooved Ware in Southern Britain: Chronology and Interpretation, in R. Cleal and A. MacSween (eds) 1999 *Grooved Ware in Britain and Ireland*, 145-76. Oxford: Oxbow Books, Neolithic Studies Group Seminar Papers 3.

Gibson, A. 2002. *Prehistoric Pottery in Britain and Ireland*. Stroud: Tempus Publishing Ltd.

Haggarty, A. 1991. Machrie Moor, Arran: recent excavations at two stone circles, *Proceedings of the Society of Antiquaries of Scotland* 121, 51-94.

Hunter, J. (ed.) 2007 *Investigations in Sanday, Orkney: Vol 1: Excavations at Pool, Sanday*. Orkney: The Orcadian Ltd.

Hunter, J. and A. MacSween 1991. A sequence for the Orcadian Neolithic?, *Antiquity* 65, 911-14.

Jones, A. 1997. Ceramics, in T. Pollard 1997 Excavation of a Neolithic settlement and ritual complex at Beckton Farm, Lockerbie, Dumfries & Galloway, *Proceedings of the Society of Antiquaries of Scotland* 127, 89-96.

Jones, A. 2005. The Grooved Ware from Barnhouse, in C. Richards *Dwelling among the monuments: the Neolithic Village of Barnhouse, Maeshowe Passage Grave and Surrounding Monuments at Stenness, Orkney*. 261-82. (McDonald Institute Monographs) Cambridge: McDonald Institute for Archaeological Research.

Kinnes I.A. 1985. Circumstance not context: the Neolithic of Scotland as seen from outside, *Proceedings of the Society of Antiquaries of Scotland* 115, 15-57.

Koestler, A. 1964. *The Act of Creation*. London: Pan Books Ltd (1975 edn.)

Mackay, R.R. 1950. Grooved Ware from Knappers Farm, near Glasgow, and from Townhead, Rothesay, *Proceedings of the Society of Antiquaries of Scotland* 84, 180-4.

MacSween, A. 1995. Grooved Ware from Scotland: aspects of decoration, in I. Kinnes. and G. Varndell 1995 *'Unbaked urns of rudely shape': Essays on British and Irish Pottery for Ian Longworth*, 41-48. Oxford: Oxbow Monograph 55.

MacSween, A. 2007. The Meldon Bridge Period: The Pottery from South and East Scotland Twenty Years On, in C. Burgess, P. Topping and F. Lynch (eds) *Beyond Stonehenge: Essays on the Bronze Age in honour of Colin Burgess,* 367-76. Oxford: Oxbow Books, 367-376.

MacSween, A. 2007. The Pottery, in J. Hunter (ed.) 2007 *Investigations in Sanday, Orkney: Vol 1: Excavations at Pool, Sanday*, 287-346. Orkney: The Orcadian Ltd.

MacSween, A. 2008. The Prehistoric Pottery, in M. Cook and L. Dunbar *Rituals, Roundhouses and Romans: Excavations at Kintore, Aberdeenshire 2000-2006, volume 1: Forest Road*, 173-89. Edinburgh: Scottish Trust for Archaeological Research.

Mercer, R. 1981. 'The excavation of a late Neolithic henge-type enclosure at Balfarg, Markinch, Fife', *Proceedings of the Society of Antiquaries of Scotland* 111, 63-171.

Murray, J.C. 2004. *Discovery and Excavation in Scotland* New Series Vol 4 (2003), 18.

Phillips, T. and R. Bradley 2004 Developer-funded fieldwork in Scotland, 1990-2003: an overview of the prehistoric evidence, *Proceedings of the Society of Antiquaries of Scotland* 134, 17-51.

Piggott, S. 1954. *Neolithic Cultures of the British Isles*. Cambridge: Cambridge University Press.

Pollard, T. 1997. 'Excavation of a Neolithic settlement and ritual complex at Beckton Farm, Lockerbie, Dumfries and Galloway', *Proceedings of the Society of Antiquaries of Scotland*, 69-121.

Richards, C. 2005. *Dwelling among the monuments: the Neolithic Village of Barnhouse, Maeshowe Passage Grave and Surrounding Monuments at Stenness, Orkney*. (McDonald Institute Monographs) Cambridge: McDonald Institute for Archaeological Research.

Rice, P.M. 1984. 'Change and conservatism in pottery-producing systems', in Van der Leeuw, S.E. and Pritchard, A.C. (eds) *The many dimensions of pottery*. Amsterdam (Universiteit van Amsterdam) 231-88.

Ritchie, J.N.G. and H.C. Adamson 1981. Knappers, Dunbartonshire: a reassessment, *Proceedings of the Society of Antiquaries of Scotland* 111, 172-204.

Schulting, R., A.S. Sheridan, R. Crozier and E. Murphy 2010 'Revisiting Quanterness: new AMS dates and stable isotope data from an Orcadian chamber tomb', *Proceedings of the Society of Antiquaries of Scotland* 140 (2010), 1-50.

Shepherd, A. 2000. Skara Brae: expressing identity in a Neolithic community, in A. Ritchie (ed.) *Neolithic Orkney in its European Context*, (McDonald Institute Monographs). Cambridge: McDonald Institute for Archaeological Research, 139-58.

Shepherd, I.A. and G.J. Barclay 2004 *Scotland in Ancient Europe: The Neolithic and Early Bronze Age of Scotland in their European Context*. Edinburgh: Society of Antiquaries of Scotland.

Sheridan, A. S. 1995. Irish Neolithic pottery: the story in 1995, in I. Kinnes and G. Varndell (eds) *'Unbaked urns of rudely shape': Essays on British and Irish Pottery for Ian Longworth*, 3-21. Oxford: Oxbow Monograph 55.

Sheridan, A.S. 1999. 'Grooved Ware from the Links of Noltland, Westray, Orkney', in R. Cleal and A. MacSween (eds) 1999 *Grooved Ware in Britain and Ireland,* 112-24. Oxford: Oxbow Books, Neolithic Studies Group Seminar Papers 3.

Sheridan, A.S. 2004. Going round in circles? Understanding the Irish Grooved Ware 'complex' in its wider context, in H. Roche, E. Grogan, J. Bradley, J. Coles and B. Raftery (eds) *From Megaliths to Metals: Essays in honour of George Eogan*, 25-36. Oxford: Oxbow Books.

Simpson, D.D.A. 1996. Excavation of a kerbed funerary monument at Stoneyfield, Raigmore, Inverness, Highland, 1972-3, *Proceedings of the Society of Antiquaries of Scotland* 126, 53-86.

Smith, I.F. 1956. The Decorative Art of Neolithic Ceramics in S. E. England and its Relations. Unpublished PhD thesis, London: University of London.

Smith, I.F. 1974. The Neolithic, in C. Renfrew (ed.) *British Prehistory: a new outline*, 100-36. London: Duckworth, second impression 1976.

Thomas, J.S. 1999. *Understanding the Neolithic*. London: Routledge.

Thomas, J.S. 2009. The return of the Rinyo-Clacton Folk? The Cultural Significance of the Grooved Ware Complex in Later Neolithic Britain, *Cambridge Archaeological Journal* 20:1, 1-15.

Van der Leeuw, S.E. and A.C. Pritchard (eds) 1984. *The many dimensions of pottery*. Amsterdam (Universiteit van Amsterdam).

Wainwright, G.J. and I.H. Longworth 1971a. The Rinyo-Clacton Culture reconsidered, in G.J. Wainwright with I.H. Longworth (eds) *Durrington Walls: Excavations 1966-1968*, 235-306. Rep Res Comm Soc Antiquaries London No 29.

Wainwright, G.J. and I.H. Longworth 1971b. *Durrington Walls: Excavations 1966-1968*, Rep Res Comm Soc Antiquaries London No 29.

Warren, S.H., S. Piggott, J.G.D. Clark, M.C. Burkitt and H.M.E. Godwin 1936. Archaeology of the submerged land surface of the Essex coast, *Proceedings of the Prehistoric Society* 2, 178-210.

Culture contact and the maintenance of cultural identity in Roman Scotland: A theoretical approach

Louisa Campbell

Introduction

In common with discussions of Neolithic Scotland (see Brophy, this volume), northern Britain has often been considered a peripheral region in Roman period studies - a marginal wilderness occupied by uncivilised, dispossessed 'barbarian' warriors (Ferris 2000) who wandered naked across the barren, inhospitable, disembodied landscape. Such concepts have been perpetuated by imperialist stances (Slofstra 1983) and an inherent reluctance on the part of Roman period archaeologists to dip their toes into the perceived murky depths of social theories. This paper seeks to re-balance the research equilibrium by proposing a theoretically informed interpretive framework for assessing the impact Roman intrusion may, or may not, have had upon the existing population of the region.

It is necessary at this early stage to highlight the negative and potentially derogatory connotations inherent in the term 'native' and its use will, therefore, be deliberately avoided herein. Iron Age societies in contact with Rome are often discussed as 'native' people (e.g. Hunter 2009), but the use of binary terms such as conquerer:conquered or Roman:native has come under heavy criticism (van Dommelen 2001). More recent approaches attempt to understand local influences and regional variability in cultural change, incorporating aspects of agency (Dobres and Robb 2000), resistance (van Dommelen 1998), adaptive practices and the accommodation of foreign objects (Lucas 2001, 51) in a culturally relevant manner (Appadurai 1986; Thomas 1991; Campbell 2011). These are critical concepts in any attempt to understand societies interfacing (Collins 2008) with the Empire.

Rome's Northern Campaigns

There is not the space here to fully document the Roman campaigns and phases of occupation of Scotland, nor the detailed debate involved, which has been eloquently summarised by numerous authors (e.g. Breeze 2007). However, a tabular summary of the consensus view, incorporating the work of Hodgson (1995) and Millett (2000), as well as Swan's (1999) suggested ceramic evidence, is provided in Table 1 for ease of reference to periods of occupation and associated terminology. The evidence confirms two main, but relatively brief (Hanson 2003), periods of Roman occupation following campaign and conquest and one aborted attempt at conquest, followed by occasional punitive campaigns in northern Britain.

AD 77-78	Agricola consolidated northern England and advanced north.
A 79-82	Agricola commenced his Scottish campaigns and reached the Tay.
AD 83	The battle of Mons Graupius signified completion of Agricola's campaign.
AD 87-105	Roman troops withdrew to the Tyne-Solway isthmus, Agricola departed Britain and troops were transferred to the Danube.
AD 122	Military disturbances brought the Emperor Hadrian to Britain and he commissioned the construction of Hadrian's Wall across the Tyne-Solway isthmus.
AD 139-142	Antoninus Pius ordered the abandonment of Hadrian's Wall and advanced north to Scotland. He commissioned the construction of the Antonine Wall across the Clyde-Forth isthmus.
AD 142-149	Construction of the Antonine Wall was completed.
AD 149-150+	Some troops returned from Mauretania and layout of the Antonine Wall and some forts was revised, some were partitioned to make annexes (eg Bearsden).
AD 158+	The decision to abandon the Antonine Wall was taken and a refurbishment of Hadrian's Wall commenced. Gradual run-down and dismantling of forts on the Antonine Wall.
AD 164-167/8	Old Kilpatrick fort was demolished to complete the decommissioning of the Antonine Wall.
AD 196-197	Clodius Albinus, Governor of Britain took troops from Britain to battle the Emperor Severus outside Lyon. Severus emerged victorious and separated Britain into two provinces, Upper and Lower Britannia.
AD 197	The Maetae and Caledonians broke a peace treaty with Rome and instigated war in the North. Due to troubles elsewhere the Maeatae were bribed to peace.
AD 208-211	More troubles brought the Emperor Severus and his sons, Geta and Caracalla, to Britain and they campaigned in Scotland. Severus died in York and his sons abandoned the northern territories.
AD 305-306	Co-Emperor Constantius conducted a campaign in Scotland with his son, Constantine. They reached the far north of Scotland before Constantius died at York.
AD 360	Troops were transferred to Britain to deal with the Scots and Picts.
AD 364	'Barbarian' raids by Picts, Scots and Saxons are recorded.
AD 367-368	A concerted attack by 'barbarians' de-stabilised the province and order was finally restored after a major campaign by Count Theodosius.
AD 369-399	General Stilicho undertook expedition against the 'barbarians' in Britain, restoring peace.

Table 1. Periods of occupation

A rich corpus of evidence, including Classical manuscripts, well-preserved epigraphic evidence, standing remains, material culture and intensive programmes of aerial reconnaissance, contributes to current understanding of Rome's northern campaigns (Keppie 1998; 2004). However, these sources are heavily Romanocentric in character and shed very little light on the experiences of the indigenous population. While Tacitus (*Agricola*) provides the most detailed and relatively contemporaneous version of events, his fragmentarily surviving account is propagandist in character, having been written for a Roman readership, and is a heavily biased veneration of his father-in-law, Agricola (Hanson 1991). Some recent commentators have even suggested that the whole account was a fabrication (Hoffmann 2004), though this rather overstates the situation.

Other accounts, for example Dio Cassius (*History of Rome*, 76), Herodian (*History of Rome*, 3) and Ammianus (*XXVII),* are non-contemporaneous, largely unsubstantiated by other sources and heavily reliant on earlier accounts (Breeze 1988), such as Tacitus and Caesar (*De Bello Gallico,* Book V, 14). Ptolemy's (*Geographia*) record of tribal boundaries and incorrect 90°bending of Scotland has caused considerable problems in correlating his locations with modern geography (Strange 1997). For example, uncertainty surrounds whether his assigned place-names refer to Roman or indigenous places (Watson 1929; Richmond 1958; Mann and Breeze 1987; Barrow 1989; Breeze 2002). This serves as a reminder that caution must be exercised when considering the evidence of ancient historiographers (Hanson and Breeze 1991, 58).

Though the reasons for Rome's failure to conquer Scotland (Breeze 1988) remain elusive, fierce resistance combined with a less than favourable climatic environment and mountainous terrain may have contributed to a lack of success in subduing the northern peoples. While a combination of the move to lands far removed from the heart of Empire (Keppie 1989, 72-5); troubles elsewhere resulting in a failure to capitalise on Roman victories; a lack of economic bounty and the combative character of northerners (Breeze 1988, 20) as well as a different trajectory in socio-politico-economic conditions (Hanson 2002, 839) probably further contributed to the lack of Roman success and eventual withdrawal from the region.

The common thread woven through past academic enquiries is a focus upon Roman experiences of events in northern Britain; however, they do not enlighten us on local perspectives - for those we must turn to the archaeological record.

Iron Age Society

The primary historical sources are frustratingly sparse on the subject of the character and political organisation of northern societies. However, all of the known accounts evoke a similar picture of competitive, highly skilled and ferocious warrior chiefdoms, social amalgamation and a democratic process of electing the most accomplished warriors as rulers, not unlike that proposed for some northern Gaulish warrior societies (Roymans 1995; 1996). Such propagandist rhetoric is commonly applied to 'barbarian' enemies of Rome (Breeze 1988, 6), a stereotypical image perpetuated through Roman art and literature to define and reinforce Rome's position in the world (Ferris 2000, 188).

Dio Cassius (*History of Rome*, 76) proposes the northerners as transient democratic groups living naked in tents and relying on livestock for subsistence while ignoring bountiful aquatic resources. However, it is easy to demonstrate the unreliability of these anthropological observations by reference to the archaeological data of sophisticated personal ornaments (e.g. Allason-Jones 1995) and elaborate structures (e.g. Main 1998) attested across the region during the early Iron Age.

Somewhat surprisingly, two opposing social models have simultaneously co-existed in academic discussions of northern Britain. The first recognises that an absence of existing infrastructures and elites to accommodate and control Roman administrative systems in the region (Clarke 1958, 42) may have restricted Roman expansion (Hanson 2002). At the same time, an unchallenged acceptance of social amalgamation and the emergence of elites (Watkins 1984, 73; Armit 1999, 583) who relied on Rome to bolster their status (Armit and Ralston 2003, 183) by restricting access to Roman exotica (Macinnes 1984) continues to permeate academic discourse of the region (e.g. Hunter 2009). These elites are said to have manipulated Roman material culture in conspicuous consumption practices (Hunter 1997, 121) to bolster their position after Roman withdrawal had resulted in a state of political fragmentation (Armit and Ralston 2003, 183). While major internal social and political changes are proposed as having led to the emergence of new power groups in the 3rd and 4th C at a time of stress, rather than amalgamation of numerous groups against Rome (Armit 1999; Hunter 2005, 238-9).

I would suggest that this latter stance stems from a basically Marxist approach (e.g. Renfrew 1982) to social structures. It imposes a modern, Westernised, hierarchical and social evolutionary (Giddens 1984) framework onto ancient societies and fails to recognise the conscious choices for action of all participants in events or the complex, situational and variable extent of contact between representatives of Rome and the inhabitants of northern Britain. The following section proposes a theoretical framework from which to consider these issues in the context of the territorial expansionist policies of Rome.

'Romanisation'

As a first step, the concept of Romanisation (Haverfield 1912), a model which is deeply ingrained within Roman studies and dominated academia for more than 60 years, requires to be addressed. The Romanisation paradigm interprets Roman material culture recovered from Iron Age contexts as signifying recipients who were embracing

Roman cultural values. Largely driven by contemporary British imperialism and an over-reliance upon exclusively Roman historical accounts, this perspective has been propagated by the reluctance of many Roman period archaeologists to incorporate social theory into their research (Slofstra 1983).

Millett (1990, 2) has proposed that 'the processes of cultural change which we call Romanisation reflect the influences brought to bear by the Roman elite on the different native peoples with whom they were dealing'. However, more recent discussions recognise reciprocity in processes of contact between two cultures as 'the processes of socio-cultural change resultant upon the integration of indigenous societies into the Roman Empire' (Millett *et al* 1995, 1). The terminology is particularly problematic because the concept of Romanisation rather blatantly implies a dominant civilising Roman culture corroding and ultimately superseding existing indigenous 'barbarian' cultures which are deemed to have become impoverished and fragmentary (Urban and Schortman 1998). Roman tastes and values are perceived as influencing patterns of consumption and production (Woolf 1998, 111), without considering individual or group agency or the potential for local resistance to such influences (van Dommelen 2005). These accounts are largely androcentric in their stance (Meskell 2010) and fail to recognise tensions, either overtly of covertly expressed, that would have inevitably been present during periods of interaction between successive incoming military forces and the existing population.

A persistent aspect of such approaches is the concept that people were involved in Romanising themselves and they are inevitably seen as having an inherent wish or need to 'become Roman' (e.g. Woolf 1998); essentially they are perceived as being 'authors of their own predicaments' (Thomas 1991, 85). This stems from the perspective that Roman identity was projected and spread across the Empire by provincial adoption and modification of Roman material culture (Hingley 2005, 72) and, further, that 'Roman culture was flexible and incorporated many within its structure' (Hingley 2005, 118). Thus, past people have commonly been reduced to cogs within an, admittedly flexible, dominant Roman socio-politico-economic engine, propelled by a primary desire to change their traditional identities and improve their status within hierarchical social structures by incorporating themselves into Romanised culture at the expense of their traditional cultural heritage (Thomas 1991, 85).

Research has predominantly focussed upon regions where Romanisation is perceived as having had a positive, successful impact, with pastoral-dominated regions, where the processes are less evident, relegated as marginal or peripheral (Roymans 1996, 102). The role of elites in facilitating successful integration of rural societies through access to and restriction of prestige Roman objects have previously been thought to have reinforced and projected an allegiance with Rome 'upon which their position now depended' and provided the impetus for control over their people (Haselgrove 1997, 139).

This current research suggests that the imposition of top-down, Westernised assumptions on the structural composition of ancient societies framed within social evolutionary stances (Giddens 1984) may not be a universally appropriate definition of ancient societies. It should be recognised that Binford's (1983) middle range theory, a relatively uniform pattern of cultural development from egalitarian to hierarchical societies, paved the way for a more anthropological approach to the study of past societies, with particular emphasis placed upon burial practices. However, Iron Age funerary evidence from Sicily cautions that social changes in prehistory can be cyclical in character and that chiefdoms need not necessarily develop into early states (Leighton 1996, 102). This serves as a cautionary reminder that each situation should be assessed in its own right in any investigation of social organisation in the past. In order to elucidate some of these issues and move the debate forward, it is necessary to consider theoretical constructs recently applied to a variety of culture contact situations.

Frontier Studies

Previously, academia has tended to focus on Roman military aspects rather than existing inhabitants of frontier regions; however, trends have altered over the last two decades and some academics have more recently sought to understand frontiers by addressing issues of contact between Roman military personnel and local peoples (e.g. Hanson 2003; Woolliscroft 2004). Hanson (2002b, 839) approached the issue by determining that there were definable 'zones of interaction' in the province of Britannia and that a northwest-southeast divide existed across the region. Up to four zones are definable during the Roman period including the southeast, where Roman cultural values, villa modes of production and material culture spread rapidly after the conquest and did not require army presence; the 'military zone' encompassing northern England where the army was a relatively fixed feature throughout the Roman period (Gillam 1970, 1); the zone beyond the frontier in northern Britain where Romans and locals may have engaged in interaction; and a fourth potential zone in the Atlantic North which saw very limited contact with the Empire.

Situated 'beyond the edge of Empire' (Hunter 2007), Scotland is often deemed marginal or peripheral (Hingley 1992, 10). However the region's occupants may be better understood as social groups that varied markedly from others encountered by Rome and for whom Roman cultural values and material culture had limited relevance (Thomas 1991; 1992; Hanson 2002b, 839). Following on from Wallerstein's world systems theory (1974), dependency theory, promoting the process of development at the core driving under-development at the periphery (Roseberry 1988, 166), has come under heavy criticism as it 'presumes a conclusion, rather than setting out a problem' (D'Altroy 1992, 16). D'Altroy's (1992) territorial-hegemonic model of imperial expansion hypothesises that the reverse is true and the high control and extraction strategies used by a dominant core leads to new socioeconomic status and land tenure systems in the periphery. Ultimately this results in increased specialisation as high volumes of low-value goods are required to be produced in the periphery for local consumption due to the escalated costs of production and transportation from a distant core (D'Altroy 1992, 21-22). Such issues have previously been addressed by combining a prestige-goods model with a core-periphery model (Haselgrove 1982) where asymmetrical patterns of exchange develop between the core and periphery leading to the development of a powerful 'high-elite' who manipulate their position at the core, thereby increasing their social status (Roymans 1990, 265).

Rather than viewing these frontier communities as the poor cousins of a core which, for Scotland, could have been situated either at Rome or southern Britain, more recent pericentric studies have defined them as being ideally suited to innovation, hybridised practices (van Dommelen 2005) and development, *precisely because* they are so far removed from the intrinsic constraints of the core or homeland (Chase-Dunn 1988). Thus, rather than traditional world systems proposals for a powerful 'core' determining the fate of a distant 'periphery' (Ortner 1984), more recent discourse recognises the role of consumer preferences in these so-called 'marginal' places in influencing production and consumption of goods (Steiner 1985; Inikori 2002).

Therefore, frontiers are now recognised as dynamic, fluid phenomena with some areas, such as northern Britain, adopting the role of boundary, frontier and periphery at various times in their lifecycle (Rice 1998, 59). This present discussion seeks to offer an alternative perspective by considering the region, not as peripheral to either Rome or southern Britain, but rather as a core of cultural belief systems with participants who utilised familiar as well as foreign material culture in their daily and ritualised practices. Indeed, the research questions the validity of terms such as 'core' and 'periphery' as these constructs impose and perpetuate a particularly unhelpful bias onto any discussion of social organisation. What is peripheral to one social group is, by implication, the centre or 'core' of another. Rather, this study promotes the apportioning of equal importance to all social groups under discussion regardless of one physical location in contrast to another.

Rice (1998, 51) promotes a move away from interpretive dichotomies in frontier and boundary situations as 'they obscure the fact that many characteristics of boundaries and the behaviour of the people within (and on both sides of) them are better seen as points along continua of variation', where some social groups can be fluid in character with some disbanding and others being newly formed (Wolf 1982). The great challenge for archaeologists dealing with frontier situations then is to holistically address a multiplicity of complex social processes, including culture contact (Lyons and Papadopoulos 2002, 6), ethnicity (Jones 1997), acculturation (Kottak 2006) and appropriating practices (Thomas 1991, 1992; Thomas 2002) when dealing with material culture in frontier regions.

Culture Contact

Postcolonialism (e.g. Benabou 1976; Said 1993) opened up conditions for the adoption of a bottom-up approach to the archaeological record to help solve the contradiction between literary sources and the realities of life for the indigenous peoples under investigation (e.g. Hill 1995; Terrenato 2001; van Dommelen and Terrenato 2007). These new interrogations serve as a vehicle to more fully immerse ourselves in the societies under scrutiny and to interact with all individual agents, rather than the previously over-emphasised upper strata of hierarchical societies. These models confirm the need to identify local variables and long term trends before, during and after conquest and to ask questions such as: why did some people wish to become assimilated into Empire while others did not? Who were these people? Why did Rome modify her approach to some communities? What was the range of choices on offer? (Vallat 2001, 106) and were the processes necessarily conscious ones?

Rather than utilising analogies of European imperialism of the 19th and 20th Centuries which had a tendency towards racist and imperialistic motivations, it is potentially more informative to consider periods of first contact between colonisers and indigenous societies using modern anthropological comparisons. Owen (2005, 14) posits that initial contact with one foreign group could have stimulated the willingness of some cultural groups to interact with additional external cultures, thereby inducing changes to both (Kottak 2006). Critically, in order to identify any long-term social changes manifest in the archaeological record or clarify multidirectional processes which can alter or transform cultures (Stein 2005, 17), equal significance must be apportioned to each site in the analysis of variation and similarities.

These complex interactions and social changes can be assessed by analysing the changing uses of imported material such as pottery. Such artefacts may initially have been viewed as unique or held some perceived prestige value. Over time and after many years of cultural interaction between groups, foreign material culture may have been 'no longer viewed as exotic imports, but as normal everyday crockery' (Owen 2005, 20). In other words, it is in the period of first contact that foreign objects are thought to have drawn some initial interest from indigenous communities. However, after an initial period of adjustment the objects may no longer have held an illusion of prestige or uniqueness and became more important for their functional and utilitarian properties.

Like Owen (2005), Sanmarti (2004) considers long term social changes before, during and after contact. Both authors posit an initial exotic or prestige status associated with incoming material culture, which they see as having been controlled by some elite individuals, and a decrease in this status over time when most of these objects became more readily available. Owen (2005) places emphasis on first contact acting as a catalyst for future wide-reaching exchange networks. However, it is equally possible that internal changes were occurring in conjunction with external contacts, not necessarily primarily as a result of them (Sanmarti 2004) and consideration must be given to changing social structures in both the expanding established and incoming societies.

There is, of course, a fairly major difference between trade contact and invasion followed by occupation. While the situation in northern Britain differs insofar as the Roman intruders were not 'colonists' in the strict sense of the word, they were an essentially static force for extended, if intermittent, periods of time. Therefore, a certain amount of autonomy with regard to interaction with local societies would have been likely, even unavoidable. Tacitus (*Agricola*, 19) touches upon this autonomy and the resultant corruption of Agricola's predecessors in southern Britain. The short timescales involved combined with the episodic character of Roman occupation in Scotland further complicates the issue of interaction and exchange between Romans and local societies.

Negotiating Identity

Rather than an uncritical acceptance of the traditionally accepted concept of Romanisation or a rather vague perception of Roman objects 'drifting' across political frontiers to less developed societies (Curle 1932, 73; Robertson 1970), consideration should be afforded to the variable methods by which indigenous peoples may have acquired foreign goods and what made them attractive objects for locally relevant consumption (Campbell 2015).

Several objects confirm cross-cultural and cross-channel exchange networks throughout the region from the early Iron Age (e.g. Harding 2004). Therefore, these communities were clearly already engaged in the exchange of material culture and it is conceivable that these established relationships facilitated the continued movement of material during the later Iron Age and Roman periods. There may well have been episodes of first contact (Owen 2005) between Rome and certain individuals who acquired Roman material culture before redistribution to the wider population, perhaps through these existing inter-cultural exchange networks.

This approach to culture contact recognise that identity is central to any discussion of people, past or present. Identity is culturally constructed, fluid and changeable throughout the life-cycle (Meskell and Preucell 2004, 125) and it is affected by a multitude of life experiences and aspects of personhood. People associate and live within a wide variety of categories throughout their lives and are required to adopt appropriate identities for the various social situations in which they engage.

Tied into identity is ethnic identity, where social groups perceive themselves as culturally distinct. Thus, ethnicity involves the reproduction of differences through the social interface and people express these differences in their daily and ritualised activities (Jones 1997). Rituality may well have been an integral aspect of identity to these ancient societies and ritual and non-ritual practices need not have been mutually exclusive (Brück 1999, 325-7). Archaeological attention might therefore be more meaningfully directed towards acquiring insights into the rationality of societies under study, the manner in which they perceived and interacted with the world around them (Brück 1999, 325-7) and the symbolic role which material culture played in that interaction (Hodder 1982; Gosselain 1999), taking account of both profane and mundane practices (Comaroff and Comaroff 1997).

The deliberate deposition of objects into ditches and angles, under broch floors or at the entrances or angles of souterrains (Hingley 1990), practices which permeate the Neolithic, Bronze age and Iron Age (Bradley 1990), may be linked to the life-cycle of structures, their inhabitants or their wider associated communities (Campbell 2011). Changes to the cultural landscape would also have altered the expectations, interpretations and perceptions of local populations (Lucas 2001, 55) whose oral traditions may have, over time, transformed culturally significant places to embody cultural tradition, identity or power (Garcia Sanjuan *et al* 2007, 1).

Therefore a strong sense of identity, combined with links to place, less centralised settlement traditions across the region and local choices for action (Knapp and van Dommelen 2008) as well as resistance (van Dommelen 1998) to external cultural impositions may have been critical components to the capacity of northern societies to resist Romanising influences. The short-lived and sporadic character of Roman occupation may also have helped in this resistance and manifest in the physical or metaphysical manipulation of the material culture of Empire resulting in hybrid practices and identities (Campbell 2012, 2016).

Conclusion

Postcolonial perspectives stimulated academic debate a long way beyond the simplistic assumption that Roman material = Romanisation and sought to identify all of the participants in situations of contact between different peoples from the past (Benabou 1976; Said 1993) by considering the perspectives of people not documented in the written sources (Dominguez 2002). This paper has sought to move that debate forward by determining that, while Roman material culture may well have been selectively adopted (Jimenez 2007, 25) by provincial societies, it functioned very differently in non-Roman contexts (van Dommelen 1998; Fincham 2001, 36) on intrinsically social, symbolic and practical levels.

Roman culture was heterogeneous and changed over time in accordance with the diverse constituent elements encompassed within it (Woolf 1997). It may therefore be more appropriate and informative to consider the multi-directional processes of interaction between Romans and provincial societies as aspects of acculturation, where changes occur in all participants (Hanson 1994; Kottak 2006). From this perspective foreign material culture was being acculturated or appropriated into recipient cultural conditions (Thomas 1991, 1992), rather than the commonly accepted proposal for provincial societies being appropriated into Empire. Thus, objects may have been used to communicate, reinforce and perpetuate social concepts (Bourdieu 1977) and local people appear to have been manipulating Roman objects in a culturally specific manner to negotiate changing social experiences resulting from contact with the Empire. This would have facilitated a degree of resistance to Romanising influence while adopting and adapting socially acceptable elements of Roman material culture. That resistance can, however, be perceived as a nuance of persistence insofar as it enabled the indigenous recipients to maintain aspects of their traditional cultural identities, a character trait that Broun (this volume) posits permeates the region's indigenous population beyond the Roman presence

Acknowledgements

A number of individuals have influenced the approach taken in this paper, including Professors Bill Hanson, Martin Millett and Peter van Dommelen. I would like to thank them for being so generous with their time and advice, their input has improved the text enormously. Special thanks are also due to Nicki Hall and Dene Wright for motivating me to publish the research.

References

Allason-Jones, L. 1995. 'Sexing' small finds, in P. Rush (ed.), *Theoretical Roman Archaeology: Second Conference proceedings*, 22-32. Oxford: Oxbow Books.

Appadurai, A. (ed.) 1986. *The social life of things: commodities in cultural perspective.* Cambridge: Cambridge University Press.

Armit, I. 1999. The abandonment of souterrains: evolution, catastrophe or dislocation? *Proceedings of the Society of Antiquaries of Scotland* 129: 577-96.

Armit, I. and I.B.M. Ralston 2003. The Iron Age, in K.J. Edwards and I.B.M. Ralston (eds), *Scotland after the Ice Age: environment, archaeology and history, 8000 BC - AD 1000*, 169-96. Edinburgh: Edinburgh University Press.

Barrow, G. W. S. 1989. The Tribes of North Britain Revisited. *Proceedings of the Society of Antiquaries of Scotland* 119: 161-3.

Benabou, M. 1976. *La resistance Africaine a la Romanisation.* Paris: Maspero.

Binford, L.R. 1983. *In pursuit of the past.* London and New York: Thames & Hudson.

Bourdieu, P. 1977. *Outline of a theory of practice.* Cambridge: Cambridge University Press.

Bradley, R. 1990. *The passage of arms: an archaeological analysis of prehistoric hoards and votive deposits.* Cambridge: Cambridge University Press.

Breeze, D.J. 1988. Why did the Romans fail to conquer Scotland? *Proceedings of the Society of Antiquaries of Scotland* 118: 3-22

Breeze, D.J. 2002. The ancient geography of Scotland, in B. Ballin-Smith and I. Banks (eds), *In the shadow of the brochs: The Iron Age in Scotland*, 11-14. Stroud: Tempus.

Breeze, D.J. 2007. *Roman frontiers in Britain.* London: Bristol Classical Press.

Brück, J. 1999. Ritual and rationality: some problems of interpretation in European archaeology. *European Journal of Archaeology* 2: 313-44.

Campbell, L. 2011. *A study in culture contact: the distribution, function and social meanings of Roman pottery from non-Roman contexts in southern Scotland*, Unpublished PhD thesis, Glasgow: University of Glasgow

Campbell, L. 2012. Modifying Material: social biographies of Roman Ceramics, in A. Kyle and B. Jervis (eds) *Make do and Mend: the archaeologies of compromise*, 13-26. BAR Brit. Ser.

Campbell, L. 2015. Negotiating Identity on the Edge of Empire, in C. Popa and S. Stoddart (eds) *Fingerprinting the Iron Age*, 211-22. Oxford: Oxbow Books.

Campbell, L. 2016. Proportionalising practices in the past: fragments beyond the frontier, in E. Pierce, A. Maldonado, A. Russell and L. Campbell (eds) *Creating Material Worlds: the uses of*

Chase-Dunn, C. 1988. Comparing world-systems: toward a theory of semipheripheral development. *Comparative Civilizations Review* 19: 29-66.

Clarke, J. 1958. Roman and Native, AD 80-122, in I. A. Richmond (ed.), *Roman and Native in North Britain*, 28-59. Edinburgh: Nelson

Collins, R. 2008. Identity in the frontier: theory and multiple community interfacing, in C. Fenwick, M. Wiggins and D. Wythe (eds), *TRAC 2007: Proceedings of the seventeenth annual theoretical Roman archaeology conference, London 2007*, 45-52. Oxford: Oxbow Books.

Comaroff, J.L. and J. Comaroff 1997. *Of revelation and revolution, Volume 2: The dialectics of modernity on a South African frontier*. Chicago: University of Chicago Press.

Curle, J. 1932 Roman drift in Caledonia. *JRS* 22, part 1: 73-77.

D'Altroy, T.N. 1992. *Provincial power in the Inca Empire*. Washington D C: Smithsonian Institute Press.

Dobres, M.A. and J.E. Robb 2000. Agency in archaeology: paradigm or platitude?, in J. E. Robb and M.A. Dobres (eds), *Agency in archaeology*, 1-18. London and New York: Routledge.

Dominguez, A.J. 2002. Greeks in Iberia: colonialism without colonisation, in C.I. Lyons and J.K. Papadopoulos (eds), *The archaeology of colonialism*, 65-9. Los Angeles: Getty Publications.

Ferris, I.M. 2000. *Enemies of Rome: barbarians through Roman eyes*. Stroud: Sutton Publishing Limited.

Fincham, G. 2001. Consumer theory and Roman North Africa: a post-colonial approach to the ancient economy, in M. Carruthers, C. van Driel-Murray, A. Gardner, L. Revell and A. Swift (eds), *TRAC 2001: Proceedings of the Eleventh Annual Theoretical Roman Archaeology Conference, Glasgow 2001*, 35-44. Oxford: Oxbow Books.

Garcia Sanjuan, L., P. Garrido Gonzales and F. Lozano Gomez 2007. The use of prehistoric ritual and funerary sites in Roman Spain: discussing tradition, memory and identity in Roman society, in C. Fenwick, M. Wiggins and D. Wythe (eds), *TRAC 2007: Proceedings of the Seventeenth Annual Theoretical Roman Archaeology Conference, London 2007*, 1-14. Oxford: Oxbow Books.

Giddens, A. 1984. *The constitution of society: an outline of a theory of structuration*. Cambridge: Polity Press.

Gillam, J.P. 1970. *Types of Roman coarse pottery vessels in Northern Britain*. Newcastle upon Tyne: Oriel Press Ltd.

Gosselain, O. P. 1999. In pots we trust: the processing of clay and symbols in sub-Saharan Africa. *Journal of Material Culture* 4(2): 205-30.

Hanson, W.S. 1991. Tacitus' 'Agricola': an archaeological and historical study. *Aufsteig und Niedergang Der Romischen Welt* II.33.3: 1741-84.

Hanson, W.S. 1994. Dealing with barbarians: the Romanization of Britain, in B. Vyner (ed.), *Building on the past: papers celebrating 150 years of the Royal Archaeological Institute*, 149-63. London: The Royal Archaeological Institute.

Hanson, W.S. 2002. Why did the Roman empire cease to expand?, in P. Freeman, J. Bennett, Z.T. Fiema and B. Hoffmann (eds), *Limes XVII: Proceedings of the 18th International Congress of Roman Frontier studies held in Amman, Jordan (September 2000)*, 25-34. Oxford: BAR Int. Ser. 1084 (I).

Hanson, W.S. 2002b. Zones of interaction: Roman and native in Scotland. *Antiquity* 76: 834-40.

Hanson, W.S. 2003 .The Roman presence: brief interludes, in K. J. Edwards and I. B. M. Ralston (eds), *Scotland after the Ice Age: environment, archaeology and history, 8000 BC AD – 1000* 195-216. Edinburgh: Edinburgh University Press.

Hanson, W.S. and D.J. Breeze 1991 The future of Roman Scotland, in W. S. Hanson and E. A. Slater (eds), *Scottish archaeology: new perceptions*, 57-80. Aberdeen: Aberdeen University Press.

Harding, D.W. 2004. *The Iron Age in Northern Britain: Celts and Romans, natives and invaders.* London: Routledge.

Haselgrove, C. 1982. Wealth, prestige and power: the dynamics of the later Iron Age political centralisation in south-east England, in C. Renfrew and S. Shennan (eds), *Ranking resource and exchange: aspects of the archaeology of early European society*, 79-88. Cambridge: Cambridge University Press.

Haselgrove, C. 1997. Iron Age societies in Central Britain: retrospect and prospect, in B. Bevan (ed.), *Northern exposure: interpretive devolution and the Iron Ages in Britain*, 169-78. Leicester: School of Archaeological Studies, University of Leicester.

Haverfield, F. 1912. *The Romanization of Roman Britain.* Oxford: Clarendon Press.

Hill, J.D. 1995. How should we understand Iron Age societies and hillforts?, in J. D. Hill and C.G. Cumberpatch (eds), *Different Iron Ages: studies on the Iron Age to Temperate Europe*, 45-66. Oxford: BAR Int. Ser. 602.

Hingley, R. 1990. Boundaries surrounding Iron Age and Romano-British settlements. *SAJ* 7: 96-103.

Hingley, R. 1992. Society in Scotland from 700 BC to AD 200. *Proceedings of the Society of Antiquaries of Scotland* 122: 7-53.

Hingley, R. 2005. *Globalizing Roman culture.* London: Routledge.

Hodder, I. 1982. *Symbols in action.* Cambridge: Cambridge University Press.

Hodgson, N. 1995. Were there two Antonine occupations of Scotland? *Britannia* 26: 29-49.

Hoffmann, B. 2004. Agricola and the role of literature in the archaeology of the first century AD, in E. W. Sauer (ed.), *Archaeology and ancient history : breaking down the boundaries*, 151-65. London: Routledge.

Hunter, F. 1997. Iron Age hoarding in Scotland and Northern England, in A. Gwilt and C. Haselgrove (eds), *Reconstructing Iron Age societies: new approaches to the British Iron Age, Oxbow Monograph 71*, 108-33. Oxford: Oxbow Books.

Hunter, F. 2005. Rome and the creation of the Picts, in Z. Visy (ed.), *Limes XIX: Proceedings of the XIXth International Congress of Roman Frontier Studies, Pecs, Hungary, September 2003*, 235-40. Pecs: University of Pecs.

Hunter, F. 2007. *Beyond the edge of the Empire: Caledonians, Picts and Romans.* Ross-shire: Groam House Museum.

Hunter, F. 2009. Traprain Law and the Roman world, in W. S. Hanson (ed.), *The army and frontiers of Rome : papers offered to David J. Breeze on the occasion of his sixty-fifth birthday, and his retirement from 'Historic Scotland'*, 28-36. JRA Suppl. 74.

Inikori, J.E. 2002. *Africans and the industrial revolution in England: a study in international trade and economic development*. Cambridge: Cambridge University Press.

Jimenez, A. 2007. A critical approach to the concept of resistance: new 'traditional' rituals and objects in funerary contexts of Roman *Baetica*. *TRAC 2007: Proceedings of the Seventeenth Annual Theoretical Roman Archaeology Conference, London 2007*, 15-30. Oxford: Oxbow Books.

Jones, S. 1997. *The archaeology of ethnicity: constructing identities in the past and present.* London and New York: Routledge.

Keppie, L.J.F. 1989. Beyond the northern frontier: Roman and native in Scotland, in M. Todd (ed.), *Research on Roman Britain: 1960-89*, 61- 73. London: Britannia Monograph Series No. 11.

Keppie, L.J.F. 1998. *Roman inscribed and sculptured stones in the Hunterian Museum University of Glasgow.* London: Britannia Monograph Series No. 13.

Keppie, L.J.F. 2004. *The legacy of Rome: Scotland's Roman remains.* Edinburgh: John Donald Publishers.

Knapp, A.B. and P. van Dommelen 2008. Past practices: rethinking individuals and agents in archaeology. *Cambridge Archaeological Journal* 18:1: 15-34.

Kottak, C.P. 2006. *Mirror for humanity: a concise introduction to cultural anthropology. 5th ed.* New York: McGraw Hill.

Leighton, R. 1996. From chiefdom to tribe? Social organisation and change in later prehistory, in R. Leighton (ed.), *Early societies in Sicily. New developments in archaeological research*, 101-16. London: Accordia Research Centre, University of London (Accordia Specialist Studies on Italy, 5.

Lucas, J. 2001. Material culture patterns and cultural change in South-West Britain, in M. Carruthers, C. van-Driel-Murray, A. Gardner, L. Revell and A. Swift (eds), *TRAC 2001: Proceedings of the Eleventh Annual Theoretical Roman Archaeology Conference, Glasgow 2001*, 51-65. Oxford: Oxbow Books.

Lyons, C.I. and J.K. Papadopoulos 2002. Archaeology and colonialism, in C.I. Lyons and J. K. Papadopoulos (eds), *The archaeology of colonialism*, 1-23. Los Angeles: Getty Publications.

Macinnes, L. 1984. Brochs and the Roman occupation of Lowland Scotland. *Proceedings of the Society of Antiquaries of Scotland* 114: 235-49.

Main, L. 1998. Excavations of a timber round-house and broch at the Fairy Knowe, Buchlyvie, Stirlingshire, 1975-8. *Proceedings of the Society of Antiquaries of Scotland* 128: 293-417.

Mann, J.C. and D.J. Breeze 1987. Ptolemy, Tacitus and the tribes of Northern Britain. *Proceedings of the Society of Antiquaries of Scotland* 117: 85-91.

Meskell, L. 2010. Romanization: a feminist critique, in A. Moore, G. Taylor, E. Harris, P. Girdwood and L. Shipley (eds), *TRAC 2009: Proceedings of the Nineteenth Annual Theoretical Roman Archaeology Conference: University of Michigan, University of Southampton*, 1-28. Oxford: Oxbow Books.

Meskell, L. and R.W. Preucel 2004. Identities, in L. Meskell and R.W. Preucel (eds), *A companion to social archaeology*, 121-34. Oxford: Blackwell Publishing.

Millett, M. 1990. *The Romanization of Britain: an essay in archaeological interpretation.* Cambridge: Cambridge University Press.

Millett, M. 2000. *Roman Britain.* London: B.T. Batsford Ltd.

Millett, M., N. Roymans and J. Slofstra 1995. Integration, culture and ideology in the Early Roman West, in J. Metzler, M. Millett, N. Roymans and J. Slofstra (eds), *Integration in the early Roman West: the role of culture and ideology,* 1-6. Luxembourg: Dossiers d'Archeologie du Musee National d'Histoire et d'Art IV.

Ortner, S. 1984. Theory in anthropology since the sixties. *Comparative studies in society and history* 26(1): 126-66.

Owen, S. 2005. Analogy, archaeology and archaic colonization, in H. Hurst and S. Owen (eds), *Ancient colonisation: analogy, similarity and difference,* 5-22. London: Duckworth.

Renfrew, C. 1982. Socio-economic change in ranked societies, in C. Renfrew and S. Shennan (eds), *Ranking, resources and exchange: aspects of the archaeology of early European society,* 1-8. Cambridge: Cambridge University Press.

Rice, P. 1998. Contexts of contact and change: peripheries, frontiers and boundaries, in J.G. Cusick (ed.), *Studies in culture contact: interaction, culture change and archaeology,* 44-66. Illinois: Center for Archaeological Investigations, Southern Illinois University, Occasional Papers no 25.

Richmond, I.A. 1958. Ancient geographical sources for Britain north of Cheviot, in I. A. Richmond (ed.), *Roman and native in North Britain,* 131-49. Edinburgh: Nelson.

Robertson, A.S. 1970. Roman Finds from non-Roman sites in Scotland: more Roman 'drift' in Caledonia. *Britannia* 1: 198-226.

Roseberry, W. 1988. Political economy. *Annual Review of Anthropology* 17: 161-85.

Roymans, N. 1990. *Tribal societies in Northern Gaul: an anthropological perspective.* Amsterdam: Universiteit van Amsterdam.

Roymans, N. 1995. Romanisation, cultural identity and the ethnic discussion: The integration of Lower Rhine populations in the Roman Empire, in J. Metzler, M. Millett, N. Roymans and J. Slofstra (eds), *Integration in the early Roman West: the role of culture and ideology,* 47-64. Luxembourg: Dossiers D'Archeologie du Musee National d'Histoire et d'Art IV.

Roymans, N. 1996. The sword or the plough: Regional dynamics in the Romanisation of Belgic Gaul and the Rhineland area, in N. Roymans (ed.), *From the sword to the plough: three studies on the earliest Romanisation of Northern Gaul,* 9-126. Amsterdam: Amsterdam University press.

Said, E. 1993. *Culture and Imperialism.* London: Vintage.

Sanmarti, J. 2004. From local groups to early states: the development of complexity in protohistoric Catalonia, Pyrenae. *Revisita de prehistoria I antiguitat de la Mediterrania occidental* 35: 17-41.

Slofstra, J. 1983. An anthropological approach to the study of Romanization processes, in R.W. Brandt and J. Slofstra (eds), *Roman and native in the Low Countries. Spheres of interaction,* 71-104. Oxford: BAR Int. Ser. 184.

Stein, G.J. 2005. Introduction: the comparative archaeology of colonial encounters, in G.J. Stein (ed.), *The archaeology of colonial encounters: comparative perspectives,* 3-31. Oxford: James Currey Ltd.

Steiner, C. 1985. Another image of Africa: toward an ethnohistory of European cloth marketed in West Africa 1873–1960. *Ethnohistory* 32(2): 91-110.

Strange, A. 1997. Explaining Ptolemy's Roman Britain. *Britannia* 28: 1-30.

Swan, V.G. 1999. The twentieth legion and the history of the Antonine Wall reconsidered. *Proceedings of the Society of Antiquaries of Scotland* 129: 399-480.

Terrenato, N. 2001. A tale of three cities: The Romanisation of northern coastal Etruria, in S. Keay and N. Terrenato (eds), *Italy and the West: comparative issues in Romanisation*, 54-67. Oxford: Oxbow Books.

Thomas, J. 2002. Reconfiguring the social, refiguring the Material, in M. Schiffer (ed.), *Social theory in archaeology*, 143-55. Salt Lake City: University of Utah Press.

Thomas, N. 1991. *Entangled objects: exchange, material culture and colonialism in the Pacific*. Massachusetts and London: Harvard University Press.

Thomas, N. 1992. The cultural dynamics of peripheral exchange, in C. Humphrey and S. Hugh-Jones (eds), *Barter, exchange and value: an anthropological approach*, 21-41. Cambridge: Cambridge University Press.

Urban, P.A. and E. Schortman 1998. Culture contact structure and process, in J.G. Cusick (ed.), *Studies in culture contact: interaction, culture change and archaeology*, 102-25. Illinois: Center for Archaeological Investigations, Southern Illinois University, Occasional Paper no 25.

Vallat, J.P. 2001. The Romanisation of Italy: conclusion, in S. Keay and N. Terrenato (eds), *Italy and the West: comparative issues in Romanisation*, 102-12. Oxford: Oxbow Books.

van Dommelen, P. 1998. Punic resistance: colonialism and cultural identities in Roman identities, in R. Lawrence and J. Berry (eds), *Cultural identity in the Roman Empire*, 25-48. London: Routledge.

van Dommelen, P. 2001. Ambiguous matters: colonialism and local identities in punic Sardinia, in C.I. Lyons and P.L.A. (eds), *The archaeology of colonialism*, 121-47. Los Angeles: Getty Publications.

van Dommelen, P. 2005. Colonial interactions and hybrid practices: Phoenician and Carthaginian settlement in the Ancient Mediterranean, in G. J. Stein (ed.), *The archaeology of colonial encounters: comparative perspectives*, 109-42. Oxford: James Currey Ltd.

van Dommelen, P. 2007. *Articulating local cultures: power and identity under the expanding Roman Republic*. Portsmouth, Rhode Island: JRA Suppl. Ser. 63.

van Dommelen, P. and N. Terrenato (eds) 1998. Punic resistance: colonialism and cultural identities in Roman identities, in R. Lawrence and J. Berry (eds), *Cultural identity in the Roman Empire*, 25-48. London: Routledge.

Wallerstein, I. 1974. *The modern world system I*. New York: Academic Press.

Watkins, T. 1984. Where were the Picts?, in J.G.P. Friell and W.G. Watson (eds), *Pictish Studies*, 63-86. Oxford: BAR Brit. Ser. 125.

Watson, W. 1929. *The history of the Celtic place-names of Scotland*. Edinburgh: Birlinn

Wolf, E.R. 1982. *Europe and the people without history*. Berkley: University of California Press.

Woolf, A. 1997. Beyond Romans and natives. *World Archaeology* 28(3) Culture Contact and Colonialism: 339-50.

Woolf, A. 1998. Romancing the Celts: a segmentary approach to acculturation, in R. Lawrence and J. Berry (eds), *Cultural identity in the Roman Empire*, 111-24. London: Routledge.

Woolliscroft, D.J. 2004. East Coldoch, Stirling (Kincardine parish), Iron Age settlement. *Discovery and Excavation in Scotland* 6.

Origins of Alba and Scotland

The origins of 'Scotland'[1]

Dauvit Broun

Until recently the standard textbook account of Scotland's origins would have told you that Scotland was born as a 'Scoto-Pictish' union in 843 when Cinaed (Kenneth) mac Ailpín led the Gaels (*Scoti* in Latin) from Dál Riata in the West and took over the Picts in the East, who inhabited most of the mainland north of the Forth (see, for example, Macquarrie 2004, 72). This new kingdom (it was said) naturally acquired a new name (*Alba*, the modern Gaelic word for Scotland), and in due course extended its bounds to embrace the English south-east of what is now Scotland, defending this recently-acquired territory successfully at the battle of Carham on the Tweed in 1018, and then acquiring the rest of southern Scotland later that century. But there is a problem. No contemporary source has anything to say about Cinaed mac Ailpín's alleged achievement. Moreover, when Cinaed mac Ailpín and his sons died they were given the title *rex Pictorum*, 'king of the Picts', and their subjects were referred to as *Picti* (Broun 2007a, 72–4). Alex Woolf has therefore offered a different scenario in which the takeover of Pictland by Gaels occurred under the successor of Cinaed's sons (Woolf 2007, 117–21, 320–2, 340–2). Unfortunately contemporary information dries up at this point, leaving this king's identity in doubt. As far as the idea of a 'union of Picts and Scots' is concerned, the earliest source which refers unambiguously to what might be construed as a Scoto-Pictish kingdom – created by Cinaed mac Ailpín – is a king-list datable to the reign of Alexander II (1214–49) (Anderson 1980, 264–89; Broun 2002, 21–3).

If we want to understand how Scotland got its name, and what this signifies, we must first wipe the old story of a 'Scoto-Pictish union' from our minds and look afresh at the issue. The question of names is, indeed, puzzling and complex. As we will see, the words used for Scotland in different languages could be taken to mean 'Britain' or 'Ireland'; when applied to northern Britain, they could refer not only to the modern country but to the mainland north of the Forth, or an even more limited region still. Not all these meanings existed simultaneously, although the different notions of 'Scotland' north of the Forth certainly did (even in the same text: Anderson 1980, 240–3; Broun 2000, 28–9). It would be too much to try to unravel and explain all this in the scope of this paper. Instead, I intend to focus on two critical changes, searching

[1] The paper given at the conference was a slightly revised version of the one I originally gave at a symposium on 'Giving Names to Medieval States', Baltic Research Centre, Frombork, 11–14 September 2006, led by Professor Przemysław Urbańczyk. As well as thanking the 'Roots of Nationhood' organisers for the invitation to speak, I would also like to thank Prof. Urbańczyk and fellow contributors on the first occasion for a memorable and stimulating gathering.

all the time for an understanding of how Scotland was used as a name by those who identified with it. One is when 'Scotland' began to be used in its modern sense for the kingdom as a whole, particularly from the modern border between Berwick and the Solway. This did not occur until the thirteenth century. More attention will be paid to the other change, which saw the earliest datable appearance of 'Scotland' in anything approximating to its modern usage in any language. This will take us to the ninth century, and possibly even earlier.

First of all, it will be useful to give some background. In the central middle ages the main languages spoken by people at large in what is now Scotland were Gaelic, spoken predominantly north of the Forth and in the West, and English. Neither of these were indigenous, of course. There were many more speakers of Gaelic and English outside of Scotland than in Scotland itself. The only language that might claim to have been unique to Scotland was Pictish. The Picts, notoriously, vanish from contemporary sources from the end of the ninth century, leaving a legacy of hundreds of remarkable sculptured stones, but only a few fragments of their language – enough to show that Pictish was closely related to Welsh (Forsyth 1997). It is a moot point whether we would think there was such a thing as a Pictish language (rather than dialect) if Bede had not included it in his famous account of the languages of Britain. It is telling, for example, that W. J. Watson, in his classic work *The History of the Celtic Place-names of Scotland* (1926), avoided the term 'Pictish', and opted for 'British' instead (Taylor 2011, 70).

Unfortunately there is no text which preserves the Pictish word for Pictland. If we want to understand what name the inhabitants of north Britain used for their country, we can only do so by considering this in both the main surviving native vernaculars. In Gaelic it was, and is, *Alba*, and in English, of course, it is *Scotland*. In Latin these became *Albania* and *Scotia*. Both names originated outside Scotland itself. *Alba* was the Gaelic/Irish word for the island of Britain (Dumville 1996), whereas *Scotland* in English denoted the island of Ireland.

The first application of *Alba* and *Scotland* to refer to northern Britain is also found in contemporary sources outside Scotland. This is not a surprise, given the almost complete loss of such material from Scotland itself. *Alba* is first found in its new sense in a record of the death of a 'king of *Alba*' in 900 that originated in the 'Chronicle of Ireland' (AU 900.6; CS 900.5; Broun 2007a, 84: on the 'Chronicle of Ireland', see now Evans 2010). The first appearance of *Scotland* in its modern guise is found not long after in the Anglo-Saxon Chronicle, in 934; the first time *Scottas*, 'Scots', is used for inhabitants of northern Britain rather than Gaels/Irish in general is in 920 (Bately 1986, 69, 70; Whitelock, with Douglas and Tucker 1961, 67, 69; Dumville 1996, 181; Broun 2005, 269). *Scotia* and *Scotti* (or forms derived from it), meaning 'Scotland' and 'Scots' rather than 'Ireland' and 'Irish', are also found on the Continent in the late tenth century (Dumville 2001, 176, 180; Dumville 2007, 165, 170).

It is not immediately obvious that the Chronicle of Ireland and the Anglo-Saxon Chronicle reflect Scottish usage. There is both textual and circumstantial evidence, however, that the Chronicle of Ireland acquired its Scottish information from Dunkeld, the centre of Columba's cult in eastern Scotland (Broun 2007a, 85–6). A more fundamental question is whether the new application of *Alba* and *Scotland* to refer to northern Britain was necessarily new at all in the tenth century. On the face of it, it is striking that in the Chronicle of Ireland and the Anglo-Saxon Chronicle the switch to the new usage is clear and permanent: both have examples of the older meanings of *Alba* and Scots in the second half of the ninth century (Dumville 1996, 181–3), meanings which are replaced in the early tenth century by what we are familiar with today.

The fact that this change affected not only *Alba* but also *Scotland* at about the same time naturally raises the question of whether they may be linked. One simple way of connecting them would be to suppose that *Alba* had always been a short-hand way of referring to Gaelic-speaking Britain (Woolf 2001, 42). If the Pictish language began to be superseded by Gaelic in the aftermath of Viking devastation in the 860s and 870s (Broun 1994; Woolf 2007, 340–1), or a Gaelic takeover shortly thereafter (Woolf 2007, 320–42), then *Alba* would naturally have expanded to embrace most of northern Britain. At the same time, the English would have had more connections with *Scottas*, that is, Gaelic-speakers, in the north of their island than with those across in Ireland, and might naturally have begun to refer to the land of the *Scottas* in Britain as *Scotland*. Such an attractively straightforward scenario is *nearly* the whole story. Yes: this must be linked to the death of Pictish and the spread of Gaelic (Broun 2005, 269, 274). But is there any positive evidence that *Alba* meant 'Gaelic Britain'? I know of no instance where this is the most natural meaning. In contrast, there are a number of cases in different contexts where *Alba* refers specifically to Pictland, or to a part of it (Broun 2007a, 75–80). One example that may be dated to the mid-ninth century (if not earlier) is a brief statement in Gaelic verse of how *Alba* was divided among the seven sons of Cruithne (Van Hamel 1932, 5, 23 n.52; Broun 2007a, 78–9). Cruithne is the Gaelic collective noun for 'Picts', and his seven legendary sons have names which denote different parts of Pictland: for example, *Caitt*, representing the northern part of the mainland, and Fife, which is still today the name of the landmass sandwiched by the firths of Forth and Tay. There is little doubt that this was intended to project a vision of Pictland as originally a single country stretching from Caithness in the far north to Fife in the south. In the longer Pictish king-list (datable to 862 × 876) this is taken a step further by using the legend to portray an image of the country as an ancient kingdom whose successor is the reigning 'king of the Picts' (Broun 2007a, 75–9: for classification of witnesses, see Miller 1982, 159–60).

The possibility that *Alba* was already used as a Gaelic word for Pictland before 900 has implications for the way we interpret the appearance in the Chronicle of Ireland of *Alba* referring to northern Britain (Broun 2007a, 84–6). There it is used specifically to refer to what had been the kingdom of the Picts. We have noted earlier how, up to the

870s, we hear of kings who are given the Latin title *rex Pictorum*: the last examples are the sons of Cinaed son of Ailpín, Causantín and Aed, who died in 876 and 878. The first person called 'king of Alba', *rí Alban*, is Causantín's son, Domnall, at his death in 900 (AU 876.1, 878.2, 900.6; CS 876.1, 900.5). The simplest explanation for the appearance of *Alba* in this new context in the chronicle is that there has been a switch from Latin to Gaelic, in which case *Alba* should be understood to mean 'Pictland' (Broun 2007a, 84–7). (The chronicle is written in a mix of Latin and Gaelic, with Gaelic becoming more predominant, particularly from the 940s: Dumville 1982, 331–2.) It may be objected that there was already another Gaelic word for Pictland: *Cruithentúath* ('the Picts' domain'). It may be recalled, however, that the chronicle here could have acquired its information on these kings from Dunkeld: in other words, the choice of *Alba* as Gaelic for 'Pictland' may reflect a Scottish preference. This could be especially significant because there is some indication that Dunkeld had close ties with Cinaed son of Ailpín and his dynasty. It would not be too rash to hazard a guess that *Alba* was how Domnall, grandson of Cinaed son of Ailpín, referred to his kingdom when speaking in Gaelic, and that Cinaed himself probably did so as well.

This still leaves us with the original conundrum of how the Gaelic word for 'Britain', *Alba*, came to be applied to northern Britain in particular. An important part of any solution must be to examine all the words for Britain or Picts used not only by the Irish, but also the Welsh, and in Latin as well as their own languages. Such a study has recently been undertaken (Broun 2005, 254–9; Broun 2007a, 81–4). The conclusion is that the Picts probably referred to their country using a word which included 'Britain' in its semantic range. (This was probably very similar to Welsh *Prydyn*, to which Latin *Britannia* is related; alternatively – although the evidence is questionable – it may have been similar to **Albid*, a Brittonic word ancestral to Welsh *elfydd*, 'world, earth; land, country, district, neighbourhood', related ultimately to *Alba*: Woolf 2007, 179–80; Broun 2005, 258 n.85.) The Welsh used *Britannia* for 'Wales' (Pryce 2001) as well as the whole island: for example, Asser described Offa's dyke as 'a great vallum between *Britannia* and Mercia' (Stevenson 1959, 12). This and similar instances of *Britannia* meaning 'Wales' have been collected and discussed by Huw Pryce, who commented that 'underlying this use of a 'British' vocabulary to describe Wales and the Welsh was surely an assumption that the country and the people *were* in a sense Britain and Britons...' (Pryce 2001, 778). The same may therefore be suggested for the Picts – that they also regarded their country and themselves as in some sense 'Britain' and 'Britons'. If so, this would explain how the Gaelic word for Britain, *Alba*, was used for Pictland, and became established as the name of the country when its inhabitants turned from Pictish to Gaelic.

In what sense could the Picts have regarded themselves as particularly British? Katherine Forsyth has drawn attention to the fact that Latin script is almost entirely absent from Pictish monumental sculpture (Forsyth 1998, 54–5). This is unparalleled, and stands in particularly sharp contrast to the edifices erected by Britons south of the Forth (Forsyth 2009, 34). James Fraser has also pointed to King Naiton's letter to Abbot Ceolfrith (preserved by Bede) where the Pictish king himself refers to the Picts as remote from *Romanitas* (Fraser 2011, section IV). The Britons, on the other hand, embraced *Romanitas*, and distinguished themselves thereby from the 'uncivilised' Picts (Forsyth 2009, 34). Although the very term *Picti* was coined pejoratively, it would appear that, by the time they began to erect sculptured stones (if not before), the Picts had espoused this view of themselves as unRomanised Britons: what Fraser has described as an 'apparently conscious non-engagement with Continental or Latin norms' (Fraser 2011). According to this scenario, Pictish identity could have taken shape around a myth that they alone were the 'true' Britons free from *Romanitas* with its origins in foreign rule (see also Woolf 2007, 180 n.6). As Christians, they would certainly have become aware, more intensely than before, of *Romanitas*, and so might have embraced this image of their 'remoteness' and a claim to be 'unRomanised Britons' not only as part of the baggage of conversion, but also in order to emphasise their distinctiveness in this new context.

It might be wondered why distinctiveness in relation to other Britons could have been so important, however. The Welsh, too, saw themselves as the remnants of the island's indigenous population. The 'other' who they defined themselves against, however, were the English, who they clearly identified as a different people. The putative 'other' in the case of the Picts, however, would (according to this scenario) have been acknowledged by them as fellow Britons: Britons of a different stamp, but Britons nonetheless. It must be suspected that, for 'Pictland' to be so clearly distinguished by its inhabitants from the rest of Britain, its identity is likely to have been rooted in something more concrete than a different imagined relationship to *Romanitas* – something which could be seen as a clear separation from the rest of the island of Britain, and which could also sustain a sense of uniqueness in the imagined world of realms and peoples under God. This 'something' was a specific topographical feature: a barrier to travel that seemed almost to divide Britain in two.

The Firth of Forth cuts deep inland, and then gives way to the River Forth which is fringed in the north by a large area of wetland as far as the hills above Loch Lomond. This was exaggerated wildly in medieval maps (Crone 1961, plates 2–8): Matthew Paris (d.1259), in his map of Britain, portrays the landmass north of the Forth as an island linked to the rest of Britain by Stirling Bridge alone. This division of Britain was a constant feature in subsequent maps, if not always so dramatically (Parsons 1958, 11). Although this may seem grossly inaccurate, it vividly conveys the difficulty of crossing this area before modern times, and how this in turn influenced the way it was imagined. Apart from Stirling Bridge and the Drip Ford nearby, the only route readily available to travellers on the move between north and south was through the River Forth at the Fords of Frew (Broun 2007a, 54). (The only other ford, at Cardross, would have required a pointless detour for nearly all traffic going any distance north or south.) The power of this geographical feature in defining *Alba*, 'Scotland', can also be seen in how it continued until the early thirteenth century to be regarded routinely by the kingdom's inhabitants as Scotland's southern limit despite the fact that it had ceased to mark a political or cultural divide for more than two centuries (Broun 1998).

If we return to the Picts, this would imply that Pictland, and their identity as Picts, was not only focused on distinctiveness in relation to *Romanitas*, but on an identification primarily with the landmass north of the Forth. The Picts saw themselves at root as the people of this landmass. Equally, this divide at the Forth could only have been regarded as a division of Britain by those who already identified with the island as a whole. In the end, therefore, the idea of separation from Roman Britain may have acquired its force because there was a powerful image of division to hand in the barrier of the Forth, an image which had the capacity to underpin a sense of country and kingdom long after the Picts as such had disappeared. By initially providing a clear demarcation from Britons to the south, it is likely to have been a key factor in Pictish identity from the beginning.

The continuing importance of the Forth as the southern limit of *Alba* / 'Scotland' has important implications for how we view the Scottish kingdom between the tenth and thirteenth centuries. Sometime about 960 Edinburgh fell to the Scots; by 1018 most of south-east Scotland had fallen; and, with the destruction of Northumbria in 1069–70 by William the Conqueror, the king of Scots gained control of all of southern Scotland, with the probable exception of Galloway (Broun 2004, 133–9). For more than two centuries after this the kings of Scots reigned undisturbed as far as the Tweed and Solway, with few exceptions. Returning to standard textbooks, it is commonplace to find maps referring to this period with 'Scotland' written across the whole area controlled by the king of Scots, as if the country and the kingdom were one-and-the-same. There is no evidence, however, that any of the king's subjects at the time thought that this was so. In their eyes the southern limit of 'Scotland' was the Forth, not the southern border of the kingdom. What, then, of the region in-between? A couple of passing comments from the late twelfth century point the way to an answer (see Broun 2007b for what follows; Broun 2004, 140–3, 167–80, deals with the diocese of Glasgow in general). In 1180 the prior of Dryburgh, not far from the border, located himself as 'in the land of England and the kingdom of the Scots' (Broun 2003, 8, 12). An even more striking statement can be found in a tract describing the topography and ancient divisions of *Albania*, 'Scotland', which should probably be dated to sometime between 1165 and 1184 (Broun 2000, 26 and n.16 for outline of evidence). It is explained there that the Firth of Forth 'divides the kingdoms (*regna*) of the Scots and the English' (Anderson 1980, 242; Broun 2007a, 53). In the eyes of one commentator, therefore, the realm of the king of Scots included part of England; as far as another was concerned, however, kingdom and country were indeed identical, but were defined not by centuries of political reality, but by geography. A fundamentally different way of thinking about kingdom and country was required before 'Scotland' could be applied to the kingdom as a whole and so assume its modern form.

The best source for this change is the chronicle written at the Cistercian monastery of Melrose only a few miles from Dryburgh in the extreme south-east of the kingdom (Broun 2007b). It was originally created sometime in 1173 and/or 1174, and was extended in fits and starts from the first decade of the thirteenth century to *ca* 1290 by as many as 40 scribes (Broun and Harrison 2007, 53–5, 78–86, 101–18). During this period a fundamental change in the scribes' identity can be detected. One of the original scribes was happy to refer to Bede as a fellow Englishman. In a passage written into the chronicle about 1220, however, events in the south-east and in Galloway were referred to as happening in 'Scotland'. But not all Scotland's inhabitants were Scots: as late as *ca* 1260 'Scots' is found referring to people from north of the Forth—people beyond the limits of Christian decency, moreover. Finally, in the last major continuation of the chronicle, datable to sometime between 1286 and (probably) 1291, it is clear that monks of Melrose regarded themselves and their neighbours in the south-east as Scots. These references to Scotland and Scots are incidental and unpredictable: they offer only a glimpse of how monks may have ordinarily used these terms. What particularly catches the eye as far as this paper is concerned, though, is the use *ca* 1220 of *Scotia*, Scotland, in its modern sense to encompass the whole of the territory ruled by the king of Scots. 'Scotland', and the sense of country which it represented, could now be sustained not by geography, but by the kingdom itself in a way that defied geography. The reason this was possible was that a new way was emerging in which the kingdom could be experienced or imagined as a single entity with clear limits. By the time that monks of Melrose finally regarded themselves as Scots, Scotland was self-consciously a land with a common law administered in the king's name. This was articulated explicitly for the first time in the Treaty of Perth in 1266 (MacQueen 1995, 10), but had its roots in an expectation that law and custom in relation to property should be the same throughout the king's territory (Broun 2007a, 9–10), and the development of mechanisms and an infrastructure to support this (Broun 2010, 98–100). This is not to say that the old geographical sense of country swiftly disappeared: the idea that 'Scotland' lay north of the Forth lived on for at least another century (for example, in an account of the Battle of Bannockburn, 1314: Shead, Stevenson and Watt 1991, 354–5), as well as in the administration of justice itself, in the justiciarship of *Scotia* (i.e., Scotland north of the Forth) established by William I (1165–1214) (Barrow 2003a, 81–8).

Scotland, then, provides a graphic instance not only of the power of geography in ideas of country in the early middle ages, but of the way the this changed so that, in the thirteenth century, it was possible for country and kingdom to be inspired and defined by the king's jurisdiction. Two aspects of this later development may finally be noted. The first is how topography (including man-made features) remained a potent force in defining boundaries wherever this was available. For the Welsh, Offa's dyke served as a clear physical limit to the applicability of Welsh law: in the law-tracts which survive from the thirteenth century, for example, to cross Offa's dyke was to leave Wales (Davies 1991, 3, 19). The second aspect to note is that, in all these cases, we are dealing with country and kingdom as ideals rather than as entities that corresponded exactly with the actual exercise of royal power 'on the ground'. 'Scotland' as the name of a country today is, first-and-foremost, a product of the experience of those whose social status allowed them to travel notable distances – royal retinues, poets, judges, clergy – which meant that they had either encountered the barrier of the Forth and its environs for themselves, or could identify with those that had. This was eventually superseded in the thirteenth century by the more intense and consistent experience of royal authority that emerged through sheriff courts and the common law, as well as the increasing economic significance of burghs, all of which made it possible, as never before, to regard the king as vital for guaranteeing the livelihoods of those with property and possessions and with goods to sell (Broun 2010, 97–100; MacQueen 2005, 249–50). This depended, above all, on royal authority expressed in documents rather than in the person of the king.

In conclusion, Scotland (Gaelic Alba) can be seen as an example of a country with a name derived from ancient ideas of geography as the basis for the highest secular authority. But these ideas were not static. A radical change was required before the term 'Scotland' could be applied to all the modern country, a change that can be traced to the thirteenth century when the highest secular authority came to be perceived more in terms of royal jurisdiction than the bare facts of topography.

Bibliography

Anderson, M.O. 1980. *Kings and Kingship in Early Scotland*, 2nd edn. Edinburgh: Scottish Academic Press.

AU: Annals of Uster (edited in Mac Airt and Mac Niocaill 1983).

Barrow, G.W.S. 2003a. *The Kingdom of the Scots*, 2nd edn. Edinburgh: Edinburgh University Press.

Barrow, G.W.S. (ed.) 2003b T*he Declaration of Arbroath: History, Significance, Setting*. Edinburgh: Historic Scotland.

Bately, J.M. 1986. *The Anglo-Saxon Chronicle. A Collaborative Edition*, gen. eds D. Dumville and S. Keynes, vol.ii, *MS A*. Cambridge: Boydell Press.

Broun, D. 1994. The origin of Scottish identity in its European context', in Crawford 1994: 21–31.

Broun, D. 1998. Defining Scotland and the Scots before the wars of independence, in Broun, Finlay and Lynch 1998: 4–17.

Broun, D. 2000. 'The seven kingdoms in *De situ Albanie*: a record of Pictish political geography or an imaginary map of Alba?', in Cowan and McDonald 2000: 24–42.

Broun, D. 2002. The Picts' place in the kingship's past before John of Fordun, in Cowan and Finlay 2002: 11–28.

Broun, D. 2003. The Declaration of Arbroath: pedigree of a nation?, in Barrow 2003b: 1–12.

Broun, D. 2004. The Welsh identity of the kingdom of Strathclyde, *ca* 900-*ca* 1200. *Innes Review* 85: 111–80.

Broun, D. 2005. A*lba*: Pictish homeland or Irish offshoot?, in O'Neill 2005: 234–75.

Broun, D. 2007a. *Scottish Independence and the Idea of Britain from the Picts to Alexander III.* Edinburgh: Edinburgh University Press.

Broun, D. 2007b. *Becoming Scottish in the thirteenth century: the evidence of the Chronicle of Melrose*, in Smith, Taylor and Williams 2007: 19–32.

Broun, D. 2010. Becoming a nation: Scotland in the twelfth and thirteenth centuries, in *Tsurushima* 2010: 86–103.

Broun, D., R.J. Finlay and M. Lynch (eds) 1998. *Image and Identity: the Making and Remaking of Scotland through the Ages.* Edinburgh: John Donald.

Broun, D. and J. Harrison 2007. *The Chronicle of Melrose Abbey: a Stratographic Edition*, vol.i, *Introduction and Facsimile Edition*. Woodbridge: Boydell Press for Scottish History Society.

Carey, J., M. Herbert and P. Ó Riain (eds) 2001. *Studies in Irish Hagiography. Saints and Scholars.* Dublin: Four Courts Press.

Cowan, E.J., and R.J. Finlay (eds) 2002. *Scottish History: the Power of the Past.* Edinburgh: Edinburgh University Press.

Cowan, E.J., and R.A. McDonald (eds) 2000. *Alba: Celtic Scotland in the Middle Ages.* East Linton: Tuckwell Press.

Crawford, B.E. (ed.) 1994. *Scotland in Dark Age Europe.* St Andrews: The Committee for Dark Age Studies, University of St Andrews.

Crone, G.R. 1961. *Early Maps of the British Isles, A.D.1000-A.D. 1579.* London: Royal Geographical Society.

CS: *Chronicum Scotorum* (edited in Hennessy 1866).

Davies, R.R. 1991. *The Age of Conquest: Wales 1063-1415.* Oxford: Oxford University Press. Originally published as *Conquest, Coexistence, and Change: Wales 1063-1415.* Oxford: Oxford University Press.

Driscoll, S.T., J. Geddes and M.A. Hall (eds) 2011. *Pictish Progress. New Studies on Northern Breitain in the Early Middke Ages.* Leiden: Brill.

Dumville, D.N. 1982. Latin and Irish in the Annals of Ulster, AD 431-1050', in Whitelock, D., R. McKitterick, and D.N. Dumville (eds) 1982. *Ireland in Early Mediaeval Europe: Studies in Memory of Kathleen Hughes*, 320–41. Cambridge: Cambridge University Press.

Dumville, D.N. 1996. Britain and Ireland in *Táin Bó Fraích. Études Celtiques* 32: 175–87.

Dumville, D.N. 2001. St Cathróe of Metz and the Hagiography of Exoticism, in Carey, Herbert and Ó Riain 2001: 172–88.

Dumville, D.N. 2007. *Celtic Essays*, vol.i. Aberdeen: Centre for Celtic Studies, University of Aberdeen.

Evans, N. 2010. *The Present and the Past in Medieval Irish Chronicles.* Woodbridge: Boydell Press.

Forsyth, K. 1997. *Language in Pictland: The Case against 'non-Indo-European Pictish'.* Utrecht: De Keltische Draak.

Forsyth, K. 1998. Literacy in Pictland, in Pryce 1998: 39–61.

Forsyth, K. 2009. The Latinus stone: Whithorn's earliest Christian monument, in Murray 2007: 19–41.

Fraser, J. 2011. 'From Ancient Scythia to the First Dundee Summer School: Thoughts on *The Problem of the Picts* and the Quest for Pictish Origins', in S.T. Driscoll, J. Geddes & M.A. Hall (eds), *Pictish Progress. New Studies on Northern Britain in the Early Middle Ages* (Leiden, Brill), 15–43.

Hennessy, W.M. (ed.) 1866. *Chronicum Scotorum. A Chronicle of Irish Affairs from the Earliest Times to A.D. 1135, with a supplement, containing the events from 1141 to 1150.* London: Rolls Series.

Mac Airt, S. and G. Mac Niocaill(eds) 1983. *The Annals of Ulster (to A.D. 1131). Part I: Text and Translation.* Dublin: Dublin Institute for Advanced Studies.

Macquarrie, A. 2004. *Medieval Scotland. Kingship and Nation.* Stroud: Alan Sutton.

MacQueen, H. 1995. *Regiam Majestatem*, Scots law and national identity'. *Scottish Historical Review* 74: 1–25.

MacQueen, H. 2005. Canon Law, Custom and Legislation: Law in the Reign of Alexander II, in Oram 2005: 221–51.

Menzies, G. (ed.) 2001. *In Search of Scotland.* Edinburgh: Polygon.

Miller, M. 1982. Matriliny by treaty: the Pictish foundation-legend, in Whitelock, McKitterick and Dumville 1982: 133–61.

Murray, J. (ed.) 2009. *St Ninian and the Earliest Christianity in Scotland. Papers from the conference held by the Friends of Whithorn Trust on September 15th 2007.* Oxford: BAR.

O'Neill, P. (ed.) 2005. *Exile and Homecoming. Papers from the Fifth Australian Conference of Celtic Studies, University of Sydney, July 2004.* Sydney: The Celtic Studies Foundation, University of Sydney.

Oram, R.D. (ed.) 2005. *The Reign of Alexander II, 1214-49.* Leiden: Brill.

Parsons, E.J.S. 1958. *The Map of Britain circa A. D. 1360 known as the Gough Map.* Oxford: Bodleian Library.

Pryce, H. (ed.) 1998. *Literacy in Medieval Celtic Societies.* Cambridge: Cambridge University Press.

Pryce, H. 2001. British or Welsh? National identity in twelfth-century Wales. *English Historical Review* 116: 775–801.

Shead, N.F., W.B. Stevenson and D.E.R. Watt (eds) 1991 *Scotichronicon by Walter Bower in Latin and English*, vol. vi. Aberdeen: Aberdeen University Press.

Smith, B.B., S. Taylor and G. Williams (eds) 2007. *West Over Sea: Studies In Scandinavian Sea-Borne Expansion And Settlement Before 1300.* Leiden: Brill.

Stevenson, W.H. (ed.) 1959. *Asser's Life of King Alfred*, with article by Dorothy Whitelock. Oxford: Clarendon Press.

Taylor, S. 2011. Pictish place-names revisited, in Driscoll, Geddes and Hall 2011: 67–118.

Tsurushima, H. 2010. *Nations in Medieval Britain.* Donington: Shaun Tyas.

Van Hamel, A.G. (ed) *Lebor Bretnach: The Irish Version of the Historia Britonum ascribed to Nennius.* Dublin: Irish Manuscripts Commission.

Whitelock, D., D.C. Douglas and S.I. Tucker (eds) 1961. *The Anglo-Saxon Chronicle. A Revised Translation.* London: Eyre and Spottiswoode.

Whitelock, D., R. McKitterick, and D.N. Dumville (eds) 1982. *Ireland in Early Mediaeval Europe: Studies in Memory of Kathleen Hughes.* Cambridge: Cambridge University Press.

Woolf, A. 2001. Birth of a Nation, in Menzies 2001: 24–45.

Woolf, A. 2007. *From Pictland to Alba 789-1070.* Edinburgh: Edinburgh University Press.

Merchants and craftsmen: a survey of the evidence for a Scandinavian presence in eastern Scotland in the eleventh to fourteenth centuries

Elizabeth Pierce

Introduction

In the final years of the eighth century AD, Scandinavian raiders arrived in Scotland from across the North Sea. At first their activities centred upon raiding, relieving monasteries such as Iona and Portmahomack of their treasures. Soon, though, the main focus turned toward settlement, including activities such as farming, fishing and trade. The most dominant Scandinavian settlement in Scotland took place in the Northern Isles, the Western Isles and the northern Scottish mainland in Caithness and Sutherland. In some areas, especially Orkney and Shetland, the Scandinavian influence was so great that it is still reflected in the culture of those islands today. In others, such as the Western Isles, the communities soon became Gaelic-speaking and focused their interactions more on the Irish Sea region. Central and southern Scotland experienced a small Norse presence, as evidenced by numerous finds of diagnostic Viking artefacts in the Clyde and Forth Valleys, the Scottish Borders and Dumfries and Galloway. Because the Norse were never the dominant cultural group here, they do not stand out in the archaeological record in these areas and disappear almost completely from discussions of the post-Viking period in Scotland. This paper aims to survey the evidence for a Norse presence in the 11th to 14th centuries outside the traditional areas of Viking settlement in Scotland, particularly in the eastern part of the country. Specifically, the paper will evaluate evidence from Aberdeenshire, Angus, Perthshire, Fife and East Lothian (fig. 1) in an effort to understand the character of the Scandinavian presence here and it's contribution to the formation of identities.

Historical and archaeological evidence for Scandinavian influence on early Scottish burghs and along the east coast of Scotland is sparse, although both Colleen Batey (2002) and Barbara Crawford (2000; 2002) have put forth evidence that could potentially be tied to a Scandinavian presence in central and eastern Scotland in the 11th and 12th centuries. Such evidence can be found elsewhere in the British Isles, so a Scandinavian presence outside the traditional Scandinavian areas of Scotland, particularly in situations which centred upon commerce, is not a far-fetched idea despite the current lack of concrete clues.

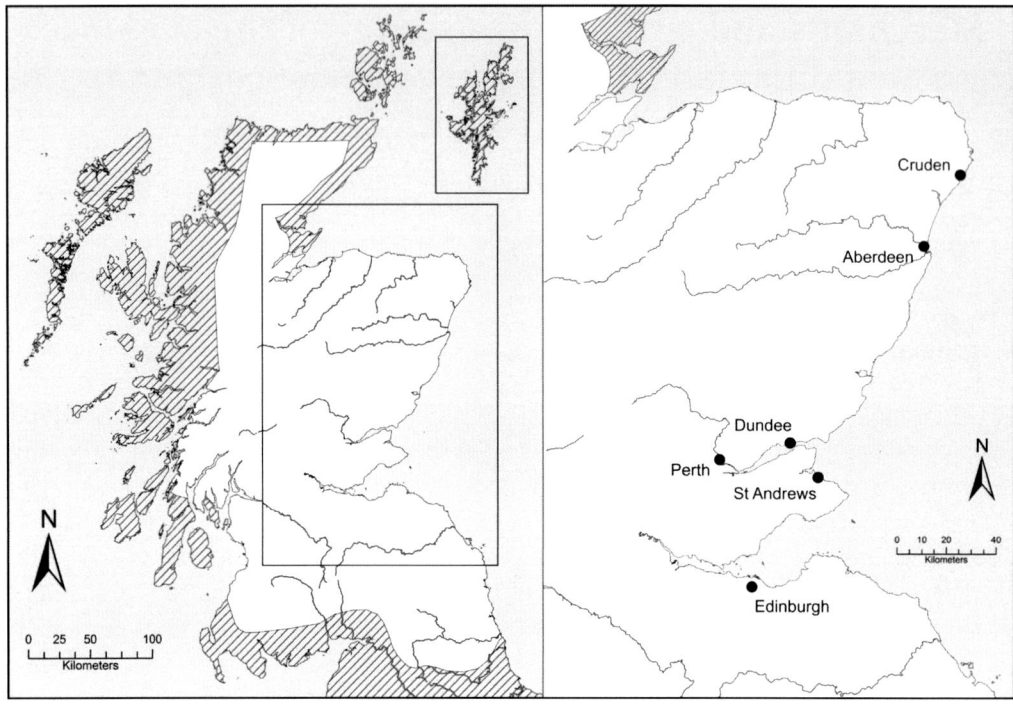

Figure 1. Settlements in eastern Scotland mentioned in the text. Map by Kirsty Millican.

'[U]rban archaeologists must be aware of the likelihood that traces of Scandinavian influence should be recognisable in the earliest levels of Scottish medieval towns: the wealth of evidence from tenth-century levels in Scandinavian York and Dublin provide a wonderful source of evidence for the richness of the culture engendered by the mobility of the Viking traders and the manufacturing centres where they operated. Should we expect this to be replicated in trading centres north of the Border?' (Crawford 2002: 1).

Finding evidence of this influence is challenging, however. Historians point out that foreigners played an important role in Scottish burghs, in part because they could take advantage of market access in exchange for their overseas contacts (Mackenzie 1949: 34-45; Ditchburn 1988; 180-183). Although Scandinavians are not specifically mentioned in early burgh charters in Scotland, foreigners from England and Flanders are, though Mackenzie (1949: 36) cautions that nationalities assigned to merchants in early charters may not always have been accurate. There were Scottish burgh residents who had Norse names, such as men named Swain in both Dunfermline and Perth (Mackenzie 1949: 36; Crawford 2002: 6), but whether these men were Anglo-Danish or had other roots is unclear. In the first two decades of the 14th century, merchants from St Andrews were trading in Norway; we know this because the Scots sought amends for them from the Norwegians when the Treaty of Perth was renewed in 1312 (Crawford 2013: 314).

Disappearing from the archaeological record

During the Viking Age, Scandinavian settlers in the British Isles left a distinctive mark in the archaeological record. Numerous pagan burials featuring boats, horses, clothing, tools and weapons have been found throughout the islands. In the ninth and tenth centuries, Norse settlers in the British Isles even created their distinctive versions of artefacts, objects considered by modern archaeologists to be 'Viking' despite their manufacture outside of Scandinavia. These objects included copper-alloy ringed-pins manufactured in Dublin (Fanning 1994) and conical shield bosses from the Irish Sea area (Harrison 2000: 68–69 & fig. 1). However, by the 12th century the Norse had long been converted to Christianity, and the material culture of everyday life was becoming more standardised and, at times, less culturally-distinctive throughout northern Europe. Many styles of annular brooches, for example, could have been manufactured anywhere from the British Isles to eastern Europe (Deevy 1998: 39–40), Grimston pottery from England was in use over a wide geographical area, and the style of leather shoes could be influenced by fashions from other places. Also, the distinctive Viking-Age long-houses with bowed walls found, for example, in the Northern Isles are not found in central and southern Scotland, which has hindered the identification of Norse settlement outside of the traditionally-recognised settlement areas. It is possible that a Scandinavian presence in Scotland has disappeared in the archaeological record in much the same way as in England, discussed below.

In Scotland, the search is further complicated by a dearth of written sources when compared to England in the same period. William the Conqueror visited Scotland only once, in 1072, when Malcolm III, king of the Scots, swore his allegiance; therefore, we lack a version of the Domesday Book for Scotland (Hall 2002: 10). Charters granted by the Scottish king David I [1124-1153] are the earliest documents we have for some locations. There is also a lack of surviving port books from medieval Scotland, hindering the study of trade and contacts (Ibid.: 21; Ditchburn 1988: 171; Stevenson 1988: 183). This is further complicated by modern publishers, who tend to separate studies of the Vikings/Norse from their contemporaries and segregate them into their own chapters or even their own volumes (see volumes by Ritchie (1993) in the *Historic Scotland* series and Owen (1999) in the *Making of Scotland* series as examples of this). This gives readers the false impression that people of Scandinavian descent in medieval Scotland were easily distinguishable and lived apart from their contemporaries.

Rather than a complete absence of Scandinavians in central Scotland in the Viking Age and later, it is most likely that they simply became less distinctive in the archaeological record as they became Christians and began using the same goods as their neighbours. Dawn Hadley (2000: 111) has argued that one problem in Viking studies is the assumption that Scandinavian settlers in Britain '...were, and long remained, recognizable as an ethnically and culturally distinctive people...', when in fact the processes of assimilation and integration could be complex and vary regionally (Hadley and Richards 2000: 3). The situation in central Scotland is not unique and can be paralleled with the situation in northern and eastern England. In the Danelaw, scholars have noted that the Danes in England seem to disappear from the archaeological record by the 11th century despite a distinctive Norse identity surviving in places like the Isle of Man (Richards 2004: 10) and Shetland (for a summary of the debate on the Scandinavian influence in England, see Hadley 2000). Rather than the Anglo-Scandinavians being driven from their former lands in the Danelaw or having been fully assimilated into a uniform 'English' culture, the people living there simply did not leave behind material culture that we can recognise today as distinctly Norse. New immigrants from Denmark continued to arrive in England in the 11th century, and they did not necessarily live in the Danelaw; such Danish arrivals could also have settled on the eastern coast of Scotland.

Hadley (2000: 116–17) argues that at the time, references to 'Danes' and the 'Danelaw' in northern England were more likely a reflection of territorial demarcation, distinctions in political conflicts or allusions to the history of an area rather than contemporary ethnic identifiers. By the 11th century, the descendants of Danish immigrants seem to have quickly become identified as 'English', as 'after a century and a half of intermarriage and social mixing the Scandinavian settlers, irrespective of their numbers, could barely have maintained a completely separate existence and identity...' (Ibid.: 118–19). Small differences and cross-cultural influences in the material culture used to represent personal identities have been noted by scholars, but only after close examination (e.g. brooches from the Danelaw in Kershaw 2013), thus raising questions about medieval identities. Chroniclers and poets of 13th and 14th century England still noted the Danes as a separate ethnic group in their writings as they strove to define the English nation (Turville-Petre 2001), but these differences cannot be seen in the archaeological record and may not have been important to the average person in daily life.

The length and nature of the survival of an important cultural marker, the language of Old Norse, in the Danelaw has been debated for nearly a century. Using place-names, personal names, inscriptions, loan-words, and phonology, scholars have estimated that Old Norse survived up to anywhere from c. 1000 to c. 1100 (Parsons 2001: 299–300). Despite the heavy Scandinavian influence in Viking-Age and medieval York, it does not appear that Old Norse took over as the dominant language. At best, there are only three rune-like inscriptions from York (compared to hundreds from Bergen, Norway) which may be Scandinavian or related Anglo-Saxon runes; meanwhile there are inscriptions from the surrounding area in Old English, and in Latin which give Scandinavian names such as *Orm* and *Gamal* on the Kirkdale sundial (Parsons 2004: 350-53). Trade in medieval York was likely conducted in a variety of languages, with Old English as the local language. Many people were probably bilingual, as was the case in Bergen, or adopted Norse names and words into English. Scandinavian street-names in York, coined by people in the 10th and 11th centuries who probably considered themselves to be English, continued to be used past the Anglo-Scandinavian phase of the town (Fellows-Jensen 2004: 371).

Even after the defeat of the Vikings by English forces at Stamford Bridge in 1066 brought an end to widespread Scandinavian incursions into England, economic contacts with Scandinavia and the northern Continent remained strong. Whetstones of schist and phyllite, probably from Norway, were found in medieval York, as well as quernstones from Germany and glassware from France, Germany, and Italy, and amber from the Baltic regions (Ottaway and Rogers 2002: 2999). Norway initially dominated trade in some of the eastern English ports in the Middle Ages, accounting for half of the total imports listed in the customs rolls at King's Lynn at one point in the 13th century (Herteig 1975: 85). Records show that up to 11 Norwegian ships were in that port at any one time (Carus-Wilson 1962-3: 185). The connections were not just with nearby Scandinavian countries, but also with the North Atlantic islands that fell under Scandinavian jurisdiction. The traffic between the North Atlantic and England may have had an impact on eastern Scottish ports, as well. Ships on their way to and from Iceland from King's Lynn would have sailed directly past Edinburgh and Dundee. The 15th century in Iceland is called the 'English Age' because of the great influence of English traders at that time (Karlsson 2000: 118–19). Direct English trade with Iceland in defiance of the German monopoly developed so quickly that by 1424, the King's Lynn 'merchants of Iceland' had elected taxation representatives in the English city (Carus-Wilson 1962-3: 199). After the mandate forbidding all but Hanseatic merchants in Iceland was reissued in 1426, the officials of King's Lynn banned ships that traded there from taking part in the Iceland route (Ibid.: 199–200). Whether Scottish ports had the same restrictions is unknown, but if they had different rules, it might have been an added incentive for Scandinavians to live and/or trade there. Woven fabric called *vaðmál* that was produced in the North Atlantic has been found at King's Lynn and in Perth and may be from Iceland, although the authors of the Perth report caution that it also could have been made in Orkney or Shetland (Clarke and Carter 1977: 375; Bennett et al. 2012: 27).

Place-names, personal names and linguistics in central Scotland

Using place-names as an indicator of settlement can be challenging, particularly in Scotland where several different languages have been used to varying degrees in different areas during the past two millennia. From the ninth to the 14th centuries, Pictish, Anglian, Gaelic, Old Scots and Old Norse were spoken in central and southern Scotland at various times, although not all languages were spoken in all areas. To add to the confusion, Old Scots and Old Norse were related, with Old Scots influenced in large part by dialects from northern England – themselves influenced by Scandinavian settlement in the Danelaw (Taylor 2007: 510). In addition, Scandinavian place-names, especially in southern Scotland, might not have been coined by Norse settlers but were familiar names brought northward from the Danelaw during a period of resettlement in the 12th century (Fellows-Jensen 2000: 141; Grant 2005: 127).

Genuine Scandinavian place-names which survived despite later linguistic changes do occur in central Scotland, all the way from Aberdeenshire, Perthshire and Fife in the east to Ayrshire in the west, but they tend to be isolated (Fellows-Jensen 2000: 135). It is worth noting, as we will see with the *–ness* names below, that Scandinavian place-names in central Scotland have not been studied with the same intensity as in other parts of the country. Fellows-Jensen's (2000) study of Scotland, for example, included the Clyde Valley and Firth of Forth north to the River Tay (Zone 4), but ignored completely anything north of that until the northern coast of Caithness.

Scandinavians are, and have been for centuries, a maritime culture, using the sea as a highway. By the beginning of the 13th century, Perth was already the *de facto* capital of Scotland, and sea-borne traffic would have travelled along the coast, perhaps between ports in England and the Northern Isles or North Atlantic. Along the eastern coast of Scotland from at least the Firth of Forth to Orkney, there is a proliferation of *–ness* place-names [ON 'headland'], but Taylor (2007: 510) points out that Old Scots also had the same linguistic element with the same meaning, so the names could alternatively be Scots. There does not appear to have been a study devoted to these names (for listing of several *–ness* names and a map, see Horne 2014: 59; fig. 2.16). Taylor (2007: 510 & fn. 38) suggests that the *–ness* names in Fife are probably relatively late given that none have become settlement names. One exception to this is Kirkness on Loch Leven in Fife, which does appear to come from Old Norse (Ibid.: 510–11). The topic of *–ness* names in eastern Scotland certainly deserves further study.

Personal names and terminology, too, might mark a Scandinavian presence. The son and grandsons of Constantine II of Alba [900-943] had elements of Scandinavian names, including one grandson named Olaf (Taylor 2004: 133–34). Although we lack charters or much other written evidence from before c. 1100, 12th and 13th century documents list Norse personal names such as Thor for people living in eastern areas of Scotland, including Perthshire and near St Andrews (Crawford 2000: 130–32). Between the 10th and 13th centuries, many administrative, legal, social and agricultural terms derived from Old Norse came into use in Scotland, some perhaps the result of links between Scotland and Northumbria during the life of Malcolm III (Crawford 2000: 130; 2002: 4–6). However there occasionally are terms that appear in Scottish documents that do not appear to have been used in England, suggesting a direct Scandinavian source. Among these are *kirset* – an administrative term for the temporary exemption of new residents from a town's financial dues; unfortunately, it is not clear exactly when this term came into use (Crawford 2000: 133; 2002: 5–6). In addition to legal terminology, ideas of medieval land partition and administration were brought to south-eastern Scotland by people from the Danelaw or perhaps by Malcolm III upon his return to Scotland from exile in 1054 (Crawford 2000: 129, 132).

Scandinavians in royal Scottish burghs?

In the Viking Age, Scotland did not yet have urban commercial centres. Scandinavian merchants, though, would have been familiar with urban centres such as Ribe in Denmark. Similar trading sites arose in other parts of the British Isles soon after

Viking settlement, most notably in Dublin and York, but it was only in the 11th and 12th centuries that urban trade and manufacturing centres began forming more widely in Scotland (Hall 2002). If Scandinavians did indeed play a role in the formation of Scottish towns as Crawford has suggested above, one of the best places to look is Perth, where major excavations were conducted in the 1970s.

Dating of the earliest layers of settlement in Perth have demonstrated that it was not a burgh founded by David I around 1128 as traditionally thought; instead, its formation dated to the late 10th or early 11th century based upon radiocarbon dates from a wattle-lined ditch which may have enclosed an earlier version of St John's church and carbonised material on pottery (Hall 2002: 10; Hall et al. 2005: 277, 280). The nature of the early settlement – whether it was religious or secular, and whether it had more than one focal point – is still unknown, although it likely had an early church (Hall et al. 2005, 280–81). Perth may even have begun as a dispersed settlement like Kirkwall in Orkney (Batey 2002: 2). It was in the 12th century that it received the status of 'royal burgh', after the town had already been in existence for at least a century (fig. 2). Becoming a royal burgh allowed a town to engage in foreign trade, unlike ecclesiastical or baronial burghs (Hall 2002: 10). Other early royal burghs in Scotland include Aberdeen, Edinburgh, Stirling and Dunfermline (Ibid.: 11).

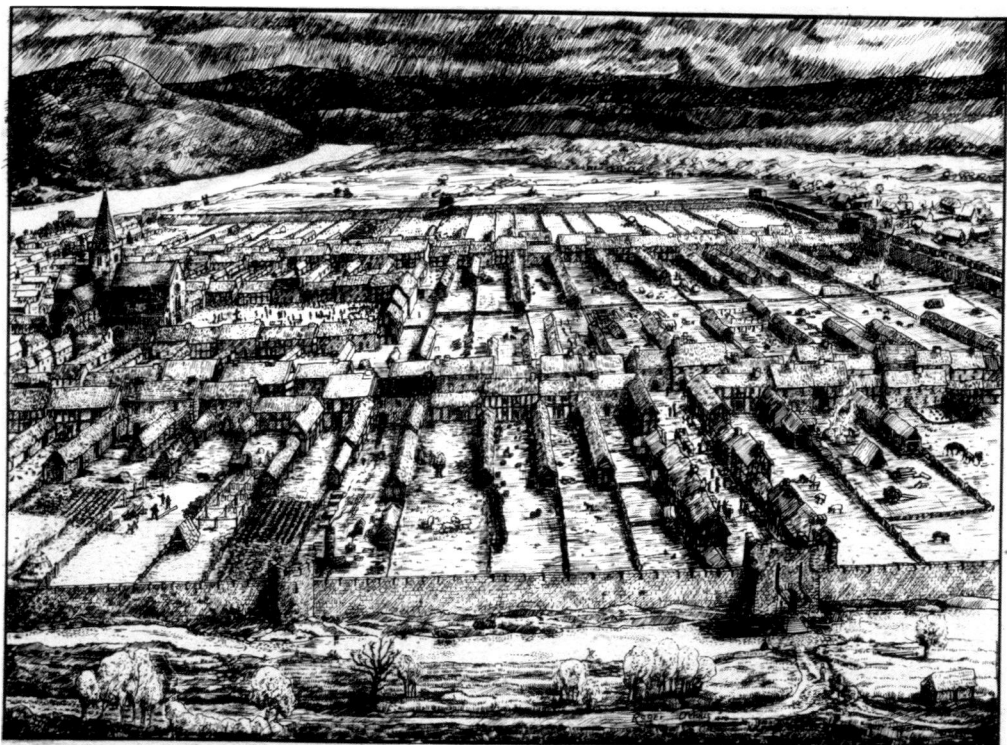

Figure 2. Artist's reconstruction of the burgh of Perth c. 13th century. Image courtesy of Perth Museum & Art Gallery, Perth & Kinross Council, Scotland.

Several pieces of timber which had been pieces of boats were found during excavations in Perth. The excavators wrote, 'All the evidence of shipping from 12th- and 13th-century Perth points, not unexpectedly, to the Scandinavian traditions of northern Europe' (Martin and Bogdan 2012: 317). Among other diagnostic finds were two short lengths of clinker-built planking held together with clench rivets were recovered from a cesspit dating to the second half of the 13th century (Martin and Bogdan 2012: 320). The boats themselves may have been built in the British Isles – the Scandinavian style of building clinker-built vessels continued into the modern period in places like Shetland – but they certainly demonstrate Scandinavian influence.

Even in the Northern Isles, where there was dense Scandinavian settlement, identifying Norse sites that were home to trade and manufacturing during the Viking Age has been difficult as many are probably buried beneath modern towns (Owen 2005: 297). Perth has revealed some parallels to York and Dublin. Off-cuts and finds of leather suggest leather-working was an increasingly prosperous business (Thomas and Bogdan 2012: 281). There was also debris from craftsmen using bone, horn and antler (MacGregor 2010: 97, 101). A few walrus ivory artefacts, including an intricate anthropomorphic handle, have been found. It is not clear whether they were manufactured nearby (Ibid.: 102). Walrus ivory at this time usually would have come from either Iceland/Greenland or northern Norway/Russia. However, excavators caution that the small amount of walrus ivory in Perth could also represent a random stranded walrus on Scottish shores or raw material imported by an itinerant craftsman (Hall in MacGregor 2010: 102). Given the challenge of identifying trade in the archaeological record, it is not surprising that we lack archaeological evidence for Norse trade, particularly on the east coast of Scotland. Matters are further complicated by the fact that many trade goods were organic. From at least the 14th century (but probably much earlier), Scotland exported wool, salted fish, animal skins, salt and other products while importing pottery, fine cloth, timber and more from the continent (Hall 2002: 21, 23).

Several finds from excavations of medieval Perth have revealed what could be construed as possible Scandinavian links. Fragments of four glass linen smoothers were found, indicating they were in use in Perth until c. 1300 (Hunter 2010: 119, 121). Similar examples have been found in Viking graves in Scotland, including from a woman's grave at Ballinaby on Islay (Graham-Campbell and Batey 1998: 124). Four complete or possible skates made from horse bones (fig. 3) have been found: two from unstratified deposits at King Edward Street, one dated to the first half of the 14th century at 80-86 High Street and what may be a broken skate also from 14th-century layers (Ford 1995: 968, 975; Moloney and Coleman 1997: 751; MacGregor 2010: 105, 111). They are similar to examples found in 11th-century layers in Anglo-Scandinavian York and in late 13th/early 14th layers in Aberdeen (Finlayson 2000: 2463; Murray 1982: 182). Examples of bone skates in the British Isles date as far back as the eighth century AD (MacGregor 1976: 65; 1985: 142--44). By the Middle Ages they need not have been a 'Scandinavian' object.

Figure 3. Bone skates found in Perth. Image courtesy of Perth Museum & Art Gallery, Perth & Kinross Council, Scotland.

Perhaps two of the more interesting objects to come from Perth are 'Viking' swords, although these weapons provide more questions than answers. One is the remains of a sword in the Perth Museum said to be from Watergate, dated to the Viking Age based upon the pattern-welding of the blade (Caldwell and Bogdan 2012: 191). The other, the hilt of a sword, is a 10th-century type but was found in deposits dating to the third quarter of the 12th century (Ibid.: 189). Neither of these is necessarily evidence of Viking activity in the area in the 9th or 10th centuries. The report authors have suggested the hilt may have been an heirloom or a rusty piece of debris when it was deposited (Caldwell and Bogdan 2012: 189). Equally, in a more intriguing hypothesis, they suggest that perhaps 'Viking'-type swords were manufactured and used in Scotland much longer than anyone has previously realised (Ibid.: 189–91). Swords with lobed pommels in the style of Viking Age swords appear on sculpture and grave slabs, particularly in the west highlands of Scotland, up through at least the 15th century (RCAHMS 1971). On the east coast, the sword appearing on one of the coped stones in Dundee (see below) has a flared five-lobed pommel reminiscent of Viking swords dating to the tenth century, especially Petersen types O or S (Peirce 2002: 18–19, 87–107), although the stone was probably carved in the 11th or 12th century.

Physical links connecting Scotland, Scandinavia and England as parts of a trade network can also be demonstrated. One example is a type of cooking pot called London Sandy Shellyware. Radiocarbon dating of food residues from similar vessels in Perth, London and Bergen found that the vessels were first used in London in the late 10th century, arrived in Perth in the late 10th or early 11th century and then came to Bergen soon thereafter before falling out of use in reverse order (Hall et

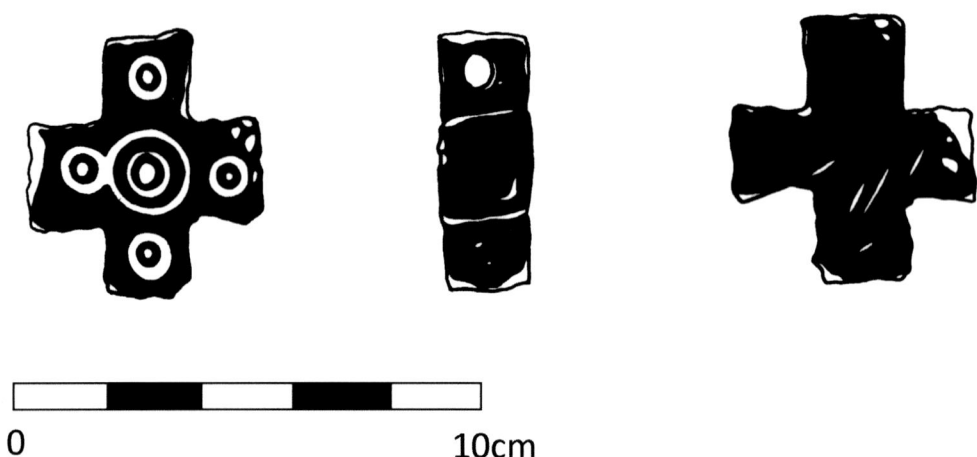

0   10cm

Figure 4. Drawing of the jet cross pendant with ring-and-dot motif found in Perth. Illustration by Alice Watterson. Image courtesy of Perth Museum & Art Gallery, Perth & Kinross Council, Scotland.

al. 2010). Another example of these links are jet cross pendants with ring-and-dot motif (fig. 4). These artefacts are especially notable because they are distinctive, and a number of identical crosses have been found in the British Isles, plus one Type A cross each in Bergen and Greenland (Pierce 2013). They were manufactured in Yorkshire, probably at Whitby Abbey in the mid-12th century, and Type A crosses have been found in Scotland in Perth and at Dairsie in Fife (Ibid.: 205, 207).

Elsewhere on the east coast there are also historical links to Scandinavia. A church near Cruden in Aberdeenshire was said to be dedicated to the Norwegian king St Olaf sometime around the 11th century and then abandoned in the 13th century because it was inundated with sand (Pratt 1857-59: 146–47; Eeles 1912-13: 470–72). Dedications to the Norwegian king and saint Olaf can be found across Scandinavia, the British Isles and North Atlantic. Recent radiocarbon dating of human bones from the church site has provided a slightly later date in the Norse period and Middle Ages. Two samples provided dates of AD 1240-1420, while a third sample dated AD 1420-1650 ([GU-1876, -1877, -1878] RCAHMS CANMORE ID 20865). The site is located near a long stretch of sand along the Bay of Cruden, and the area where the Water of Cruden empties into the bay at modern Port Erroll provides a small sheltered place with sandy areas. Such a location could potentially have played host to temporary beach markets in the Norse period. Cruden was said to be the site of one of the last battles between Scottish and Scandinavian forces (Cock 1791-99: 431–33). No evidence for a battle or a beach market has been reported in the area by metal detectorists to Treasure Trove Scotland (N. Ferguson, *pers. comm.*), but the possibility of a Scandinavian presence and commerce at sites such as this cannot be discounted.

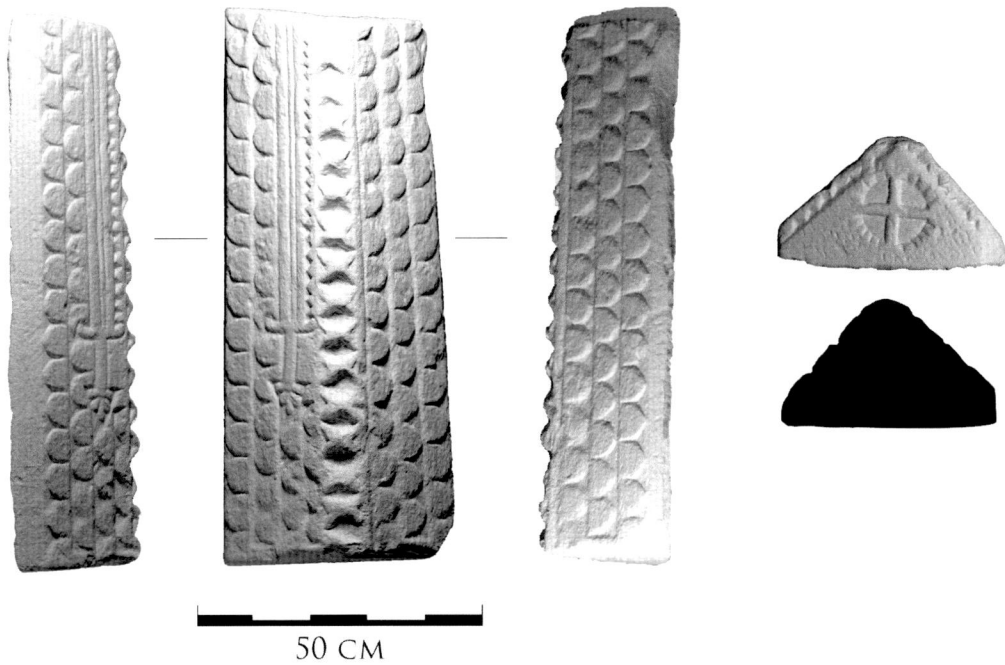

Figure 5. Laser scan of the 'Fish Scales stone' from Dundee. Copyright Dundee City Council.

Dundee also may have been an important location for trade and political manoeuvring as early as the mid-11th century. It was granted royal burgh status in the 12th century by King William I (Crawford 2002: 4; McManus 2013: 4). Excavations at St. Mary's church in central Dundee discovered a defensive ditch which pre-dated the late-12th century foundation of the church, although no datable material was found in the ditch fills which could prove that the enclosure was from the Viking period (Brown and Roberts 2000: 70; 73–75). Additional evidence for a Scandinavian presence includes the fact that the first parish church in Dundee was dedicated to St Clement, a saint popular in Denmark and Danish urban areas of eastern England (Crawford 2002: 4).

Recently rediscovered and put on display are two coped monuments from the churchyard which appear to be related to the other hogback/coped recumbent monuments in Scotland (see below). One stone, called the 'Fish Scales stone' (fig. 5), features the roof-tile decoration, or *tegulation*, seen on many hogback/coped stones and a five-lobed sword incised in the top row parallel to the rows of tegulation on one side (McManus 2013: 6–7). This is one of many swords depicted on medieval stones from the churchyard. The other coped stone features a lattice design on its sloped side that may be a stylised representation of the roof-tile motif and a pair of wool shears carved in relief, now very worn (Ibid.: 18–19). Were the people who commissioned these monuments perhaps Scandinavians who had seen the similar monuments in areas of commerce in southern Scotland and England? Representations of both weapons and tools of trade are unusual on hogback/coped stones in Scotland. While no one artefact can be definitively labelled as evidence for a Scandinavian (or Scotto-Scandinavian) presence in eastern Scotland at this time, the types and combinations of artefacts found hint at some Scandinavian presence in the region.

Set in stone? The sculptural evidence

The Dundee stones are part of a larger group of related stones called hogbacks and coped monuments (hereafter *HCMs*) that are found in the British Isles, particularly in England and Scotland, and only later, and rarely, in Scandinavia. Although HCMs are difficult to date and there are still many questions surrounding them, they appear to have originated in Anglo-Scandinavian Yorkshire sometime in the 10th century (Lang 1972-4: 206; Ritchie 1999: 16). Traditionally they have been associated with Anglo-Scandinavians (e.g. Bailey 1980; Lang 1972-4; 1984) because of their art styles and their distribution relative to other markers of Scandinavian influence; in England, they are especially concentrated in Cumbria and Yorkshire. However, more recently scholars have debated whether this ethnic association is valid. In Scotland, there are a number of HCMs along the Clyde and Forth corridor and in the Scottish borders which appear to be closely related to the stones from northern England, perhaps most notably the four hogbacks at Penrith and the five hogbacks at Govan (fig. 6). In the area of eastern Scotland covered by this paper, there are HCMs at Meigle, St Vigeans, St Andrews, Dunkeld and Dundee. Anna Ritchie (2004: 8–9) categorises these types of stones as 'coped' stones and generally dates them to the 11th and 12th centuries. It is also notable that in the 12th century these recumbent monuments began to appear in Scandinavia such as the Botkyrka stone, carved into the shape of a church but reminiscent of the shape of some HCMs, in the Swedish History Museum in Stockholm and two coped stones now housed in the National Museum of Denmark [D1679 and DLXVIb].

Whether or not these stones in Scotland had Anglo-Scandinavian connections, the link between HCMs and commerce is not a new one. On the Wirral peninsula in south-west England, at least seven Viking Age sculptures, including hogbacks, are located within a mile of the coast in an arc that centres upon the 10th-century beach market site of Meols (Bailey et al. 2006: 350). In Lincoln, 80% of what is termed 'Hiberno-Norse' sculpture is concentrated around two churches: St Marks and St Mary-le-Wigford. These were new churches at the edge of the city in the Viking Age, and it has been suggested that they represent the Anglo-Scandinavian elite who traded at the newly-established port (Stocker 2000: 187–89). Stocker (2000: 206–7) also noted similar patterns in Yorkshire.

It's the small things: stray finds

A survey of stray finds of Viking or possibly-Viking objects from Scotland and northern England has demonstrated that objects with Scandinavian links are found to a greater

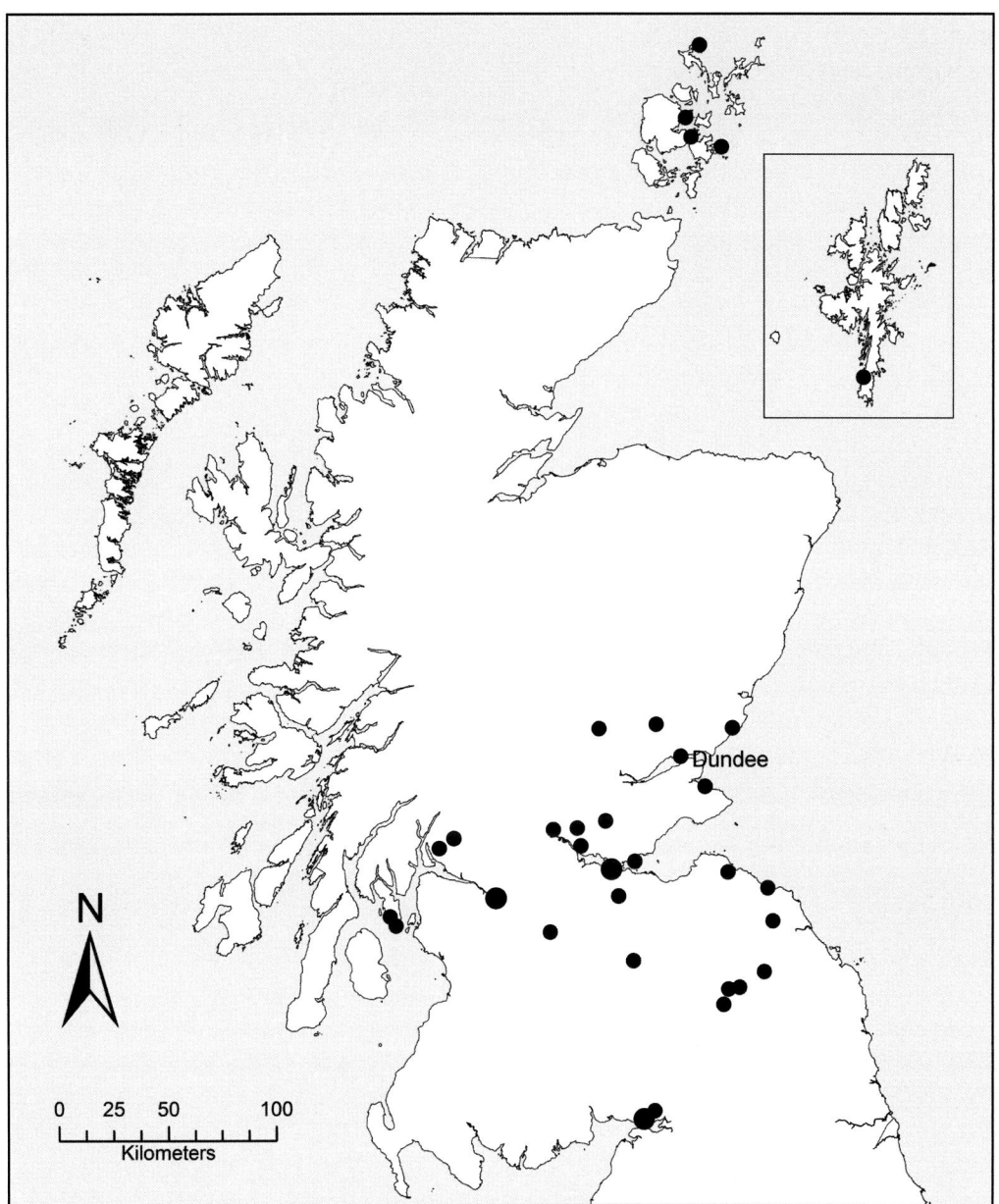

Figure 6. Distribution of HCMs in Scotland, including examples which have been lost since they were recorded. Larger dots mark several stones at one site. Map by Kirsty Millican

or lesser degree across all of Scotland (Buchanan 2012: esp. table 4.2). In the 10th century, Scandinavian settlement was encouraged on a small-scale by Scottish kings, especially as a buffer on the borders of their kingdoms (Taylor 2004: 134). Even after the end of the Viking Age, the kings of Alba and later Scotland had close links with both the Norwegian earldom of Orkney and the Danish kingdoms in eastern England, particularly in the 11th century when the future king Malcolm III lived in exile in Northumbria (Crawford 2000: 128–9).

Outside of the major excavations undertaken in Perth, smaller items which suggest Scandinavian connections have been found. A copper-alloy, Hiberno-Norse kidney-ringed pin found at Whitehills, Aberdeenshire is similar to pins from 11th and 12th century contexts in Ireland (Shiels 2005: 14), while a spiral-headed copper-alloy pin, which shares characteristics with other Hiberno-Norse pins, as well as a find from 13th-century levels in Novgorod, was found in the same area (Shiels 2007: 12). At Inchaffray Abbey in Perthshire, an 11th-century crest from a bell shrine was found which featured Irish Ringerike-style decoration (Graham-Campbell and Batey 1998: 104).

Coins are also an indicator of trade and movement. A now-lost gold dinar was minted in Morocco by Emir Yusuf ibn Tashfin c. 1097 and found at Monymusk, Aberdeenshire (Buchanan 2012: 113–14; citing Graham-Campbell 1995: 87). More substantially, a hoard of approximately 16 Hiberno-Norse coins deposited c. 1025 was found near Dull in Perthshire in 1989 (Bateson 1993: 213–14). Two other 11th-century hoards have been found in this part of the country: the hoard of Anglo-Saxon coins from Lindores, Fife, and a possible hoard of ten Hiberno-Norse coins from Fife that was sold at auction at Sotheby's in the 1920s (Ibid.: 213–14).

Discussion

Combining the clues provided by place-names, historical records and the distribution of archaeological finds, a case can be argued for the presence of a Scandinavian or Scotto-Scandinavian minority in eastern Scotland from the Viking Age until at least the 13th century, although there is certainly room for additional evidence. Who these people were and where they came from is still unclear. There is evidence to suggest they had links with the Hiberno-Norse in Ireland and western Britain, the Anglo-Scandinavians in eastern England and directly with Scandinavia. Most likely, people from all three areas were present. Some may have received land grants in the area in the 10th to 12th centuries or inherited property gained during the Viking period, but many were likely craftsmen and merchants attracted to the commercial opportunities found in Scotland's emerging urban centres. The presence of so many people with Norse connections may have been important for encouraging the presence of Anglo-Danish traders because they would have had powerful local protectors and the right connections for trade with Scandinavia (Crawford 2002: 4).

Although this paper has focused on the Scandinavian presence in eastern Scotland, it is important to remember that any Scandinavians would have lived side-by-side with Scots, English, Flemish and other foreign neighbours. Personal and social identities were fluid concepts that could change with each new situation. They likely would have dressed like their neighbours, with perhaps only slight nuances in style and decoration (e.g. Kershaw 2013: 216-50 for the Danelaw), lived in similar houses and were probably bilingual or had worked out a mutually-intelligible language since Old Scots and Old Norse were so closely related. Unlike Orkney and Shetland, where the Scandinavian influence can be seen even today, it is not immediately obvious in eastern Scotland, and thus often overlooked. The legacy they left behind may not have been so much a distinctive 'Scandinavian' influence as a legacy of assisting in the growth of Scotland's first urban centres through their efforts in manufacturing and commerce. A Scandinavian presence in areas not typically associated with Norse settlement in Scotland is a topic worth considering, and perhaps more evidence will be found once we start looking for it.

Acknowledgements

I am very grateful to several scholars who were able to provide me with digital copies of their work and other research for this paper when I could not do the research in person. They are, in no particular order, Drs Simon Taylor and Ryan McNutt of the University of Glasgow, Mark Hall of Perth Museum and Art Gallery and Dr Tom Horne. Thanks also to Dr Natasha Ferguson of Treasure Trove Scotland for the information she provided on reported finds. Dr Colleen Batey kindly commented on an earlier draft of this paper. Any remaining mistakes are mine alone.

Bibliography

Bailey, R. 1980. *Viking Age Sculpture*, Glasgow: William Collins Sons.

Bailey, R., J. Whalley, A. Bowden and G. Tresise 2006. A miniature Viking-Age hogback from the Wirral, *The Antiquaries Journal* 86, pp. 345–56.

Bateson, J.D. 1993. A Hiberno-Norse hoard from Dull, Perthshire, *The Numismatic Chronicle* 153, pp. 211-14.

Batey, C.E. 2002. Scandinavian Influence? I: Archaeological Background, an abstract of a paper given at a Tayside and Fife Archaeological Committee conference in Perth in March 2002. Available at: http://www.tafac.org.uk/category/conferences/ [last viewed: 17/02/2015].

Bennett, H., P.Z. Dransart and N.Q. Bogdan 2012. Loom-woven textiles, *Perth High Street Archaeological Excavation 1975-1977 Fascicule 3 The textiles and the leather*, Perth: Tayside and Fife Archaeological Committee, pp. 7–42.

Brown, G. and J. Roberts 2000. Excavations in the medieval cemetery at the city churches, Dundee, *Tayside and Fife Archaeological Journal* 6, pp. 70–86.

Buchanan, C. 2012. *Viking Artefacts from Southern Scotland and Northern England: Cultural Contacts, Interactions, and Identities in Peripheral Areas of Viking Settlement*, unpublished PhD thesis, University of Glasgow.

Caldwell, D. and N.Q. Bogdan 2012 The weapons, *Perth High Street Archaeological Excavation 1975-1977 Fascicule 2: The Ceramics, the Metalwork and the Wood*, Perth: Tayside and Fife Archaeological Committee, pp. 189–94.

Carus-Wilson, E. 1962-3 The medieval trade of the ports of the Wash, *Medieval Archaeology* 6-7, pp. 182–201.

Clarke, H. and A. Carter 1977. *Excavations in King's Lynn 1963-1970*, Society for Medieval Archaeology monograph series no. 7, London: Society for Medieval Archaeology.

Cock, A. 1791-99. Parish of Cruden, County of Aberdeen, *First Statistical Account,* vol. 5, number 30, pp. 431–39.

Crawford, B.E. 2000. The Scandinavian contribution to the development of the kingdom of Scotland, *Acta Archaeologica* 71, pp. 123–34.

Crawford, B.E. 2002. *Scandinavian influence II: Historical background*, an abstract of a paper given at a Tayside and Fife Archaeological Committee conference in Perth in March 2002. Available at: http://www.tafac.org.uk/category/conferences/ [last viewed: 19/02/2015].

Crawford, B.E. 2013. *The Northern Earldoms: Orkney and Caithness from AD 870 to 1470*, Edinburgh: Birlinn.

Deevy, M. 1998. *Medieval Ring Brooches in Ireland: A Study of Jewellery, Dress and Society*, Wordwell monograph series no. 1, Bray: Wordwell.

Ditchburn, D. 1988. Trade with Northern Europe, 1297--1540, in M. Lynch, M. Spearman and G. Stell (eds.), *The Scottish Medieval Town*, Edinburgh: John Donald Publishers, pp. 161--179.

Eeles, F. 1912-13. Ecclesiastical remains at Cruden and St Fergus, Aberdeenshire, *Proceedings of the Society of Antiquaries of Scotland* 47, pp. 470–88.

Fanning, T. 1994. *Viking Age Ringed Pins from Dublin*, series B, vol. 4, Dublin: Royal Irish Academy.

Fellows-Jensen, G. 2000. Vikings in the British Isles: The place-name evidence, *Acta Archaeologica* 71, pp. 135–46.

Fellows-Jensen, G. 2004. The Anglo-Scandinavian street-names of York, in R. Hall (ed.), *Aspects of Anglo-Scandinavian York,* Archaeology of York: Anglo-Scandinavian York 8/4, York: Council for British Archaeology, pp. 357–71.

Finlayson, R. 2000. Excavation at 22 Piccadilly, in A. Mainman and N. Rogers, *Finds from Anglo-Scandinavian York,* Craft, Industry and Everyday Life, The Archaeology of York, The Small Finds 17/14, York, Council for British Archaeology, pp. 2462–63.

Ford, B. 1995. Bone and antler objects, in D. Bowler, A. Cox and C. Smith, Four excavations in Perth, 1979-84, *Proceedings of the Society of Antiquaries of Scotland* 125, pp. 917–99.

Graham-Campbell, J. 1995. *The Viking-Age Gold and Silver of Scotland (AD 850-1100)*, Edinburgh: National Museums of Scotland.

Graham-Campbell, J. and C. Batey 1998. *The Vikings in Scotland: An Archaeological Survey*, Edinburgh: Edinburgh University Press.

Grant, A. 2005. The origin of the Ayrshire Bý names, in P. Gammeltoft, C. Hough and D. Waugh (eds.), *Cultural Contacts in the North Atlantic Region: The Evidence of Names,* Lerwick: NORNA, Scottish Place-name Society and Society for Name Studies in Britain and Ireland, pp. 127–40.

Hadley, D. 2000. 'Cockle amongst the wheat': The Scandinavian settlement of England, in W. Frazier and A. Tyrrell (eds.), *Social Identity in Early Medieval Britain*, London: Leicester University Press, pp. 111–35.

Hadley, D. and J. Richards 2000. Introduction: interdisciplinary approaches to the Scandinavian settlement, in D. Hadley and J. Richards (eds.), *Cultures in Contact: Scandinavian settlement in England in the ninth and tenth centuries*, Turnhout: Brepols, pp. 3–15.

Hall, D. 2002. *Burgess, Merchant and Priest: Burgh life in the Scottish medieval town.* Making of Scotland series, G. Barclay (series ed.), Edinburgh: Birlinn and Historic Scotland.

Hall, D., G.T. Cook, W. Hamilton 2010. New dating evidence for North Sea trade between England, Scotland, and Norway in the 11th century AD, *Radiocarbon* 52(2-3), pp. 331–36.

Hall, M., D. Hall and G. Cook 2005. What's cooking? New radiocarbon dates from the earliest phases of the Perth High Street excavations and the question of Perth's early medieval origin, *Proceedings of the Society of Antiquaries of Scotland* 135, pp. 273–85.

Harrison, S. 2000. The Millhill burial in context: artifact, culture, and chronology in the 'Viking West', *Acta Archaeologica* 71, pp. 65–78.

Herteig, A. 1975. The excavation of Bryggen, Bergen, Norway, in R. Bruce-Mitford (ed.), *Recent Archaeological Excavations in Europe*, London: Routledge and Kegan Paul, pp. 65–89.

Horne, T. 2014. *The Most Praiseworthy Journey: Scandinavian Market Networks in the Viking Age*, unpublished PhD thesis, University of Glasgow.

Hunter, J. 2010. The medieval glass, in *Perth High Street Archaeological Excavation 1975-1977 Fascicule 4: Living and Working in a Medieval Scottish Burgh, Environmental Remains and Miscellaneous Finds*, with N. Q. Bogdan and G. Dalgleish, Perth: Tayside and Fife Archaeological Committee, pp. 119–25.

Karlsson, G. 2000. *The History of Iceland*. Minneapolis: University of Minnesota Press.

Kershaw, J. 2013. *Viking Identities: Scandinavian Jewellery in England*. Oxford: Oxford University Press.

Lang, J. 1972-4. Hogback monuments in Scotland, *Proceedings of the Society of Antiquaries of Scotland* 105, pp. 206–35.

Lang, J. 1984. The hogback: a Viking colonial monument, *Anglo-Saxon Studies in Archaeology and History* 3, pp. 86–176.

MacGregor, A. 1976. Bone skates: a review of the evidence, *Archaeological Journal* 133, pp. 57–74.

MacGregor, A. 1985. *Bone, Antler, Ivory & Horn: The technology of skeletal materials since the Roman period*, Beckenham, Kent: Croom Helm.

MacGregor, A. 2010. The worked bone, *Perth High Street Archaeological Excavation 1975-1977 Fascicule 4: Living and Working in a Medieval Scottish Burgh, Environmental Remains and Miscellaneous Finds*, with N. Q. Bogdan, M. Hall and C. Smith, Perth: Tayside and Fife Archaeological Committee, 97–117.

Mackenzie, W.M. 1949. *The Scottish Burghs*, Edinburgh: Oliver and Boyd.

Martin, C. and N.Q. Bogdan 2012. The boat timbers, *Perth High Street Archaeological Excavation 1975-1977 Fascicule 2: the Ceramics, the Metalwork and the Wood*, Perth: Tayside and Fife Archaeological Committee, 317–22.

McManus: Dundee's Art Gallery and Museum (2013), *Dundee's Medieval Carved Stones.*

Moloney, C. and R. Coleman 1997. The development of a medieval street frontage: the evidence from excavations at 80-86 High Street, Perth, *Proceedings of the Society of Antiquaries of Scotland* 127, pp. 707–82.

Murray, J.C. (ed.) 1982. *Excavations in the Medieval Burgh of Aberdeen 1973-81*, Society of Antiquaries of Scotland Monograph Series no. 2, Edinburgh: Society of Antiquaries of Scotland.

Ottaway, P. and N. Rogers 2002. *Craft, Industry and Everyday Life: Finds from Medieval York*, The Archaeology of York, The Small Finds 17/15, York: Council for British Archaeology.

Owen, O. 1999. *The Sea Road: A Viking Voyage Through Scotland*, The Making of Scotland series, Edinburgh: Canongate Books.

Owen, O. 2005. Scotland's Viking 'towns': a contradiction in terms?, in A. Mortensen and S. Arge (eds.), *Viking and Norse in the North Atlantic: Select Papers from the Proceedings of the 14th Viking Congress, Tórshavn*, Tórshavn, Føroya Fróðskaparfelag, pp. 297–306.

Parsons, D. 2001. How long did the Scandinavian language survive in England? Again, in J. Graham-Campbell, R. Hall, J. Jesch, and D. Parsons (eds.), *Vikings and the Danelaw: Select Papers from the Proceedings of the 13th Viking Congress*, Oxford: Oxbow Books, 299–312.

Parsons, D. 2004. The inscriptions of Viking-Age York, in R. Hall (ed.), *Aspects of Anglo-Scandinavian York*, Archaeology of York: Anglo-Scandinavian York 8/4, York: Council for British Archaeology, pp. 350–56.

Peirce, I. 2002. *Swords of the Viking Age*, Woodbridge: Boydell Press.

Pierce, E. 2013. Jet cross pendants from the British Isles and beyond: forms, distribution and use, *Medieval Archaeology* 57, pp. 198–211.

Pratt, J. 1857-59. Note of the recent excavation of a cairn on the High Law, and of other antiquities in the parish of Cruden, Aberdeenshire, with additional notes by J. Stuart, *Proceedings of the Society of Antiquaries of Scotland* 3, pp. 144–49.

RCAHMS 1971. *Argyll: an inventory of the Ancient Monuments. vol.1, Kintyre*, Edinburgh: HMSO.

Richards, J. 2004. *Viking Age England*, first published 1991, Stroud: Tempus.

Ritchie, A. 1993. *Viking Scotland*, Historic Scotland series, reprinted 1996, London: T T Batsford and Historic Scotland.

Ritchie, A. 1999. *Govan and its Carved Stones*, Balgavies: Pinkfoot Press.

Ritchie, A. 2004. *Hogback Gravestones at Govan and Beyond*, Glasgow: Friends of Govan Old.

Shiels, J. 2005. Whitehills (Boyndie parish): Viking kidney-ringed pin, *Discovery and Excavation in Scotland* new series 6, R. Turner (ed.), Edinburgh: Council for Scottish Archaeology, pp. 14.

Shiels, J. 2007. Whitehills: early-historic/later spiral-headed bronze pin, *Discovery and Excavation in Scotland* new series 8, R. Turner (ed.), Edinburgh: Council for Scottish Archaeology, pp. 12.

Stevenson, A. 1988. Trade with the South, 1070--1513, in M. Lynch, M. Spearman and G. Stell (eds.), *The Scottish Medieval Town*, Edinburgh: John Donald Publishers, pp. 180--206.

Stocker, D. 2000. Monuments and merchants: irregularities in the distribution of stone sculpture in Lincolnshire and Yorkshire in the tenth century, in D. Hadley and J. Richards (eds.), *Cultures in Contact: Scandinavian settlement in England in the Ninth and Tenth Centuries*, Studies in the Early Middle Ages 2, Turnhout: Brepols, pp. 179–212.

Taylor, S. 2004. Scandinavians in central Scotland – *bý*-place-names and their context,'in G. Williams and P. Bibire (eds.), *Sagas, Saints and Settlements*, Leiden: Brill, pp. 125–45.

Taylor, S. 2007. The Rock of the Irishmen: an early place-name tale from Fife and Kinross, in B. Ballin Smith, S. Taylor and G. Williams (ed.), *West* Over Sea: Studies in Scandinavian Sea-Borne Expansion and Settlement before 1300, Leiden and Boston: Brill, pp. 497–514.

Thomas, C. and N.Q. Bogdan 2012. The other leather finds, *Perth High Street Archaeological Excavation 1975-1977 Fascicule 3: The textiles and the leather*, Perth: Tayside and Fife Archaeological Committee, pp. 261–98.

Turville-Petre, T. 2001. Representations of the Danelaw in Middle English literature, in J. Graham-Campbell, R. Hall, J. Jesch, and D. Parsons (eds.), *Vikings and the Danelaw: Select Papers from the Proceedings of the 13th Viking Congress*, Oxford: Oxbow Books, pp. 345–55.

Local and foreign clergy: the provision of clergy in the late mediaeval diocese of Sodor

Sarah Thomas

In late mediaeval Scotland, the idea of national identity and what it meant to be Scottish was bound up with the kingdom of Scots and the king, who they were ruled by. Scotland did not have a common language – indeed there were four main languages spoken – English or Scots, Gaelic, French and Norse. However, a person's sense of belonging may have been more locally defined both by language and kinship. In terms of the Church, we might imagine that within the kingdom of Scotland it was possible for clergy to move relatively freely between dioceses. However, a study of the clergy of the diocese of Sodor, which after 1387 encompassed the Hebrides, Arran and Bute, reveals that clergy not native to the Hebrides or to Argyll were exceedingly rare. In the neighbouring diocese of Argyll, the prevalence of lowland Scots clergy holding benefices increased particularly in the fifteenth century (for the diocese of Argyll see MacDonald, 2008). This paper examines the factors that ensured, despite the increasing centralisation of papal power over clerical appointments and the growth of royal power over ecclesiastical benefices, that the vast majority of clergy in Sodor were inherently local and the only thing 'foreign' about them was that they did not always belong to the island on which they held a parish church.

It is possible primarily through papal sources to identify 211 fourteenth and fifteenth century clergy associated with churches in the diocese of Sodor. When a cleric sought a benefice in a papal petition, the diocese he came from was stated so we are able to use this to analyse geographic origin of the clergy. Thus, in Sodor, there were 197 clerics who came from that diocese, 7 from the diocese of Argyll, 2 from Ross, 1 from Moray, 2 from Glasgow, 1 from Dunblane, 1 from St Andrews and 1 from Raphoe in Ireland. In contrast, in the same period, the diocese of Argyll had approximately 30 clerics from the diocese of Glasgow and 23 from St Andrews diocese alone (MacDonald 2008, 87).

Why is it that clerical provision to Hebridean benefices seems to have been so inherently local? What factors ensured that the vast majority of Hebridean clerics hailed from that diocese? The prime reason seems to have been MacDonald patronage of the majority of parish churches within the diocese of Sodor. The MacDonald Lordship of the Isles incorporated the Hebrides, Kintyre, Ardnamurchan, Morvern, Moidart, Knapdale and Lochaber (Steer and Bannerman 1977; Bannerman 1977; MacGregor 1998; Oram 2006). In the Hebrides, there were 43 parish churches of which 27 had the Lords of the Isles as patrons (Thomas forthcoming). Patronage of parish churches gave the patron the power to decide which priests could serve and receive income from the parish. The majority of the remaining 16 were appropriated to the monastery of Iona with a few appropriated to the nunnery of Iona, the priory of Oronsay and the bishop of Sodor (Thomas 2009b, 75-78). Appropriation usually meant that the part of the income of the parish church, primarily gained through tithes paid by the parishioners, was diverted to the appropriator. None of the parish churches were appropriated to either secular or ecclesiastical organisations outside the diocese of Sodor. Despite the attempts of James I to extend his control over ecclesiastical benefices in the west, it was not until the sixteenth-century, after the forfeiture of the Lordship, that the Crown obtained control over ecclesiastical benefices in the Hebrides. Fourteen of the Sodor parish churches are recorded in Crown grants of benefices in the sixteenth century in the Registers of the Privy Seal: Kilarrow, Islay (RSS i, 68), Kilchrist, Skye (RSS i, 163), Kilchoman, Islay (RSS i, 261), Kilchattan, Gigha (RSS i, 331), Eynort, Skye (RSS i, 352), Uig, Skye (RSS i, 365), Benbecula (RSS ii, 301), Barvas on Lewis, Kilmaluag of Skye and Kilconan of Skye (RSS ii, 301), Benweall in Uist (RSS ii, 739), Harris (RSS ii, 753), Kildalton, Islay (RSS iii, 413) and Eye on Lewis (RSS v, 138). There were also four parish churches, two apiece on Arran and Bute, which were in the patronage of the Stewarts. However, this paper is going to focus on the Hebridean clergy and therefore will not consider the Arran and Bute parishes further.

The degree of potential control over ecclesiastical benefices wielded by the Lords of the Isles is unusual compared with the rest of Scotland. In the diocese of Aberdeen, 95% of parish churches were appropriated to a secular or ecclesiastical institution and overall in Scotland the average was 86.5%, in contrast in the Lordship of the Isles the appropriation rate was only 36% (Cowan 1972, 43-44; Cowan 1978-80, 26-27). That the appropriated churches in the diocese of Sodor were overwhelmingly appropriated to local monastic and episcopal institutions is a point worth emphasising. There is one case in the fourteenth century of a parish church in the Hebrides appropriated to a monastic institution outside the diocese of Sodor: in 1380, Ardchattan priory in Lorn in mainland Argyll tried to get their annexation of Kirkapoll parish church on Tiree confirmed by the pope and their petition implies that they had held it for at least a hundred years (*CPL Clement VII*, 46). This church of *Sancte Columbe de Thiriach* has often been identified as Soroby, the other parish church on Tiree, but this is an oft-repeated error which seems to stem from the belief that Kirkapoll was in the possession of the bishop prior to 1397 and that therefore Ardchattan's possession had to be Soroby (MacPhail 1914, 138-40 & 168; RCAHMS 1980, 166-7; Cowan 1967, 185; McDonald 1997, 93-94). However, a papal letter regarding Kirkapoll from 30 October 1397 clearly indicates that it was Kirkapoll which Ardchattan had sought to confirm possession of in 1380 (CPL Benedict XIII, 79). In 1397, the bishop of Sodor seems to have successfully annulled Ardchattan's appropriation and instead acquired the benefice for himself (CPL Benedict XIII, 79). There was one other recorded grant to a monastic institution outside Sodor: the chapel of the Holy Trinity in North Uist was granted to Inchaffray abbey in Perthshire by Christina, daughter of Alan MacRuairi, and confirmed by Godfrey of the Isles, and lord of Uist, in 1389 and by Donald, Lord of the Isles, in

1410 (Munro 1986, 13-14 & 28-29). Patronage of the parish churches was thus held firstly predominantly by the Lords of the Isles and secondly by local ecclesiastical institutions, not by outsiders.   It has been possible to identify the geographical and social origins of approximately 25% of the Sodor clergy and through that we can analyse the patterns of patronage. The percentage of identified clergy is relatively low because of the inconsistent naming patterns; a cleric can be recorded by first name and patronymic, first name only or first name and surname (Thomas forthcoming). For example, in August 1441 a cleric called *Alexander Tarleti Ferchardi Macgillcan* sought provision to the rectory of Kilchoman on Islay (CSSR iv, 193) whilst in the same year a *Dominicus Patrici* sought provision to the parish churches of St Conan's of Vaternish and Uig on Skye (CSSR iv, 1999). The first cleric can be identified as a MacLean, both by the surname and also by the distinctive names of his father and grandfather. However, the second cleric is harder to identify – no surname and neither the first name nor the father's name is particularly distinctive.

We will begin by looking at the identity of the clergy provided to the 27 parish churches in the patronage of the Lords of the Isles. In the fourteenth and fifteenth centuries, 15 of these parish churches feature in petitions to the papacy usually regarding a cleric's provision to or removal from a specific benefice: for example, Kilchoman on Islay (*CSSR* iv, 76), Kildalton on Islay (*CSSR* iii, 31), Kilarrow on Islay (*CSSR* iv, 107), Kilchattan on Gigha (*CSSR* iv, 76), St Columba's of Eye, Lewis (*CSSR* iv, 189), St Conan's of Vaternish, Skye (*CSSR* iv, 199), St Conan's of Uig, Skye (*CSSR* iv, 199), St Peter's of Uist (*CSSR* iv, 203), St Comgan of Duirinish, Skye (*CSSR* iv, 307), Kilchrist of Strath, Skye (*CSSR* ii, 203), St Christopher's, Uig, Lewis (*CSSR* v, 85), St Columba's, Howmore, Uist (*CSSR* v, 422), the parish church of Barra (*CPL Clement VII*, 394); Kilmaluag of Trotternish, Skye (ACSB, 97).

The parish church which features most frequently in the papal petitions is Kilchoman on the west coast of Islay. Archdeacon Monro's account of 1595 stated that 'in the town of Kilchomain the Lords of the Isles dwelt offtymes' (Monro 1999, 310). The parish church would therefore appear to be an important benefice and the pattern of provision and the amount of late medieval grave-slabs at the church suggest that that was indeed the case. Amongst those who either held or sought to hold the rectory were an illegitimate MacDonald, Angus *Johannis de Insulis* (CSSR v, 166), a MacLean of Lochbuie, Alexander *Tarleti Ferchardi* MacLean (CSSR iv 193 & v 91), a MacEachern from Kintyre, Andrew MacEachern (*CPL Clement VII*, 79 & 189) and a cleric, Andrew Dunoon, from the diocese of Ross (CSSR v, 174). All four of these clerics either had close personal or familial connections to the Lords of the Isles (Thomas, forthcoming; as regards Andrew Dunoon see also MacDonald 2008: 89 n.464). Andrew Dunoon is perhaps the most intriguing because he does not seem to have been ideally suited for a Hebridean benefice given that he had admitted in an earlier petition of 1441 that he did not 'speak the dialect intelligibly'(CSSR iv, 206). He seems to be a clear case of a cleric from the diocese of Ross benefiting from the Lords of the Isles' expansion eastwards with their attainment of the earldom of Ross (Thomas, forthcoming).

At Kildalton at the south-east end of Islay, we also find clerics with connections to the Lordship. For example in the 1450s and 1460s, the rector was Duncan Ó Brolchán who was a member of the kindred of stone masons involved in the restoration of the abbey of Iona in mid fifteenth century (Steer and Bannerman 1977, 107; Glas. Mun., 61; CSSR v, 351). Duncan also seems to have acted as a public notary and to have been a witness for at least one lordship charter (Munro 1986, 92). Another Ó Brolchán, Neil, appeared in 1382 as rector of the parish church of Kilarrow in central Islay, another church in the patronage of the Lords of the Isles (DN 7, no.313). The social and geographic origins of many of the clerics recorded in connection with Kilarrow cannot be identified, although one John son of Mauritii may have been MacMhuirich – a member of the poetic kindred (Steer and Bannerman 1977, 39; CSSR iii, 203; Thomas forthcoming).

We not only find clerics with lordship connections at churches in the heartland of the Lordship – that is Islay – they are also identifiable at churches in Skye. For example, the presence of Cristinus MacMarkys, a cleric from the MacMhurcuis kindred based in Kintyre, at the parish church of Kilmaluag at Trotternish in northern Skye strongly implies the influence of the lordship (CPL viii, 14; Thomson 1968, 73; O Baoill 1976, 183). Additionally, a cleric, John Hector MacLean, who would later rise to be bishop of Sodor, seems to have begun his ecclesiastical career at Kilchrist in Strath in southern Skye (CSSR iii, 251). In addition to Andrew Dunoon, there is a second cleric to originate from north-east Scotland, John Beollan from the diocese of Moray, sought to hold Kilchrist (CSSR v, 88). According to Alexander Grant, seventeenth-century historians such as Hugh MacDonald believed that O'Beólan was the surname of Fearchar Mac-an-t-Sagairt until he was created earl of Ross in circa 1220 (Grant 2005, 120). John Beollan may have been related to the earls of Ross, although, according to Grant, it was a fairly common Gaelic name (Grant 2005, 119). However, it seems to be a fairly tenuous link to the fifteenth-century earls of Ross, the Lords of the Isles.

However, in general, the further we get away from the heartland of the lordship the harder it becomes to identify clerics with clear unambiguous links to the lordship and indeed it is easier to identify local clerics. By this we mean that clerics by-and-large can be identified, not so much with the Lords of the Isles, but with the local landowners. Thus, for example, in northern Skye, we can identify clerics whose names would suggest that they were members of the MacLeods of Harris. Thus, in 1450, the rector of St Comgan's of Duirinish was a John son of Tormod – the names John and Tormod were both used by the MacLeods of Harris (CSSR v, 85; Steer and Bannerman 1977, 100). This parish church also seems to have been served by rectors bearing the name MacCormack; *Nonnas* or Naomhan MacCormack was recorded as having been the rector of this church until his death in 1406 (CPP i, 631). John MacCormack had been rector of this church until his death sometime before August 1445 (CSSR iv, 307). MacCormack or MacCormick seems to have been a relatively common surname across the Gaidhealtachd with MacCormacks found from Kirkcudbrightshire to the Highlands (Black 1996, 476). It may be that these particular MacCormacks were local to Skye and in this respect we must also recall the early fourteenth century archdeacon of Sodor, Cormac son of Cormac, who was closely associated with Skye and the church of Snizort (Thomas 2009a, 145-163).

In Lewis, it is clear that the MacLeods of Lewis must have had some influence over clerical provision to the parish churches on their island. For example, in 1450 a Finlay MacLeod was rector of the parish church of St Columba of Eye – a church which was the main place of burial for the MacLeods of Lewis (CSSR v, 85). Nine years earlier there was one cleric who sought to hold St Columba's of Eye who may be indicative of Lordship patronage; in 1441, John Alexander Kenothson or Kennochson, a clerk of the diocese of Ross, sought to remove Martin *Duncani* on the grounds that he had held the benefice without dispensation or canonical collation for at least four years (CSSR iv, 189). This man failed to gain possession; a point stated in a petition of 1454 regarding the treasurership of the diocese of Ross (CSSR v, 151). Indeed he seems to have been involved in litigation over not only the treasurership, but also the role of subchanter (Watt and Murray 2003, 364 & 369-370). The name, Kenothson or Kennochson, suggests that he may have been a MacKenzie, possibly the MacKenzies of Kintail. It is worth noting that in his 1441 petition he stated that he was 'of a noble race of earls'; this may suggest that he claimed a relationship with the earls of Ross, although it is hard to see without more documentation how he might have been related to them (CSSR iv, 189). Given that the MacKenzies were 'the most powerful kindred in Ross' who from 1411 onwards 'consistently opposed' the Lords of the Isles, John Kenothson seems an unlikely candidate for Lordship patronage (Bannerman 1977a, 205). The appearance of Torquil MacLeod of Lewis as a charter witness in Lordship charters in the 1430s and 1440s would suggest that they were on reasonably good terms with the Lord of the Isles (Munro 1986, 41 & 53). It may be that John Kenothson simply saw St Columba's of Eye as a benefice worth challenging for, but found without the local connections that physical possession was impossible.

If the Lords of the Isles in exercising their right to present priests to 27 parish churches were on the whole choosing local candidates with strong kindred links to the Lordship, what types of clergy were presented to the appropriated parish churches? In the introduction, it was noted that 36% of Hebridean parish churches were appropriated to ecclesiastical institutions within the diocese of Sodor. Appropriation, usually of the rectory of the parish church, meant that the appropriator had the right to present their candidate for the benefice to the bishop. None of the perpetual vicarages of the parish churches appropriated to monastic institutions were occupied by clerics from outwith the diocese. Instead, it is a picture of the appointment of local clergy either with ties to the area of the parish church or connections to appropriating institution. For example, the perpetual vicarage of Kilcolmkil in northern Mull, whose rectory was appropriated to the monastery of Iona, had been held prior to 1391 by Maurice *Macsiri* or MacSherry who was a member of a branch of the MacKinnons based on Mull (CPL Clement VII, 170; Black 1996, 563). The MacSherries or MacSiris appear in northern Mull in the seventeenth century in papers connected with the Campbells' campaign to gain the lands of the MacLeans of Duart. For example, in 1675 a Ferquhar *McSheri* was named in a list between men holding lands in Balliemoir and Derryvyll which suggests that he too lived in northern Mull (MacPhail 1914, 301). In the same document, a John *McShirie* was listed at Ledmore which was probably towards the southern boundary of the parish of Kilcolmkil (MacPhail 1914, 302). This therefore seems to be a case of very local provision where the perpetual vicar came not only from the island, but the very parish he served.

There is further evidence from southern Mull of local clerics serving as perpetual vicars of local parish churches. In 1431, Felan, son of John, was perpetual vicar of the parish church of St John the Evangelist in Ardnish, later known as Killean, in Mull (CSSR iii, 167). Patrick, son of Felan, until his death in circa 1467, held the perpetual vicarage of Kilfinichen on Mull (CSSR v, 421). This Patrick might well have been the son of the Felan of 1431; they may well have been members of a hereditary ecclesiastical lineage which was based in Mull but not necessarily attached to a specific parish church.

On Coll, the rectory of the parish church was appropriated to the nunnery of Iona and its perpetual vicarage was in the possession of a MacKinnon cleric in the 1430s (CPL viii, 469). In April 1433, there was an attempt made to deprive Finguine, son of Finguine MacKinnon, of the church of Killunaig on Coll because he had held it for over a year without being ordained as a priest (CPL viii, 469). This attempt clearly failed since Finguine was still perpetual vicar in October 1441 when he supplicated to oust the incumbent of the rectory of St Columba of Kirkapoll on Tiree (CSSR iv, 201). Finguine's 1441 supplication described him as the 'son of a great noble, unmarried, and an unmarried woman' (CSSR iv, 201). This Finguine may be the same man as the monk of that name of 1421 who had sought to hold a parish church (CSSR i, 272). However, Finguine was a common MacKinnon name and the cleric of 1433 and 1441 makes no reference to being a monk.

Not only were the appropriating institutions based in the Hebrides, but the men and women in charge of the monastery of Iona, the nunnery of Iona and Oronsay Priory were also local. It must have been a significant factor for the appointment of clerics to appropriated churches that all of these institutions remained under the control of Gaels. The monastery of Iona's abbots in the fourteenth and fifteenth centuries were all Gaelic speakers and all were probably native Hebrideans or at most from Argyll. Amongst their numbers are two MacKinnons, a MacAlasdair and a Gille-Coinnich (Watt and Shead 2001, 111-115). The MacKinnons were closely connected to the monastery of Iona, having supplied an infamous abbot, the so-called Green abbot – Finguine MacKinnon – from circa 1357 until 1405 (MacQuarrie 1984-6, 355-375). They continued, as we shall see, to be associated both with the abbey and its ecclesiastical possessions in the fifteenth century. The Benedictine prioresses of the nunnery of Iona are less well-recorded; a possible prioress in the fifteenth century was Cristina *Dominici* (Watt and Shead 2001, 116). The only other recorded prioresses are from the sixteenth century and both were MacLeans, probably from Kingairloch in Morvern (Watt and Shead 2001, 116). The priory of Oronsay was principally held by men from families closely connected with it; in particular, the MacDuffies, the MacMhuirichs and the MacIans (Steer and Bannerman 1977, 68; Watt and Shead 2001, 166). The absence of any lowlanders in charge of religious houses in the Hebrides reduces further the possibility that lowland secular clergy would gain possession of Hebridean ecclesiastical benefices.

Additionally, the bishops of Sodor had three parish churches appropriated to them, but they were also unlikely to give openings to lowland clergy since from the split of the diocese in 1387 all the bishops of the Scottish diocese of Sodor seem to have come from the Hebrides. In particular, from the mid 1420s, the bishop, Angus, was a nephew of the Lord of the Isles and his successor was a MacLean, possibly of Duart (Thomas 2010, 34-37). The bishops had the rectories of three parish churches – Snizort in Skye, St Moluag's on Raasay and Kirkapoll on Tiree. No clergy are recorded for St Moluag's, but there are fifteenth-century papal petitions surviving for the perpetual vicarages of Snizort and Kirkapoll. Kirkapoll was also associated with the MacKinnons. The MacKinnon priest whom we encountered at Killunaig on Coll also tried to expand his possessions to include Kirkapoll. The MacKinnon links to Tiree and to Kirkapoll specifically are highlighted by the cross and grave-slab from that church which commemorate and make reference to Abbot Finguine (Steer and Bannerman 1977, 100-102). Whether the Finguine priest of 1433 successfully gained possession of Kirkapoll is not recorded, but the MacKinnon association with the church of Kirkapoll suggests that they also had relationships with the bishops of Sodor as well as the abbey of Iona.

An alternative interpretation might be that the bishops were relatively weak and whilst they had successfully taken Kirkapoll from the previous appropriator, Ardchattan priory, they were unable to break this association between MacKinnons and Kirkapoll. The evidence for a long-standing link between this kindred and the church comes from 1374; in November of this year a priest called Niall MacFinnlaech claimed in a petition to the papacy that the church of St Columba of Kirkapoll was vacant after the incumbent, Aed *MacPeter,* had been deprived by the bishop for falsifying papal letters (Reg. Aven. 195 fo.465-465v). However, ten months later, in September 1375, Aed made a counter-claim stating that Niall had made false representations to the pope and was illegally occupying the church (DN 7 no.293). The outcome of the investigation, ordered by the pope, by the bishop of Argyll is unfortunately not recorded. However, a significant point from these two petitions is the identity of Niall MacFinnlaech; Finnlaech is a MacKinnon name which appears in the MacKinnon genealogy in *MS 1467* (Steer and Bannerman 1977, 103). Niall MacFinnlaech may have been a member of a branch of the MacKinnons who were descended from the Finnlaech in the *MS 1467* genealogy. We therefore have an earlier link between the MacKinnons and the parish church of Kirkapoll.

Whilst Kirkapoll came into the possession of the bishops of Sodor late in the fourteenth century, the rectory of the parish church of St Columba's of Snizort may have been in the possession of the archdeacons of Sodor much earlier and after the split of the diocese it may have passed to the bishops of the new Scottish diocese of Sodor (Thomas 2009a, 151). Snizort seems to have been adopted as the episcopal seat of the Sodor bishops after the 1387 split even if it was not a universally happy choice (CSSR iv, 25). The parish church was served by perpetual vicars; however, only two appear on record, a Michael Maccoyle and a Martin son of Donald, both in 1441 (CSSR iv, 188). Martin son of Donald was described as coming from the diocese of Argyll; however, both names are so common that it is difficult to identify his origins. A cleric from further afield, from the diocese of St Andrews, was Robert Thom who sought to hold the perpetual vicarage of Snizort in May 1450. He claimed that the incumbent, Martin son of Donald, had been excommunicated by a local official (CSSR v, 87). His petition does not state whether he had the support of the patron, the bishop, in seeking Martin's removal. However, he seems to have failed to obtain physical possession of the benefice which might suggest that the bishop had not supported him. His failure to obtain possession is attested by his reappearance in 1459/60 when he was still seeking a benefice in Skye and still described as hailing from the diocese of St Andrews (CPL xii, 60). However, the fact that he was clearly determinedly seeking a benefice in Skye suggests that the designation 'of the diocese of St Andrews' may be misleading. Is it possible that he was actually from Skye? It is highly speculative, but possible that he had been a student at the University of St Andrews and had been ordained a cleric in St Andrews and was therefore designated 'of that diocese'. However, his two names, Robert and Thom, are not ones used by kindreds in Skye. It is possible, nevertheless, that Robert was used in place of the name *Ruairi* and that Thom is an abbreviation of Thomas or *Támhas*, which was a name used by kindreds in the Hebrides (for the use of Robert for Ruairi, see Steer and Bannerman 1977, 136 n.21). The bishop may not have supported Robert Thom in 1450, but on the second occasion Thom had been provided by the bishop to the benefice of St Comgan of Duirinish in Skye and the patron had also supported him (CPL xii, 60).

This last example is perhaps a warning that the designation of their diocesan origin should not always to be taken at face value. Robert Thom's failure to obtain physical possession of Snizort in 1450 may well demonstrate the limitations of episcopal and patronal power against a well-entrenched incumbent. At face value, Robert Thom was foreign to the Hebrides, but the evidence from 1459/60 suggests that he was not quite as foreign as he seemed. Foreign clergy were indeed a rarity in the Hebrides.

There were two other factors, language and poverty, which probably also deterred foreign clergy from seeking Hebridean benefices. The issue of language concerned the ability of clergy to speak the local language, in this case Gaelic. One of the most important skills for the clergy was the ability to communicate with lay society. If the clergy can be said to have been there for two main functions, the worship of God and the instruction of lay society in Christianity, then they had to be able to understand lay people and vice-versa. Thus, one statute of Bishop Russell of 1350 stated that the clergy were expected to 'teach and instruct them to understand the Apostles' Creed in their mother tongue' (Oliver 1862, 204). The mass and probably the sermon would have been in Latin, but Bishop Russell's statute makes it clear that there was an expectation that the clergy should be able to communicate in their parishioners' dialect or language. The fourth Lateran Council's ruling of 1215 on annual confession for the laity also has implications on language – in order for the priest to hear his parishioners' confessions he would need, in the Hebrides, to understand Gaelic (Thomson 1998, 209). The late mediaeval Church had become increasingly concerned about the issue of language and theoretically the inability to speak the language of the diocese might bar a priest for taking up a benefice. Canon nine of the Fourth Lateran Council concerned language and communication with parishioners – it ordered that where there were people of different languages, the bishop was to provide 'suitable men who will, according to the different rites and languages, celebrate the divine offices for them, administer the sacraments of the Church and instruct them by word and example' (http://www.fordham.edu/halsall/basis/lateran4.html). There are examples of papal provisions where provisos are given that the cleric must speak the language of the parish or diocese; this seems to be particularly the case for provisions made by Pope Urban V. For example, in 1366 he granted John *Dugaldi* a benefice in Dunkeld on the proviso that he spoke the language well (Barrell 1995, 90). Andrew Barrell has argued that 'an incumbent's lack of fluency in Gaelic frequently led to attempts to bring about his deprivation' (Barrell 2003, 28).

There are no examples of any non-Gaelic speaking clergy in the Hebrides, whereas for example in Argyll the Pope ordered the removal of John Arous from the vicarage of Kilcalmonell specifically because he did not speak the local language (CPL viii, 470). However, we have already encountered the Ross-shire cleric, Andrew Dunoon; in 1441 he sought a dispensation because:

'although (that) he speaks and understands the dialect of the city and diocese of Sodor, he doubts if he speaks it well enough for preaching and other public acts according to the constitution promulgated thereanent by the Pope; therefore, for his greater safeguard and for the peace of his conscience he supplicates for the apostolic letters to be expedited with dispensation and concession because he does not speak the dialect intelligibly' (CSSR iv, 206).

We must be aware that this supplication was probably intended to protect Andrew Dunoon from litigation, but it is a telling statement – not that he did not speak Gaelic, but that he did not speak it well enough to preach in that language. Lowland clergy who did not have Gaelic might well have found it impossible to obtain the support of the patron and even if they had such support, they would have been likely to have faced opposition from local clergy who presumably would not have hesitated to use those grounds to petition the papacy for their removal.

Additionally, the value of benefices and therefore the income available to the clergy may also have rendered Sodor benefices unattractive to outsiders. Neither the diocese of Sodor nor the neighbouring diocese of Argyll have any recorded surveys of the values of ecclesiastical benefices. We are therefore dependent on papal supplications in which on some occasions the values of individual benefices are given. We must acknowledge that there may have been a tendency to undervalue the benefices because the wealth of the benefice determined the amount of tax which would be due to the Apostolic Camera (Barrell 2003, 34). Based on the possibility of undervaluation, Barrell urges cautious use of the valuations (Barrell 2003, 34). The values of benefices given in papal petitions is the amount of annual income of that church due either to the rector or perpetual vicar as stated. This annual income was presumably made up of the teind or the proportion allocated to the vicar. In the diocese of Sodor, the bishop was entitled to one third of the parochial revenues and the remainder was presumably divided between the rector and vicar (Cowan 1978-80, 19). The rector or vicar was supposed to receive at least £10 in addition to the house and glebe attached to the church (CSSR v, 147-148; Davies 2003, 103). However, devaluation combined with failures to pay indicate that the reality was much bleaker for parish clergy.

The highest value for a Sodor benefice was only 13 merks sterling for Kilchoman on Islay (CSSR iv, 193), and the lowest value was 0.5 merk sterling for St Christopher's of Uig on Lewis (CSSR v, 85). The majority of parish churches seem to have had an average value of between five and nine merks sterling; for example, the rectory of Kilchrist on Strath was consistently valued between six and eight merks sterling (CSSR ii, 203-4). Devaluation can be seen in the mid-fifteenth century where the values of benefices dropped noticeably. For example, the value of the perpetual vicarage of St Columba's of Snizort slumped from nine merks sterling in 1441 to six merks sterling in 1450 (CSSR iv, 188; CSSR v, 87). St Christopher's of Uig was valued at three merks sterling in 1433, but fell to 0.5 merk sterlings by 1450 (ACSB, 112). Unsurprisingly, perhaps, poverty is a common complaint in letters to the papacy as exemplified by Adam son of Dominicus who in 1427 sought papal permission to hold jointly the perpetual vicarages of St Kenneth's and St Eugenius's both on Mull on account of 'the penury of the fruits of the above perpetual vicarages' (CSSR ii, 184). There is a case to be made for these complaints to be seen in the context of clerics seeking consent to hold more than one benefice, but in comparison to lowland benefices Sodor benefices were not well remunerated. According to a statement by Bishop John of Moray in June 1454, prior to devaluation, it was acceptable to pay a vicar in his diocese an annual sum of six merks sterling, but post-monetary devaluation ten merks sterling was not even sufficient for the cleric (CSSR v, 148). However, in the Hebrides, ten merks sterling equalled a wealthy benefice; only Kilchoman of Islay and St Columba's of Eye had income which was higher than ten merks.

A late mediaeval cleric would therefore find it easier to obtain a benefice in the Hebrides if he or his kindred had links either to the Lords of the Isles or to one of the appropriating ecclesiastical institutions like Iona. The provision of clergy in the Sodor diocese was inherently local and was brought about through the MacDonald Lordship of the Isles' control of benefices and to a lesser extent the issues of language and poverty. The absence of Crown control over any benefices must also provide some explanation for the absence of any lowland clergy. The fact that the bishops of Sodor in the fifteenth century were also native to the Hebrides must also have been a factor in clerical provision. The apparent struggles of Andrew Dunoon, a Ross-shire Gaelic speaker, to make himself understood, illustrates the challenges that lowland clergy would have faced. The inclusion of the Hebrides into the Kingdom of Scotland after 1266 did not necessarily mean that mainland Scots were able to take up ecclesiastical benefices in the islands.

Moreover, in terms of ideas of nationhood, whilst the bishop might be described as 'episcopus Sodorensis in Scotia' (DN 17 no.35) – the bishop of Sodor in Scotland – patronal, linguistic and economic issues prevented the diocese from being fully integrated as regards clerical personnel. This may lead us into the debate about the nature and extent of Hebridean and Lordship independence since the local ecclesiastical evidence indicates a strong tendency to localism. Elsewhere, localism also seems to have been the case in the diocese of Lincoln; Nicholas Bennett's study of clergy in north-east Lincolnshire revealed that in the period 1290-1340, 79% of the incumbents came from the diocese and from the remaining 21% only one was not English (Bennett 2005, 47-48). Bennett concludes that the comparatively low value of these benefices, circa £6 13s 4d in the 1291 Taxation, may have discouraged foreign clergy who would also have needed the support of the patrons, nearly two-thirds of whom were local (Bennett 2005, 46). However, north-east Lincolnshire's figures for local clergy still contrast with Sodor where 92% of clergy came from Sodor diocese. Until there are broader studies of clerical provision across Scotland and other countries to determine whether the Hebrides is unusually local, this conclusion about the nature of Hebridean ecclesiastical integration has to be tentative.

Acknowledgements

This paper was originally given at the Roots of Nationhood conference on Sunday 29th November 2009. I have to thank all those who asked questions or made comments after that paper. My thanks also go to my Ph.D. supervisors at the University of Glasgow, Martin MacGregor and Stephen Driscoll, who gave valuable advice and guidance. I am grateful to Nicholas Evans for his assistance, patience and proof-reading skills. Iain MacDonald kindly allowed me to read his Ph.D. thesis and I must thank him for the stimulating discussion in our shared office. All remaining mistakes and errors are of course my own.

Bibliography

Bannerman, J. 1997. The Lordship of the Isles: Historical Background, in K.A. Steer and J.W.M. Bannerman, *Late Medieval Monumental Sculpture in the West Highlands*, Edinburgh: RCAHMS. [Bannerman 1977a]

Bannerman, J. 1997. The Lordship of the Isles, in J.M. Brown (ed.), *Scottish Society in the Fifteenth Century*, London: Edward Arnold, pp.209-240. [Bannerman 1977b]

Barrell, A.D.M. 2003. The church in the West Highlands in the late middle ages, *The Innes Review*, 54, pp.23-46.

Barrell, A.D.M. 1995. *The Papacy, Scotland and Northern England, 1342-1378*, Cambridge: Cambridge University Press

Bennett, N. 2005. Pastors and Masters: the Beneficed Clergy of North-East Lincolnshire, 1290-1340, in P. Hoskin, C. Brooke and B. Dobson (eds), *The Foundations of Medieval English Ecclesiastical History*, Woodbridge: The Boydell Press, pp.40-62.

Black, G.F. 1996. *The Surnames of Scotland: their origin, meaning and history*, Edinburgh: Birlinn

Bliss, W.H. (ed.) 1896. *Calendar of Entries in the Papal Registers relating to Great Britain and Ireland – Petitions to the Pope vol.1 1342-1419*, London: HMSO. [abbreviated *CPP*]

Bliss, W.H. et al (eds.) 1893. *Calendar of Entries in the Papal Registers relating to Great Britain and Ireland: Papal Letters,* London: HMSO. [abbreviated *CPL*]

Burns, C. (ed.) 1976. *Calendar of Papal Letters to Scotland of Clement VII of Avignon, 1378-1394*, Edinburgh: Scottish History Society [abbreviated *CPL Clement VII*]

Cameron, A.I. (ed.) 1934. *The Apostolic Camera and Scottish Benefices, 1418-88,* Oxford: Oxford University Press. [abbreviated *ACSB*]

Cowan, I.B. 1978-80. Medieval Church in Argyll and the Isles, *Records of the Scottish Church History Society*, 20, pp.15-29.

Cowan, I.B. 1972. The Church in the Diocese of Aberdeen, *Northern Scotland*, 1 pp.19-48

Cowan, I.B. 1967. *The Parishes of Medieval Scotland,* Edinburgh: Scottish Record Society

Davies, R. 2003. The Church, in R. Griffiths (ed.), *The Fourteenth and Fifteenth Centuries*, Oxford: Oxford University Press.

Dunlop, A.I. et al (eds.) 1934-1997. *Calendar of Scottish Supplications to Rome*, vols.i, ii and iii, Edinburgh: Scottish History Society and vols. iv and v, Glasgow: University of Glasgow Press

Glasgow University, Scottish History Department, Ross Fund Collection, *Registra Avinionensia* 195

Grant, A. 2005. The Province of Ross and the Kingdom of Alba, in E.J. Cowan and R.A. McDonald (eds.), *Alba: Celtic Scotland in the Middle Ages*, Edinburgh: Tuckwell Press, pp.88-126.

Innes, C. (ed.) 1854. *Munimenta Alme Universitatis Glasguensis*, Glasgow: Maitland Club

Lange, C.A. et al (eds) 1847-1995. *Diplomatarium Norvegicum*, 20 volumes, Christiania: University Press

Livingstone, M. (ed) 1908-1982. *Registrum Secreti Sigilii Regum Scotorum,* 8 volumes, Edinburgh: H.M. General Register House

MacDonald, I.G. 2008. *The Secular Church and Clergy in the Diocese of Argyll from circa 1189 to 1560,* Unpublished Ph.D. thesis, University of Glasgow.

MacGregor, M. 1998. Church and Culture in the late medieval Highlands, in J. Kirk (ed.), *The Church in the Highlands*, Edinburgh: Scottish Church History Society, pp.1-36.

MacPhail, J.R.N. (ed.) 1914. *Highland Papers*, 4 volumes, Edinburgh: Scottish History Society

MacQuarrie, A. 1984-6. Kings, Lords and Abbots: Power and Patronage at the medieval monastery of Iona, *Transactions of the Gaelic Society of Inverness* 54, pp.355-375.

McDonald, R.A. 1997. *The Kingdom of the Isles, Scotland's Western Seaboard, c.1100-c.1336*, Edinburgh: Tuckwell Press

McGurk, F. (ed) 1976. *Calendar of Papal Letters to Scotland to Benedict XIII of Avignon, 1394-1419*, Edinburgh: Scottish History Society [abbreviated *CPL Benedict XIII*]

Monro, D. 1999. A Description of the Occidental, i.e. the Western Islands of Scotland c.1549, in R.W. Monro (ed.), *A Description of the Western Islands of Scotland*, Edinburgh: Birlinn

Munro, J. and Munro, R.W. (eds.) 1986. *Acts of the Lords of the Isles, 1336-1493*, Edinburgh: Scottish History Society

O Baoill, C. 1976. Domnhall Mac Mharcuis, *Scottish Gaelic Studies* 12, pp.183-193

Oram, R. 2006. The Lordship of the Isles: 1336-1545, in D. Omand (ed.), *The Argyll Book*, Edinburgh: Birlinn, pp.123-139.

RCAHMS, 1980. *Argyll: an inventory of the Ancient Monuments, volume 3: Mull, Tiree, Coll and Northern Argyll*, Edinburgh: RCAHMS

Steer, K.A. and Bannerman, J.W.M. 1977. *Late Medieval Monumental Sculpture in the West Highlands*, Edinburgh: RCAHMS

Synodal Ordinances of Bishop Russell A.D.1350, in J.R. Oliver (ed.), *Monumenta de Insula Manniae*, Douglas: Manx Society, 1862

Thomas, S.E. (forthcoming), Bishops, Priests, Monks and their patrons: the Lords of the Isles and the Church, in R. Oram (ed.), *The Lordship of the Isles*

Thomas, S.E. 2010. The diocese of Sodor between Niðaróss and Avignon - Rome, 1266-1472, *Northern Studies*, 41, pp.22-40

Thomas, S.E. 2009. Rival bishops, rival cathedrals: the election of Cormac, archdeacon of Sodor, as bishop in 1331, *The Innes Review* 60:2, pp.145-163 [Thomas 2009a]

Thomas, S.E. 2009. *'From Rome to the ends of the habitable world': the provision of clergy and church buildings in the Hebrides, circa 1266 to circa 1472*, Unpublished Ph.D. thesis, University of Glasgow [Thomas 2009b]

Thomson, D.S. 1968. Gaelic Learned Orders and Literati in Medieval Scotland, *Scottish Studies*, 12, pp.57-78

Thomson, J.A.F. 1998. *The Western Church in the Middle Ages*, London: Oxford University Press

Watt, D.E.R. and Murray, A.L. (eds.) 2003. *Fasti Ecclesiae Scoticanae medii aevi: ad annum 1638*, Edinburgh: Scottish Record Society

Watt, D.E.R. and Shead N. F. (eds.) 2001. *Heads of Religious Houses in Scotland from twelfth to sixteenth centuries*, Edinburgh: Scottish Record Society

Canon 9 of the Fourth Lateran Council of 1215 from the *Internet Medieval Sourcebook* at http://www.fordham.edu/halsall/basis/lateran4.html (viewed 06.08.08)

Forging Scotland's Identities at Home and Abroad

Pictish, Celtic, Scottish: The Longing for Belonging

Steven Timoney

This paper focuses on data from three case studies:

Tarbat Discovery Centre is a museum located in the former parish church of Portmahomack, Easter Ross (Figure 1), and is run by the Tarbat Historic Trust. It is adjacent to the site of a Pictish monastic settlement dating from the 6 century, which was the focus of intensive excavation and analysis from 1996 to 2007 (Carver 2008). The museum tells the story of the monastic site, and displays artefacts from the excavations, alongside exhibits relating to the later history of the area.

Urquhart Castle (Figure 2) is located on the banks of Loch Ness, south-west of the Highland capital Inverness. The site comprises the ruined remains of a medieval castle with later additions. It was developed in the late-1990s to provide a new visitor centre,

Figure 1. Tarbat Discovery Centre at the former parish church of Portmahomack, Easter Ross

including shop, café and museum. Today the Castle is in the care of Historic Scotland, and attracts hundreds of thousands of visitors per year.

The *Antonine Wall* (Figure 3) is a Roman turf and earth wall constructed in the 2 century AD across the Forth-Clyde isthmus in central Scotland. The Wall is c.60km long, terminating in the east near Bo'ness, with the western end located at Old Kilpatrick (Robertson 2001). The Wall was built c.AD142 by the occupying armies of the Roman Empire in central Scotland, under the order of the Emperor Antoninus Pius. Today the Antonine Wall survives as a series of pockets of archaeological remains, due to its location in the most populous area of Scotland, and is in the care of various local authorities, alongside Historic Scotland.

Figure 2. Urquhart Castle, located on the banks of Loch Ness

Figure 3. The Antonine Wall

Research data was collected through in-depth interviews, sometimes referred to as semi-structured interviews, using open and non-leading questions. Excerpts from some of these interviews used to highlight specific ideas and beliefs about identity which developed from this research. As is standard with this kind of research pseudonyms are used to maintain participants anonymity.

Through the case studies a number of key themes emerged. One of these overarching themes was a sense of identity, at the same time collective and yet unique, influenced by the present and perceptions of identity, as well as ideas and (pre)conceptions about the past. Archaeological sites on the ground have a central role in creating and reinforcing these perceptions of identity, bound up within notions of romance, landscape, belonging, and authenticity.

These constructed identities exist amongst the Scottish diaspora, but are also created by those who live within Scotland. This article illustrates the complex ways members of the public identify with archaeological sites, and how knowledge and interactions with these sites and the tangible remains of the past are used to construct and promote identities. It also looks at what terms such as Pictish, Celtic and Scottish mean to members of the public on an individual as well as collective basis, when considering archaeology and identity, past and present.

Identity and sites on the ground

Identities are not fixed in time or space, but rather are socially constructed, and are constantly being evaluated at multiple levels (Ballesteros and Ramirez 2007; Brewer and Gardner 2004; Peil 2005; Tong and Chang 2008). Archaeological sites as relics of the past are used in the present through incorporation into the construction of identities on various levels: individual; group; local; regional; national (Goulding and Domic 2009; Jones and Graves-Brown 1996; Gruffudd *et al.* 1998; Jones 1997; Jones 2004; MacClanahan 2004; Macdonald 1997; Merriman 2000). The historic environment is an important factor in forming identities for two reasons: 'it is ubiquitous [....] and it is infinite in its variety' (Graham *et al.* 2000, 204).

A paradox exists in the role of archaeological sites and identity. Where identity is the sharing of a common set of beliefs, sites identified as of, for example, national importance and therefore used to create a national identity, are often atypical, unique, or special. The association of heritage with national identity often reflects this positive bias, with the selective interpretation of aspects of the past used to promote communality (Graham *et al.* 2000; Jones 1997; Merriman 2000; Moser 2003; Piggott 1976) and specific 'pasts' (Goulding and Domic 2009; Gruffudd *et al.* 1998; Light and Dumbraveanu-Andone 1997; Walsh 1992). Research into the role of national identity was recognised as key in the development of World Heritage, under the auspices of the UNESCO World Heritage Convention (Herrman 1989, 31).

Identities are also created and promoted for consumption by others, particularly within the context of heritage tourism (Tunbridge and Ashworth 1996; Uzzell 1998; Cohen 1988; Ballesteros and Ramirez 2007; Gonzales 2007). This has an effect on both visitors and local perceptions of theirs and others identities (Ballesteros and Ramirez 2007; Vidal Gonzalez 2008; Medina 2003), which can lead to the creation of staged identities (MacCannell 1976; Medina 2003). This process can lead to the commoditisation of certain aspects of a culture, society or community (Cohen 1988), which can result in the destruction of the inherent identity of local products and activities, instead transforming them into 'staged authenticity' (MacCannell 1979; Cohen 1988).

At the case study sites perceptions and beliefs about identity were discussed in a variety of ways, sometimes complimentary, but also more complex, and at times conflicting. These are presented under a number of broad headings, but as the excerpts reflect, perceptions of identity are ultimately multi-layered, and can at the same time be personal, communal, regional and national.

Personal identities

An interesting theme that developed from the interviews was the importance of sites, and the past more generally, in relation to the construction of some participants' personal identities. These are obviously very individual interpretations, but what they reflect is the way that ideas of identity and the past are negotiated by the individual, to create something personal (Dierking 1998; Falk and Dierking 1992; Moscardo and Pearce 1986).

At Tarbat Discovery Centre, the Christian origins of the site were important for a number of participants. The site's role in the early spread of Christianity was significant for some in making the visit, as Robert, a retired male visitor from the Moray area, discussed:

Robert *I suppose I'm interested in the early church, origin of how Christianity arrived and how the division between Rome and Christianity.... Anyway, from that we can understand the political divisions and all the warfare that took place. I think that Christianity bears a big responsibility for a lot of the ills of the present age. [....] I'm just fascinated by the origins of Christianity.*

Robert identified the site as a 'Christian' site, and made a connection through religion to wider issues and events, both in the past and the present. The Christian faith was an important factor for a number of visitors. In particular, some participants acknowledged the link between their visits and the central role their faith had in their everyday lives. Paul, a mid-40s American visiting with his family, identified himself as an active Christian, and discussed the importance of the link with Iona in their experience:

Paul   *We're pretty active church musicians, and the Iona community now is a source of a lot of more modern sacred music and we've played and sung music from a number of the composers there. So that was kind of the connection* [to Tarbat]*, and then it had the long history, St Columba connection.*

The connection with St Columba and Iona was important in influencing a number of people to visit the site. The excavations of the early-medieval monastery, and the wider landscape analysis which took place through the Tarbat Discovery Programme, have resulted in an interpretation of the site as an 'Iona of the East' which was arguably as important as Iona in the early-medieval period (Carver 2004).

Tarbat was also seen as an important site in the construction and reaffirming of other aspects of personal identity. For Andy, a male visitor in his late 30s from Aberdeenshire, discussion of the Picts reflected a concept of his own north-eastern Scottish identity, in particular through perceptions of a separate language and culture:

Andy   *I've got a great affinity for the things* [Pictish stones]*. And I feel myself that I'm a Pict, and not a Celt. I don't feel Celtic. I went to Ireland and I didn't feel part of it, you know?*[....] *'Cause I used to think that our language* [Doric] *was kind of bastardised English and we were a bit thick in the north-east and got words wrong. But it's not. We've always had a separate language.* [....] *And if you take a line between Forres and Nairn, that's exactly where Doric changes to Highland. It's exactly that area. So I think it's always been a distinct separate kingdom.*

Andy's ideas reflect perceptions of his own identity and his beliefs about a hidden regional identity. His separation of the Picts from other late Iron Age groups in the north, and the misleading dichotomy of the Picts compared to the 'Celtic' other, were used to create and define separate cultural identities, which were, for Andy, an ancient mirror which could be held up to reflect his modern context.

The regional variations within modern day Scotland were viewed as having a much more important historical legitimacy and legacy, to the point where Andy identified himself as Pictish. Although Andy had very strong convictions in relation to his Pictish heritage, his comments also reflected a sense of romanticising the past which conformed to other Pictish stereotypes.

Andy's comments also reflected understandings or beliefs in regional identities.

Heritage is key in the development of local or regional identities as, by its very nature, heritage has the capacity to be unique (Frodsham 2004; Graham *et al.* 2000). The growth of heritage and tourism has led to local communities being encouraged to construct a 'sense of place' (Jones 2004; Lumley 2005, 20). The very nature of this process brings in to question whether perceptions of what is local heritage are altered to create an image for the other (Jones 2004; Lumley 2005; Said 1978).

Local and regional identities

In contrast to Andy's comments, the majority of respondents interviewed at Tarbat had little or no knowledge of the Picts prior to their visit. A number acknowledged they had heard of *the Picts* but were unaware of what the term meant or to whom it referred, as reflected in the thoughts of Claire, a middle-aged female visitor from England, who was visiting friends in the area:

Claire   *I've heard of the Picts but I've not....didn't know much about them to be honest. And then we just came here this afternoon. [....] Also, I think, until you come up here [to Scotland], I don't think you really, especially where we're from, London, you don't hear a lot about the Picts.*

This type of response was a common one through many of the interviews. Although participants had often heard of the Picts, they knew little more about them, although certain commonly held beliefs continue. The common perceptions of the Picts, developed and augmented since the classical writings of Eumenius (Ritchie 1994), continues to reflect them as painted savages, within a period of post-Roman, pre-Enlightenment darkness.

Representations of heritage are often used to promote aspects of identity which are valued by a community: As McDonald states, 'a heritage representation is, intentionally, a cultural explicating device' (Macdonald 1997, 156). In this way people have always used the past in the present to create and reinforce identity (see for example Bradley 1987; Driscoll 1991; 1998; Gosden and Lock 1998; Hingley 1996; Isbell 2004; Jones 1996; .Jones and Graves-Brown 1996; van Dyke 2004). Claire's comments reflected a belief that the Picts were viewed as of local or regional interest and importance, rather than of a wider national identity. This response reflected a perception of the Picts as of regional rather than national (Scottish or British) interest, and may echo a lack of interest in, or identity with, what is perceived to be a regional Scottish group. It also reflects an absence of informative processes through which knowledge and understanding of who the Picts were may be accessed by a wider audience, for example in the current educational curricula throughout the United Kingdom.

Sites and artefacts can often have a role in the creation of local and regional identities. The area of Easter Ross has already been the focus for much heated debate over the role and rightful location of the Hilton of Cadboll stone (Jones 2004; 2005). The importance of local heritage and the belief that artefacts should remain within the local community was a key issue for a number of respondents. Sarah, an artist from Angus who was on holiday in the area and interested in Pictish art reflected:

Sarah   *I think that it is quite important that things [artefacts] stay if they are going to represent what was going on in a community. Because it's got less meaning to that place if it's taken away somewhere else to be exhibited. There are times where it's maybe important to have a travelling exhibition to show what's available in different places. But I think that things... should be displayed or returned to where they belong because it's part of that heritage.*

Sarah discussed a popular and growing opinion about the need for artefacts to remain at or return to their original locations (see Jones 2004; Lumley 2005). She also discussed the belief that artefacts played a role in representing community – rather than being inanimate objects, they played a role in the construction of identities. These beliefs reflected the importance of place in creating both identity and value for objects, and vice versa.

In this way the artefacts from the excavations were viewed as an intrinsic part of the local community and the heritage of the area, and therefore 'belonged' to that community rather than being sent to a centralised institution for conservation and display. Charles, a local resident who had retired to the area from the south of England, had strong views on this issue:

Charles *Because it's part of this community. It's here, it's got a right to be here. Like the people that live here have a right to be here. Whatever you find has a right to be here as well. And I don't think that the people in this area should have to travel to see something that's found on their doorstep. I feel pretty strongly about that. [....] And if you guys [the archaeologists] hadn't dug it up it would still be here. All right, we couldn't see it. A lot of people, if it's taken away, they don't see it anymore than they would if it was still under ground. It's a link to this district's history. And I think it should be displayed in this district.*

In this way the artefacts were part of the site and were seen as crucial in providing the area with, at least part of, its uniqueness, difference and identity. A key value of the artefacts was in their geography, their literal place in the landscape. To remove them was to take away the place's identity. Charles' beliefs in this 'belonging' were so strong that if the artefacts were removed from the site, he felt they would be of as much benefit to the local community as if they had never been discovered.

At times through the interviews there was an element of unease about the removal of artefacts from the site with no sign of them returning. Some of these discussions were influenced by the developments over the neighbouring Hilton of Cadboll stone (see Jones 2004; 2005; 2006), and these issues were raised again with regards to the rights of the local community in Portmahomack. Although more commonly discussed with regards to indigenous communities in other parts of the world, such sites are increasingly viewed as important in perceptions of sense of place and local identity (ibid; Lumley 2005). Through its role in creating and reinforcing other forms of identity, whether as a symbol of local identity, or seen as a reflection of a (pre-) Scottish heritage, the site was imbued with multiple values and roles.

Concepts of identity are also important in the creation and endurance of heritage resources (Macdonald 1997). Issues relating to identity were important not just in terms of the local community, but also for some visitors who projected meanings onto the site and artefacts, as well as using them and the wider area to create identities.

The presentation of sites, and information about the past, were seen as crucial, not just for those who identified themselves as Scottish, but with regards to the importance of maintaining a connection with the past to inform modern perceptions of identity, as May, a middle-aged female visitor from England, who was visiting friends in the area, discussed:

May   *I think it's great that people do things like this* [the Tarbat Discovery Centre], *because otherwise the past would be lost, wouldn't it. And I think that would be a great shame. We should all know where we came from, shouldn't we.*

From May's point of view, 'the past' was something which had to be remembered and (re)presented otherwise it would be lost.

National identities: Scottish

The importance of the development of sites such as Tarbat and their links to the creation or presentation of identities and *Scottishness*, were also discussed by those looking for a link to their own past, as a way of becoming part of this positive construction, and at the same time part of the growing enthusiasm with genealogy.

Reflecting on why they had chosen to visit the Centre, Rhona, a 60+ year old female visitor from the Highlands who had visited the site with her husband and grandsons, discussed perceptions of heritage and history, viewing it as an important part of the development of her grandchildren:

Rhona   *To keep them* [her grandsons] *interested in their history as well. To let them know what was in their native land before they appeared you know?*

The 'history' was both part of their own personal development, and part of their own national identity. In this way the centre played a role in communicating specific values to younger generations, in the form of identity and Scottishness.

This role of interpreting and presenting sites, and by extension, the past, is one of selection and promotion (Timothy and Boyd 2003), with the concept of a fixed, immutable past no longer valid (Crew and Sims 1991; Copeland 2004; Merriman 2000; Walsh 1992). This process of selection often highlights aspects of a place's heritage which are generally favourably viewed at that time, and can be derived from pre-existing biases and beliefs (Jones 2006; Jones and Graves-Brown 1996; Merriman 2000). Preconceptions and stereotypes are often bound up within heritage sites and the identities which they project, and have imposed upon them.

In this way castles are perceived to assimilate within broader perceptions of Scotland, for example through a continuation of the Victorian reimagining of the Scottish Highlands as a location of mystery and wonderment (McCrone *et al.* 1998; McCrone 2001). Urquhart Castle plays an active role within this construction of identity, with its ruined state, reaffirming for visitors these preconceived ideas of Highland Scotland, and by extension, Scotland as a whole. These are aspects which have been selected and actively promoted as identifiers of Scotland. These themes were developed in some interviews, with Scotland identified as a location for castles, lochs and mountains:

Gordon *Well, Scotland's famous for castles; it's famous for castles from the Middle Ages so we thought we'd have a look. We've only just arrived in Scotland yesterday so we thought we'd come here and it's the first castle we've visited.*

Gordon was a middle-aged visitor from Australia who discussed these well worn clichés of Scotland. In this way, parts of Scotland were therefore perceived as 'more Scottish' than others, as they assimilated with these well worn and commonly recognised stereotypes. Richard, a retired American visitor on a three week holiday to Scotland, raised this point:

Richard*I've always been fascinated with Scotland, and the scenery, and Glasgow and places like that don't give me the feeling you're in Scotland. It feels you're in Scotland when you're in the Highlands. It's different.*

While visitors to Scotland discussed these types of site as important parts of what they thought they knew about Scotland, a number of Scottish participants discussed the importance of learning about sites such as Urquhart Castle, as key to instilling a sense of identity for Scottish people more generally. Alison, a retired female visitor from Aberdeenshire, discussed this:

Alison   *You must remember the people of my generation we were never taught Scottish history at school. It wasn't allowed. [....] I think a lot of the Scottish history that I know I've only read since I've been an adult. [....] So I think there is a lot to be done in education for young people.*

Conversely, as well as being cultural clichés, these sites were still viewed as important in instilling a sense of national identity for Scots young and old, in connecting them to the past.

Scottish and *un-Scottish* heritage

While certain sites and types of site were seen to be identifiers of Scotland and a Scottish heritage, others were viewed as having little place in concepts of a 'Scottish' past. A number of participants spoke about the Antonine Wall in this way. Respondents discussed the concept of value in a number of ways, and the issue of whether the Wall has a value as part of 'Scottish' heritage was discussed:

Sandy   *The Celts all left Scotland for all their various reasons in the Clearances, and the Americans, and Canadians, and Australians would be more Scots than a lot of the Scots are. And their family connections and lots of stuff. And they would come and see Bannockburn as part of a tour I would imagine. They may come to see, if it was added on, the Antonine Wall, but they wouldn't be coming over, I wouldn't have thought, for that purpose.*

Sandy, a visitor in his late 40s from Tayside, reflected a number of interesting beliefs with regard to identity. Identifying himself as Scottish, he discussed a popular perception that members of the Scottish diaspora often tended to 'be more Scots than a lot of the Scots are' with regards to perceptions of identity and a sense of belonging. His rationale that members of the diaspora would come to visit certain sites but not others reflected wider perceptions of what represents Scottish heritage.

In some circumstances this can be extended to identify certain sites within Scotland as in a sense '*un*-Scottish', in particular Roman sites. This was viewed in stark contrast to England, where the Roman heritage was perceived to be something which was valued and embraced, as David, a retired local resident and member of a local history society, explained:

David   *I don't think there is a national consciousness in Scotland about it. There is in England, because they see it as dividing them from the barbarians to the north. Whereas in Scotland it's almost the other way around, it could be seen as sort of an intrusive feature in our national consciousness.*

In this way, the notion of the Romans as being linked to perceptions of English heritage and identity have led to the belief that anything Roman represents the English *other* when compared to perceptions of Scottish identity and heritage (McCrone 2001; McIntosh *et al.* 2004). This connection between the Romans and the English may create issues in terms of individuals and communities appreciating the Antonine Wall as in any way 'Scottish'.

The belief that the Romans never conquered Scotland is an important aspect of many people's perceptions of Scottish identity and the unconquered nation. In this way, the Romans are viewed as outsiders or invaders, and the remains of their activities in modern Scotland are often viewed in this way. Whether the inscription of the Antonine Wall as a World Heritage Site will change these perceptions remains to be seen.

This is reflected in the response of Michael, a 19 year-old university student, who identified himself as half-Scottish and half-English when discussing his perceptions of heritage:

Michael   *Well....obviously because I live in Scotland, and I'm half Scottish and half English so I've got the half Scottish and the idea of the Picts living here so I'm sort of descended from them. But also because I'm half English I have the Anglo-Saxon and Roman side to it. So since a lot of the Romans will actually be English and so they'll be the ones invading Scotland. So I have the kind of mixed, I have both sides essentially, of people defending their homeland, but I also have the, my people trying to extend their homeland. So I like to think that while they're not directly related to me, both sides are part of my heritage. So it just enables me to believe in both sides and that what both sides were doing was right and wrong at the same time.*

Michael's ideas reflect an interesting interpretation of the Romans in Northern Britain which at once reflects national and personal identities. This frequent connection of the Romans as 'English' was not generally contested by participants. In this way modern identities were inextricably linked to those of the past, with geography playing a crucial role in the development of these identities and perceptions of the past.

British heritage

A few participants discussed the Wall in terms of its importance in *British* history. Heritage is a key factor in the construction of a British identity, but this is achieved through a disregard for regional differences within the British Isles to achieve a homogenous whole (Gruffudd *et al.* 1998). In this way the concerns over what was or was not Scottish or English could be bypassed when the monuments were considered in the broader context of the British Isles, which Liz, a local resident who had moved to Scotland from America, discussed:

Liz   *But it is an amazing part of British history, isn't it? Because the Romans got here, in my book they didn't leave much trace, but they got this Wall and retreated. And when you think about that, that's the northern, it's not the edge of the world but it's getting there.*

Whilst the Antonine Wall may not have been seen by some participants as having a role to play in Scottish or local identities, it does still play a number of roles in the area today. In this way, sites, and the past more generally, can be absorbed and reinterpreted within space and place to less or more obvious effect, as is reflected in the Antonine Housing Co-operative in Kirkintilloch (Figure 4), and the Antonine Shopping Centre in Cumbernauld (Figure 5). The Antonine Wall, and many archaeological sites, therefore have the potential to play a variety of roles in shaping identity into the future, as well as in (re)presenting the past.

Summary

On reflection, archaeological sites play an important role in the development of identity and the construction of identities at various levels. They are also important because they often provide a physical connection to 'the past', providing legitimacy for the creation of particular narratives on the past.

Figure 4. Antonine Housing Co-operative in Kirkintilloch

Figure 5. Antonine Shopping Centre in Cumbernauld

Archaeological sites can be used in the construction of identities, but can also have meanings and values placed upon them. With the case studies discussed, participants recognised the role of artefacts and sites in the landscape in the construction or reaffirming of identities on various levels. These roles were varied and at times conflicting, a reflection of the complexities of identity. But it is interesting to note that alongside the clichés and stereotypes of Scotland, there were other, less obvious, but equally valid, personal interpretations of sites and associated constructions of identity, and in turn we should be cautious when we look to consider just what sites mean and represent to people.

Bibliography

Ballesteros, E. and Ramırez, M. 2007. Identity and community: reflections on the development of mining heritage tourism in Southern Spain *Tourism Management* 28 (3), 677–687.

Bradley, R. 1987. Time regained: the creation of continuity. *Journal of the British Archaeological Association* 140, 1-17.

Brewer, M. and Gardner, B. 2004. Who is this 'we'? Levels of collective identity and self representations, in Hatch, M and Schultz, M (eds) *Organizational Identity: a reader*. Oxford University Press, 66-80.

Carver, M. 2004. An Iona of the east: The Early-medieval monastery at Portmahomack, Tarbat Ness. *Medieval Archaeology* 48, 1-30.

Carver, M. 2008. *Portmahomack: Monastery of the Picts*. Edinburgh University Press.

Cohen, E. 1988. Authenticity and commoditization in tourism. *Annals of Tourism Research* 15, 371-86.

Copeland, T. 2004. Presenting Archaeology to the Public: Constructing insights on-site, in Merriman, N. (ed) *Public Archaeology*. London: Routledge, 132-144.

Crew, S. and Sims, J. 1991. Locating Authenticity: Fragments of a Dialogue, in I. Karp, I. and S. Lavine (eds) *Exhibiting Cultures: The Poetics and Politics of Museum Display*. Washington: The Smithsonian Institution Press, 159-75.

Dierking, L. 1998. Interpretation as a social experience, in D. Uzzell R. Ballantyne (eds) *Contemporary Issues in Heritage and Environmental Interpretation: problems and prospects*. London: The Stationary Office, 56-76.

Driscoll, S. 1991. The archaeology of state formation in Scotland, in Hanson, W. and Slater, E. (eds) *Scottish Archaeology: New Perceptions*. Aberdeen: Aberdeen University Press, 81-111.

Driscoll, S. 1998. The Past in the Past: The Reuse of Ancient Monuments, *World Archaeology* 30 (1), 142-158.

Falk, J. and Dierking, L. 1992. *The Museum Experience*. Washington D.C: Whalesback Books.

Foster, S. 2004. *Picts, Gaels and Scots: Early Historic Scotland*. Batsford/Historic Scotland: London/Edinburgh.

Frodsham, P. 2004. So much history in the landscape, so much confusion, so much doubt, in P. Frodsham (ed) *Interpreting the Ambiguous: Archaeology and interpretation in early 21 century Britain*. Oxford: Archaeopress, 1-26.

Goulding, C. and Domic, D. 2009. Heritage, identity and ideological manipulation: the case of Croatia. *Annals of Tourism Research* 36 (1), 85–102.

Gosden, C. and Lock, G. 1998. The past in the past: the reuse of ancient monuments, World Archaeology 30 (1), 2-12.

Graham, B., Ashworth, G., and Turnbridge, J. 2000. *Geography of Heritage: Power, Culture and Economy*. London: Arnold.

Gruffudd, R., Herbert, D. and Piccini, A. 1998. Learning to think the past: Heritage, identity and state education in Wales. *International Journal of Heritage Studies* 4 (3), 154-167.

Herrman, J. 1989. World archaeology; the world's cultural heritage, in H. Cleere (ed) *Archaeological Heritage Management: Principles and Practice*. London: Unwin Hyman, 30-37.

Hingley, R. 1996. Ancestors and identity in the later prehistory of Atlantic Scotland: the reuse and reinvention of Neolithic monuments and material culture. *World Archaeology* 28 (2), 231-43.

Hunt, S. 2002. `Neither here nor there': the construction of identities and boundary maintenance of West African Pentecostals. *Sociology* 36 (1), 147–169.

Isbell, W. 2004. Mortuary Preferences: A Wari Culture Case Study from Middle Horizon Peru. *Latin American Antiquity* 15(1), 3-32.

Jones, S. 1996. Discourses of identity in the interpretation of the past, in Graves-Brown, P. Jones, S. and Gamble, C. (eds) *Cultural Identity and Archaeology: The construction of European communities*. London: Routledge, 62-80.

Jones, S. 1997. The Archaeology of Ethnicity: Constructing identities in the past and the present. London: Routledge

Jones, S 2004. Early Medieval Sculpture and the Production of Meaning, Value and Place: The case of the Hilton of Cadboll. Edinburgh: Historic Scotland.

Jones, S. 2005. 'That stone was born here and that's where it belongs': Hilton of Cadboll and the negotiation of identity, ownership and belonging, in Foster, S. and Cross, M. (eds) *Able Minds and Practised Hands: Scotland's early medieval sculpture in the 21 century*. Society for Medieval Archaeology Monograph 23, 37-53.

Jones, S. 2006. "They made it a living thing didn't they': the growth of things and the fossilisation of heritage', in Layton, R. Shennan, S. and Stone, P. (eds) *A Future for Archaeology: the past in the present*. London: UCL Press.

Jones S, and Graves-Brown, P 1996. Introduction: Archaeology and cultural identity in Europe, in Graves-Brown, P. Jones, S. and Gamble, C. (eds) *Cultural Identity and Archaeology: The construction of European communities*. London: Routledge, 2-24.

Light, D. and Dumbraveanu-Andone, D. 1997. Heritage and national identity: exploring the relationship in Romania. *International Journal of Heritage Studies* 3 (1), 28-43.

Lumley, R. 2005. The debate on heritage reviewed, in Corsane, G. (ed) *Heritage, Museums and Galleries: an introductory reader*. London: Routledge, 15-25.

MacCannell, D. 1976 (1999). *The Tourist: A New Theory of the Leisure Class*. London: Macmillan.

MacCannell, D. 1979. Staged Authenticity: Arrangements of Social Space in Tourist Settings, *American Journal of Sociology* 79, 589-603.

McClanahan 2004. The Heart of Neolithic Orkney in its Contemporary Contexts: A case study in heritage management and community values. Unpublished report for Historic Scotland.

Macdonald, S. 1997. A people's story: heritage, identity and authenticity in Rojek, C. and Urry, J. (eds) *Touring Cultures*. London: Routledge, 155–176.

May, J. 1996. In search of authenticity off and on the beaten track. *Environment and Planning D: Society and Space* 14, 709-736.

McCrone, D., Stewart, R., Kiely, R., and Bechhofer, F. 1998. Who are we? Problematising national identity. *The Sociological Review* 46, 629–652.

McCrone, D. 2001. Understanding Scotland: the sociology of a nation. London and New York: Routledge.

McIntosh, I., Sim, D. and Robertson, D. 2004. 'We hate the English, except for you, cos you're our pal': identification of the 'English' in Scotland. *Sociology* 38 (1), 43–59.

Medina, L. 2003. Commoditizing culture tourism and Maya identity. Annals of Tourism Research 30 (2), 353–368.

Merriman, N. 2000. The crisis of representation in museums, in. F. McManamon and A. Hatton, A. (eds) *Cultural Resource Management in Contemporary Society: Perspectives on Managing and Presenting the Past*. London: Routledge, 300-309.

Moser, S. 2003. Representing archaeological knowledge in museums: Exhibiting human origins and strategies for change. Public Archaeology 3, 3-20.

Moscardo, G. and Pearce, P. 1986. Historic theme parks: an Australian experience in authenticity. *Annals of Tourism Research* 13, 467-479.

Peil, T. 2005. Estonian heritage connections - people, past and place: the Pakri Peninsula. *International Journal of Heritage Studies* 11 (1), 53–65.

Piggot, S. 1976. Ruins in a Landscape: Essays in Antiquarianism. Edinburgh: Edinburgh University Press.

Ritchie, A. 1994. Perceptions of the Picts : from Eumenius to John Buchan. Rosemarkie: Groam House Museum Trust.

Robertson, A. 2001. *The Antonine Wall: A Handbook to the Surviving Remains*. Glasgow: Glasgow Archaeological Society.

Timothy, D. and Boyd, S. 2003. *Heritage Tourism*. Harlow: Pearson Education Limited.

Tong, E. and Chang W. 2008. Group entity belief: An individual difference construct based on implicit theories of social identities. *Journal of Personality* 76 (4), 707-732.

Tunbridge, J. and Ashworth, G. 1996. *Dissonant heritage: the management of the past as a resource in conflict*. Chichester: J. Wiley.

Uzzell D. 1998. Interpreting our heritage: a theoretical interpretation, in Uzzell, D. and Ballantyne, R. (eds) *Contemporary Issues in Heritage and Environmental Interpretation: problems and prospects*. London: The Stationary Office, 11-25.

van Dyke, R. 2004. Memory, Meaning, and Masonry: The Late Bonito Chacoan Landscape. *American Antiquity* 69 (3), 413-431.Vidal Gonzalez, M. 2008 Intangible heritage tourism and identity. *Tourism Management* 29 (4), 807–810.

Walsh, K. 1992. *The Representation of the Past: museums and heritage in the post-modern world*. London: Routledge

'The Different Fruits of all the World' -
The Early Colonial Connections of Glasgow
(c.1660-1740)

Stuart Nisbet

Questions about Glasgow

The development of the Scottish city of Glasgow in the 1660-1740 period depended increasingly on overseas trade. Despite this, the colonial end of the trading cycle has rarely been of serious interest in Glasgow. For a city which depended on overseas trade to fund its early development, Glasgow's history has been surprisingly inward looking.

When we consider the colonial merchants who led the development of the city from the seventeenth century, one of the few remaining physical connections is their country houses and gardens. We will see below how, by the 1780s, they cultivated exotic fruits, well beyond those normally possible in the Scottish climate, including 'peaches, apricots, nectarines, and the different fruits of all the world' (Semple 1782, 10). Such exotic fruits characterised the wide ranging transatlantic connections of the city's merchants.

Perhaps the most tangible remnant of the merchant's country houses are those properties which endure as tourist attractions. Beyond their basic survival, do such heritage attractions truly acknowledge the origins of their founders? Three recent personal encounters illustrate the growing demand for more information, or the lack of appreciation of the resources available, and not just from academics or residents of Glasgow.

The first was with a Glaswegian, whose family originated from West Africa, who recalled his own impression after visiting such a merchant's country mansion (Nisbet & Welsh, 1992). The pedimented frontage and symmetrical wings of the house all attested to money and status, while the improved country setting added to the impression of wealth and culture. Less tangible, was the background and source of fortune of the mercantile founder of the property. The focus inside the mansion was more on antique furniture, of uncertain provenance, than on history. Although occasional paintings of ships adorned the walls, overseas trade was only hinted at. Enquiries to staff about the source of fortune of the original owner resulted in increasingly vague answers.

Soon after, a history of the property was located in a local library. This revealed that the founder of the mansion traded across the Atlantic with the Americas. From the 1740s his trade goods included not only sugar, tobacco and cotton, but human cargoes of enslaved Africans. In the house itself, young black boys were kept as personal servants, including one named 'Negro John'.

Today, this living human story of the mansion's founder and his chattels was invisible, replaced by a selective and celebratory history. The human heritage was buried under a fuzz of vague, over-arching terms, such as 'merchant', 'trade' and 'colonies'. The reasons for the apparent subterfuge was puzzling. Did the property owners believe that the public were unable to cope with the full scope of Glasgow's mercantile identity? Was the truth too radical for those who spend their leisure time touring such country mansions and tearooms?

The second encounter which challenged Glasgow's colonial origins came through meeting a young student named John, recently arrived in Glasgow as a postgraduate from West Africa. John had known the word 'Glasgow' for as long as he could remember, and his native country is still scattered with heavy machinery and ironwork stamped 'made in Glasgow'. Before flying to Glasgow, John had read about Glasgow's background history. A phrase which stuck in his mind was Glasgow's claim to have been 'Second City' of the British Empire.

At home in West Africa, this connection with Empire raised darker curiosities. John had visited the stone forts dotted along his coast, with their cellar doors pointing to the Americas. From these prisons, untold numbers of his countrymen had been forcibly carried across the Atlantic to work on British sugar plantations. Glasgow's claim to be 'Second City' hinted at a deeper and earlier link, beyond the more innocent 'Glasgow' brand on rusting machinery. The implication was that as 'Second City', Glasgow was originally built on the labour of John's enslaved countrymen. Yet, when John came to Glasgow, he could find nothing in the streets or in print to illuminate this connection between his home country and the city of Glasgow.

The third encounter was during a tour of Georgian warehouses on the banks of the River Lune, in the northern English 'port city' of Lancaster. One visitor was following the trail of Britain's Atlantic ports which had traded with his home country in the eighteenth century. As an African-American, he had a related interest in the human connection between these ports and transatlantic slavery. When asked if he was also visiting Glasgow, the American replied that Lancaster was as far north as his tour reached. He was aware of Glasgow's industrial heritage, but not about Glasgow's Atlantic connections in the early colonial period. One of the best internet source for information on the slave trade in Britain is the 'Port Cities' website. Although it features the leading English slave ports, Glasgow is prominent by its absence.

These three examples suggest that there is an active demand for more information on Glasgow's mercantile foundations, or lack of awareness of the connections. The demand is not just for a passive celebratory pastime for its residents, but through a wider, more modern desire from visitors from much further afield, including those seeking to understands slavery from a British perspective.

In line with the far reaching-theme of this volume, this paper considers the potential of linking the less visible parts of Glasgow's overseas connections, during its early mercantile period (c. 1660-1740). During this period, the River Clyde had trading connections with the Caribbean (Smout 1963). This was long before Glasgow's better-know tobacco links with North America (Devine 1976). Along with Bristol and Liverpool, Glasgow was one of three leading British Atlantic 'Port Cities'. All three grew rapidly from the seventeenth century, to become world leading ports. By the 1811 census, Glasgow had become the largest of the three, to be christened 'Second City' of the British Empire.

Most of what we know about Glasgow from the late seventeenth century has come through its traditional written history (McUre 1860; Brown 1795). In recent decades, this has been revisited and affirmed, mainly from an economic history background (Devine 1995). Unfortunately the study period is a 'dark age' historically, with relatively few documentary sources available. Scotland also suffers from a common misconception of being excluded from this early stage of the British Empire, due to political restrictions such as the English Navigation Acts (MacInnes 2008).

Beyond the limitations of archive-based history, an alternative way of exploring Glasgow's early colonial connections is from a more physical approach. This respects written sources, but seeks a deeper connection in the landscape of both Glasgow and its transatlantic connections. These are sought through physical connections (though specifically not via archaeology, which was the original aim of this paper, but was not possible to bring into its wide ranging framework). It is hoped also to dig deeper, to shed light on the individuals who populated Glasgow's colonial landscapes.

By seeking to transcend the constraints of written sources, the paper will explore Glasgow's early mercantile period through a world-wide framework, linking two basic 'triangles'

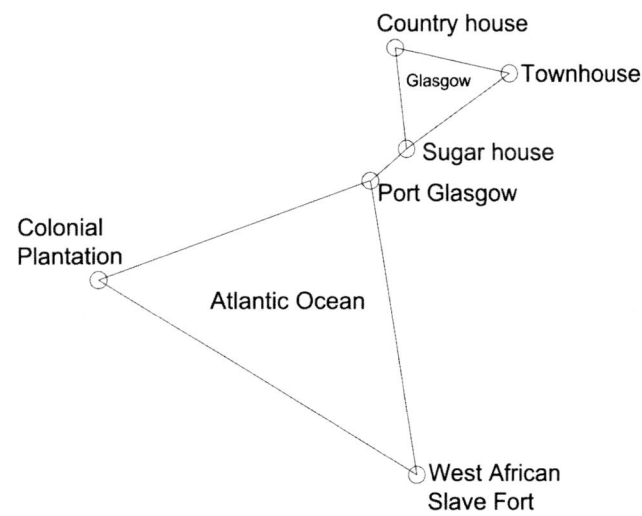

Figure 1. Triangular Framework of Glasgow's Atlantic Connections (author).

(Figure 1). The first triangle comprises a Glasgow mercantile trio of the sugar houses, town houses, and country houses of the city's sugar merchants. The second is the classic Atlantic 'triangular trade' of British Atlantic ports, Caribbean sugar plantations and West African slave forts. The background to this framework is ongoing research and fieldwork on early Glasgow sugar planters in the West Indies (Nisbet 2009). However, the theme in this paper extends beyond specific studies, to provide a more focussed framework for further research.

It is patently obvious that all six points of the sugar triangles were mutually dependent. The sugar (later tobacco and cotton) had to be grown somewhere, and the intensive system of cultivation depended on labour brought forcibly to the Caribbean from West Africa. The sugar was transported across the Atlantic to the Clyde, where it was processed in Glasgow's early sugar houses. The profits from the sugar houses funded the merchants' townhouses and country estates. To date most Glaswegians (if prompted) recognise a distant or 'secondary' link between their city and colonial trade, through the activities of well-known merchants. However, as the component parts of the trading cycle become more distant, they are less tangible, and have been easy to ignore in Glasgow.

The key to the big changes which occurred in the west of Scotland in the pre-1740 period was external markets. These generated enormous wealth, many times what could readily be achieved at home. In the early sugar period, some Glasgow merchants ventured beyond the mid-Atlantic to become sugar planters (Nisbet 2009). Within the general 'merchant' theme, these 'planters' give Glasgow a personal place in the Atlantic sugar cycle, well beyond any token or 'secondary' link.

Unfortunately, compared with the more familiar identity of the colonial 'merchant', the role of 'planter' is much more elusive in Glasgow. This is partially due to the parochial character of city histories (Eyre-Todd 1934), where distant events were of less interest to traditional historians, no matter how important they were to the city's development. From a Glasgow perspective, it is almost as if any merchant who headed permanently beyond the mid-Atlantic, somehow dropped off the edge of the known world. Yet those who ventured further as planters provide the missing link, personally tying Glasgow to all six points of the sugar cycle.

The purpose here is to investigate the surviving physical fabric from the time of each of the six points of Glasgow's sugar triangles. This includes the landscapes of urban gardens, country estates and sugar plantations, which were all linked by common ownership. It will be suggested that, only once we consider these seemingly diverse Atlantic worlds, not least through being visited, worked or owned by Glasgow merchants, can we move a step further to begin to understand the hitherto invisible folk who populated these spaces and forged a global city.

On the Scottish side of the Atlantic the least visible but most important part of the sugar triangle was the Glasgow sugar house. The sugar house received, processed and sold the refined sugar, and also made rum from the waste molasses (Defoe 1726). The income from the sugar house was the basis of the merchant's business, livelihood and social position.

Glasgow had at least four sugar houses in the seventeenth century (Smout 1962). These are often regarded as the city's earliest factories, and pioneers of its subsequent boiling and chemical industries (Clow 1952, 515). Much later,

Figure 2. Easter Sugar House, Glasgow (Source: Scran).

Glasgow also became a world leading manufacturer of sugar machinery (Oakley 1937, 271). Thus, the sugar trade had wider implications for a place which later matured from a merchant city into a world centre of manufacturing.

Glasgow's sugar houses were scattered around the growing Merchant City from the 1660s, in the Stockwell and Candleriggs area (Figure 2). Though long-demolished and built over, at the time their steam, smoke and smell ensured a dominant place in the early city. In the 1730's Glasgow's early historian John McUre described:

> 'Stately and lofty buildings belonging to the King Street Sugar-House, consisting of a large court, high and low apartments, cellars, store-houses and distilling-houses' (McUre 1830, 131).

One or two sketches of the sugar houses survive (Gordon 1872, 543), but repeated redevelopment has virtually wiped their location from Glasgow's popular history, particularly compared with the later 'Tobacco Lords' (Devine 1975). The only physical hint of the location of the sugar houses is the enduring 'Glasgow Grid' of streets. However, compared with the Tobacco trade, the sugar houses remain much less well known.

The merchant's base in Glasgow was his townhouse. Although dozens were built in Glasgow from the late seventeenth century and through the eighteenth, the townhouses are almost as invisible as the city's sugar houses.

The townhouses made a strong physical statement through their architecture and their urban presence. They also defined a wider sense of social refinement, through their walled gardens. In the seventeenth century, these gardens were country estates in miniature, located on the fringes of the medieval town, in what later became the 'Merchant City'. The enduring theme of the merchants' gardens was their orchards, located in what is now the heart of Glasgow. One of the earliest merchants, George Elphinstone, who became provost of Glasgow from 1601 (McUre, 53), had a garden in the city with its trademark orchard. It is apt that this family had a tangible physical link, through patronage of the Tron steeple, one of the very few surviving icons of post-medieval Glasgow.

> 'The townhouses fronted the merchants' gardens, providing a bond between colonial trade and architecture. It is already well-established in Glasgow that much of the most important architecture was funded through overseas trade, buoyed up on a wave of mercantile activity........to show that cultural innovation was the fashionable corollary of foreign trade' (Walker 1999, 19).

Beyond wealth and commerce, the merchant's gardens played an active role in the social and cultural life of the Atlantic port city. In their controlled environment, space and images of antiquity were manipulated through earth, gravel, statues, urns, steps, paths and plants, to define a wider sense of social refinement. Sher and Hook (1995) noted how 'The trading link made an interweaving of Scottish and American culture almost inevitable' and,

> 'Glasgow's commercial prosperity also provided opportunities for the development of notions of enlightened progress and improvement, in all aspects of the polite civic culture of an increasingly civilized modern world. Progress could be seen in economic life, stimulating the dissemination of new, progressive ideas' (Sher and Hook 1995).

Glasgow's most celebrated townhouse, the Shawfield Mansion, described as a 'great and stately lodging, orchard, and gardens' (Gordon 1872, 374; Nisbet 2012 (2)), was built at the West Port in 1711 by a merchant and sugar importer Daniel Campbell (Figure 3) (McUre, 129). When the second, and longest, owner, Colonel McDowall, purchased Shawfield in 1726 on returning from the Caribbean, he was quite specific that he was acquiring both the house and gardens (National Library of Scotland 1726-35, Col. Wm McDowall, London, to Cousin Crichan, Edinburgh, 22 Nov 1726). One of the main purposes of his purchase was to accommodate and entertain his friends and associates from London and Bristol.

Figure 3. The Shawfield Mansion, Glasgow (Nisbet).

Shawfield was the prototype of dozens of merchant's town and country villas which would follow over the next century. Beyond Glasgow's history, its influence stretched far beyond Glasgow, appearing in the second volume of Vitruvius Britannicus, described as being wholly without precedent in Britain (Walker, 1999, 25). Built on what was the very fringes of Glasgow at the time, beside the West Port, Shawfield was just as important for its setting, and its ornamental gardens, which stretched the full length of modern Glassford Street (Gordon 1872, 955). A rare glimpse of the garden is achieved in the aftermath of the Shawfield riots in 1725. After wrecking the interior of the house, the crowd:

> 'Made the same havoc in my garden by breaking my statues, pulling up my trees, shrubs and hedges by the roots and breaking down two pavilions in it' (Hill 2007, 73).

Regrettably, a physical sense of the merchant townhouse in Glasgow today is almost non-existent. The Merchant City today is largely a Victorian rebuild from the foundations of its seventeenth century namesake (McKean 1990). Very few eighteenth century buildings survive, and even fewer from the seventeenth century. The grand two-storey colonial merchant villa simply did not stand a chance of surviving against the onslaught of six-storey Victorian warehouses. The gardens and orchards in the city are even more elusive.

Yet they are important links to the wider Glasgow mercantile landscape, both in the Scottish countryside and spanning the Atlantic to the Caribbean. The merchant's townhouses were mirrored, in building materials, style and architecture, by their country houses. The merchants' town and country houses are also the physical spaces in Britain with the most identifiable link to their slaves. The slave boys and black servants roamed the corridors and rooms of the mansions and slept in the basements and garrets.

The closer we come to Glasgow, the less visible become the labour force of the city's merchants. The slave boys were among the few publicly visible Africans in eighteenth century Glasgow (Whyte, 2006, 13). These boys would be seen accompanying the merchant to and from his townhouse. The owner of Shawfield brought back two young African boys to accompany his son to school in Glasgow (National Library of Scotland 1726-35, Col. Wm McDowall, Edinburgh to Major Jas Milliken, St Kitts 8th Dec 1727). One of the very few Africans whom we know anything about in Glasgow, was named 'Cato'. Cato lived at both Shawfield and Castle Semple giving a unique personal link. Cato seems to have been born shortly after 1700 in the Congo and was transported to St Kitts, where he was purchased by Colonel McDowall of the Shawfield Mansion. Cato was employed as a sugar boiler, valued at £75, and was later brought to Glasgow. Although the Africans brought to Glasgow may have had a less physically demanding life than in the plantations, they did not necessarily fit easily into domestic servitude. In January 1748 Cato ran away, and the following advert appeared in the Glasgow press:

> 'Run away from Colonel McDowell of Castle-Sempill, upon the 30th of January, a Negro man, named CATO, alias JOHN: he is middle aged, pretty tall, ill-legs, with squat or broad feet. Any person who apprehends him, or gives any information of him to Colonel McDowell, or to Mr. Alexander Houston Merchant in Glasgow, shall have a sufficient reward paid him' (Glasgow Journal 25th January 1748).

The importance of such brief glimpses of the hitherto invisible Africans who laboured to fund the early development of Glasgow, cannot be overemphasised. Near another Atlantic Port City, on Sunderland Point, downstream from the northern English slaving port of Lancaster, a single grave of an African survives. As one of the few physical remnants of a trade which involved thousands, this remote spot has become a focal point to remember Africans in Britain (Figure 4). Perhaps if Glasgow had even such modest physical remains, it would allow a better understanding of the city's human relationship with its plantations.

By the time Glasgow matured into a merchant city, well beyond our study period, the merchants' gardens in the city centre were built over and transposed to the

Figure 4. Grave of West Indian, Sunderland Point, Lancashire (Nisbet).

surrounding suburbs and countryside (Nisbet and Welsh 1992). The wealth and influence of the colonial merchant was now transferred for posterity to his country house and estate. Unlike the sugar house and town house, many of the merchants' country houses survive, retaining a much more tangible sense of physical heritage as demonstrated by their architecture and building materials. Yet the remoteness of the country house from the city tends to blur its close relationship with the metropolitan trading cycle.

Much of what we know about the physical development of Glasgow derives from its numerous histories, published from the Victorian era (McUre 1830). Typical of their time, they take a celebratory approach to the city's mercantile success. Their antiquarian style may now be dated, but they are still a principal source for Glasgow's history, and their factual content is rarely questioned. The traditional histories describe the landscapes of the city which have gradually disappeared under suburban sprawl.

A prime example is *The Old Country Houses of the Old Glasgow Gentry* (Mitchell 1870). Today it is quite difficult to find a part of Glasgow that did not at one time feature the country house and estate of a retired colonial merchant. The joint names of the merchants and their estates such as Houston of Jordanhill, Campbell of Blythswood, Hamilton of Aikenhead, Maxwell of Pollok and McDowall of Castle Semple still roll off the tongue, giving a solid sense of culture and tradition to the west of Scotland landscape. Many estate remnants appear on the first edition Ordnance Survey maps, but were soon swallowed up thereafter by suburban development.

The Old Country Houses makes numerous references to the city's sugar merchants, dubbing them 'Glasgow's Old West Indians'. They are described in a celebratory manner, as 'magnates' with large plantations in the Caribbean, where they made great fortunes through 'social and commercial supremacy'. This is one of the very few admissions in Glasgow's histories that the identity of the city's merchants was indelibly linked with their role as sugar planters. However, the book continues, claiming that 'there is not one Glasgow man left that ever owned a slave'. This is amplified with the claim that:

> 'Whatever faults our West Indians had, it must always be remembered to their credit that they kept aloof from the slave trade - Glasgow was clean handed in this matter' (Mitchell 1870, 83).

Despite the initial admission in the book of a physical link with the Caribbean through personal ownership of plantations, this denial of Glasgow merchants' involvement in slavery, particularly plantation slavery, means that the landscape of the Glasgow planter remains empty, devoid of any sense of the Caribbean population whose labour directly funded the development of the city.

Quite how Glasgow men could have operated as sugar planters without a labour force defies common sense. This quote exemplifies more than anything else the modern difficulties with the city's early colonial identity.

Beyond the published reputation of the city's merchants, their enduring physical heritage is the country houses at the heart of their estates, especially those which survive as tourist attractions (Nisbet and Welsh 1992). The country houses were set in an improved landscape, transposing the merchant's early gardens from the city centre to the countryside. By the 1780s it was universal for the merchants' country estates to have 'orchards and gardens abounding with plenty of the most excellent fruit' (Semple 1782, 10). It was on Colonel McDowall's country estate at Castle Semple in Renfrewshire that he grew fruits in hothouses, described as being second only in Scotland to those of the Duke of Argyle (Semple 1782, 153). The technology of hot walls and glasshouses provided a home from home with his Caribbean plantations, growing:

'peaches, apricots, nectarines, and the different fruits of all the world, melons, grapes, pineapples and tobacco' (Semple 1782, 10).

On a par with the orchards and gardens were the water features at Castle Semple, including 'diverted rivulets, cascades, ponds, and subterranean passages' (Semple 1782, 153-4). Directly in front of the new Palladian mansion, a 500-acre loch was drained. This was partly an economic enterprise, to create new farmland, but was equally a cultural achievement to create canals with views for leisure trips. This reflected the seafaring side of the merchant's life, where guests in the 1730s were entertained by trips in an elaborate boat ordered from London, decorated with a family crest. The boat was to be:

> 'as light and neatly contrived as possible to hold about six people.... let it be fairly painted with a square stern for a coat of arms.... and a flag staff and.... will provide something extraordinary' (National Library of Scotland 1726-35, Col. Wm McDowall, Castle Semple to Thos Truman, London, 20th June 1727).

Merging with this use of the landscape as a status symbol, were more practical agricultural enclosures and improvements (Semple 1782, 11). After developing intensively worked, regulated and enclosed sugar plantations the planters returned to make radical changes to the Scottish landscape, in the form of enclosed and managed estates. In some cases the pre-improvement landscape was overlaid with a vast rectangular grid, akin to a sugar plantation (BCA Survey of Milliken Estate 1731). As on the sugar plantation, at its heart was the mansion house and offices. Further out was the enclosed farmland.

On his return from the Caribbean, at his country estate of Castle Semple, Colonel McDowall sought not only to alter the landscape (BCA Survey of Castle Semple Estate 1728), but to attempt to command and control his estate tenants through physical measures, including enclosure, closing of roads and bridges, large-scale drainage schemes and canals. This created widespread opposition. He had a very low opinion of his tenants, writing,

> 'such is the temper of the creatures here that they choose to live upon potatoes and oat meal on their own dunghills' (NLS 1726-35, Col. Wm McDowall, Castle Semple to Daniel Smith, St Kitts, 12th May 1731).

He considered them to be, a stumbling block to his ambitions, calling them

> 'a parcel of unruly and barbarous people, who were enemies to the laudable spirit of improvement'.

Unlike his enslaved workforce in the Caribbean, the Colonel's estate tenants in Scotland took resort to the law, ultimately resulting in defeat of some of his most radical schemes (NAS GD 124/6/221 1733).

It hardly takes a great leap of the imagination to see that, for Glasgow men who served much of their life in the colonies as sugar planters, improvements at home and the control of underlings (whether slaves or tenants), were less a novelty, than simply based on a lifetime of experience in a system of intensive agriculture. Many of the planters spent apprenticeships and careers learning intensively operated cultivation, nearly a century before it was common in Scotland. The staples and climate were radically different, but the principles were the same.

Beyond wealth, what impact did such experience in the Caribbean have on Scottish estate improvements in later life? Was it a coincidence that periods of more intense land acquisition and improvements at home coincided with expansion in the Caribbean? Such big questions remain to be answered, They entail a responsibility for Glasgow historians and fieldworkers, and are far too wide-ranging to explore simply from a home base, when the main players operated on the international stage. In the end, their groundwork forms the basis for the great swathe of wider, more popular, writing in the city, ranging from poetry, to anthologies, to Glasgow's literature in the 'Glasgow novel' (Burgess 1998).

The River Clyde connected the Broomielaw in Glasgow with the quayside at Port Glasgow (Figure 5). Port Glasgow was the gateway to Glasgow's much bigger 'sugar triangle' which spanned the Atlantic. This was where the ubiquitous Glasgow merchant morphed into a seafarer and planter. Port Glasgow was the landing point for sugar from the Caribbean (NAS, E504/28, Customs Accounts, Port Glasgow). It is no coincidence that Port Glasgow was founded in the same decade as Glasgow's sugar houses, but the connection is rarely made.

Figure 5. View of Port Glasgow in the 1760s (Nisbet Collection).

Today the public image of Port Glasgow is of a post industrial town which, until a few decades ago, was dominated by shipyards and giant cranes. Like the city of Glasgow, this latent image of heavy industry and shipbuilding has obliterated Port Glasgow's much earlier heritage. Three hundred years ago, Port Glasgow was a thriving Atlantic port. Until well beyond the study period, oceangoing vessels could not reach Glasgow. The city's trade was carried out indirectly via Port Glasgow (Gibb 1983, 66), but its one-step removal from Glasgow has added another layer of invisibility.

Although any history of Glasgow's mercantile origins mentions the founding of Port Glasgow in 1668 (Gibb 1983, 44), little else tends to be said about the town. The physical sense of seventeenth century Port Glasgow is now even less well preserved than that

Figure 6. Eighteenth Century Custom House and Warehouses, Lancaster (Nisbet).

of the city of Glasgow. Its sugar houses and warehouses are all gone. Any remaining maritime heritage was destroyed in the 1960s when the harbour was filled in to build a bypass. Again, other port cities such as Lancaster have much more surviving infrastructure, giving a much more tangible sense of survival of Georgian buildings and riverside warehouses, contemporary with the slavery era (Figure 6).

Despite being administered as a detached portion of Glasgow, Port Glasgow has a rich history of its own. From its founding in 1668, feuars were given permission to 'build wharf or breast work down on the shore within the sea water mark opposite ground which the town has allowed them to build upon' (Nisbet 1992, 24). As development gradually spread up Custom House Lane, a planned grid was established from 1718, mirroring the 'Glasgow grid' of the Merchant City. No decent maps survive of Port Glasgow before the late eighteenth century, although it has been possible to piece together a layout from a jigsaw of hundreds of burgh deeds (Nisbet 1992, 25). One of the merchants, Robert Allason, who lies in the kirkyard typifies the multi-layered mercantile experience in Port Glasgow. Each layer of his career can be seen in isolation, but together they provide the key to Glasgow's mercantile success (Nisbet 1992, 26). In addition to the big Glasgow merchants who traded through the town, the development of Port Glasgow became dominated by several dozen entrepreneurs. Buying up plots, they invested in manufacture and shipping, and developed a small empire, supporting and participating in overseas trade (Nisbet and Welsh 1992). One of their few tangible links is the graves of the town's merchants and seafarers in Port Glasgow kirkyard. Some of these merchants played an active role in the plantation trade, their ships left the Port Glasgow quayside, and they owned property, warehouse and industries in the town. As Port Glasgow was Glasgow's deepwater port through the slavery era, most Africans who were brought to Scotland as servants were landed there.

One of the merchants, Robert Allason, who lies in the kirkyard typifies the multi-layered mercantile experience in Port Glasgow. Each layer of his career can be seen in isolation, but together they provide the key to Glasgow's mercantile success (Nisbet 1992). From a Glasgow apprenticeship and burgessship, he and his brothers moved downstream to Port Glasgow, where they developed a property empire. Success in manufacturing and supply to shipping in the port, led to shares in ships, then to outright ownership, and personal involvement in trade. Again the most deeply hidden parts of mercantile success are the overseas ones. In the common Glasgow pattern, Allason did not simply sit on the quayside trading with passing ships. A younger brother went to sea and captained the family's ships, including slavers (Eltis 1999), and died of fever in the leading African slave port of Old Calabar. An older brother was the family agent in America, where his wealth arose, by his own admission (Nisbet and Welsh 1992), from dealing in enslaved Africans. Ultimate financial and social success was expressed in the purchase of unimproved farmland and the development of a country estate south of Glasgow. His country house survives as the National Trust for Scotland attraction which was featured in the introduction to this paper.

The countless crossings of the Atlantic will always be the most elusive part of the Glasgow sugar cycle, leaving no tangible remnant. The sugar of Colonel McDowall of the Shawfield mansion was transported home to Britain on thousands of vessels, some of which he personally owned, and were captained by his brother David and other relatives. From his slave trading exploits, all that remains are accounts of odd voyages, gleaned from documents and newspapers (Nisbet 2012 (1); NLS Letters of Col. McDowall 1726-35; Eltis 1999). Colonel McDowall entered the slave trade in 1726 by purchasing a slave ship, named the Fair Parnelia. After loading 273 enslaved African men, women and children in Guinea, heading for St Kitts, the ship apparently disappeared. Initially it seemed to have been taken by pirates. However, a full report in the London press in January 1727 provided the full tragic account, via the testament of the surviving Scots Captain, Thomas Gillespie. In the mid Atlantic, the Fair Parnelia was struck unexpectedly by a whirlwind. The ship overturned, drowning all the enslaved men, women and children chained below deck. Only the captain and two others survived, after an arduous month drifting in a small boat. Beyond its Glasgow ownership and direct link to the Shawfield Mansion, the Fair Parnelia was named after the daughter of another Glasgow sugar planter, Major James Milliken. The 'figurehead' of this Glasgow slave ship has one of the few tangible slave trading links to Glasgow, as she died in Glasgow two years later of smallpox, and was buried under the choir of Glasgow Cathedral (Nisbet 2012 (1)).

From a global perspective, Glasgow's participation in the sugar trade linked the city right back to the development of the earliest European colonialism by the Portuguese in the fifteenth century. Sugar came via the Mediterranean, to the islands of Madeira and the Canaries, then across the Atlantic to the Caribbean (Thomas 1997). By the study period, sugar was the jewel in the crown of the early British Empire (Sheridan 2001, 403), long before North American tobacco came to the fore. From the 1660s, sugar cultivation in the Caribbean was an intensive industrial process. Each plantation was worked by around 200 enslaved Africans in deplorable conditions. They were forced to work in the scorching cane fields and central boiling works, to produce partly-refined sugar, to be shipped back for final processing in Glasgow's sugar houses (Dunn 1972). The fortune of each Glasgow sugar planter literally came directly from the personal ownership and mortality of several hundred enslaved African men, women and children.

Perhaps the biggest omission from Glasgow's history is that Glasgow's sugar houses needed sugar. This sugar came not through some distant secondary connection, but through a direct personal link. Some of Glasgow's most celebrated characters transcended the over-arching 'merchant' label and spent their careers as 'planters'. This role extended far beyond Port Glasgow and the mid-Atlantic, to participate personally in the intensive cultivation of sugar in the Caribbean sugar islands.

The estates of Glasgow's sugar planters were artificial landscapes originally created from jungle. They combined the planter's great house, sugar works, mill, rum distillery, cane fields and slave accommodation. As the physical core of the plantation, the sugar works has been the target of much physical research to date, often under the label of 'Industrial archaeology' (Wright 1991). While this raises lasting Glasgow connections through sugar machinery and steam engines, stamped 'Made in Glasgow', such surviving sugar plant postdates the study period by two centuries (Figure 7). Again Glasgow's later industrial identity confuses and obscures the earlier colonial reality, escaping any concrete part of the city's heritage. Other investigations have looked at the landscape organisation of plantations, slave villages and slave burials, but not from a Scottish perspective (Hicks, 2007).

Not only was the sugar plantation just as crucial to the Atlantic sugar triangle as Glasgow's sugar houses. The planter's great house was one of a set or trio of houses, including his country house and townhouse in Scotland. It was also part of a much wider property empire taking on the Caribbean islands, London and Bristol. Apart from plantation houses, Colonel McDowall owned houses in Basseterre (capital of St Kitts), Charlestown (capital of Nevis), and Bristol; plus lodgings in Edinburgh and London (NLS Letters of Col. McDowall). Such a spread of property introduces a much wider mix of architectural influences, hitherto barely imagined in Glasgow. All the

Figure 7. Sugar 'Mill Roll', Nevis, by P. Stewart & Co., London Road, Glasgow, 1859 (Nisbet).

houses were a leading sign of social success. In the St Kitts, Colonel McDowall's house was later rented out to the Governor.

Today, numerous former plantation houses survive, converted to luxury hotels, belying their original purpose as the centre of an intensive sugar empire. Even more pertinent to the memory of Glasgow's sugar planters is the sugar works, invariably lying forgotten in vegetation directly behind the luxury hotel. Scattered around the works such as at Canada Hills, St Kitts (Nisbet 2009) are numerous artefacts and structures, from boiling coppers to complete windmills (Figure 8). In fact, much more physical remains of the sugar cycle survive in the Caribbean than in Glasgow. Beyond physical remnants, the least visible memory is of the labour force who dominated the landscape and worked the mills, boiling coppers and cane pieces. The design of the landscape was geared not only towards the economics of sugar production, but also towards the management and control of the slave population. The site of the slave villages, whether marked on maps, or evident on the ground, gives us a tangible link to the lives of the slaves who inhabited them.

Like the orchards, gardens and country estates in and around Glasgow, the sugar plantation was an artificial landscape which had cultural as well as functional overtones. In the 1720s, a parish minister on St. Kitts was able to wander amongst

Figure 8. Windmill, Canada Hills, St. Kitts (Nisbet).

a 'parallel universe', in a valley due north of the plantation of Glasgow's Colonel McDowall. The valley was:

> 'plentifully stocked with wild palm and other fragrant trees; in the cool shade, upon the mossy banks of a transparent river, we regaled ourselves with some of the sweetest water I ever drank, and indulged our souls with soothing discourse on the happiness of a retired state of life, concluding that we wanted nothing just then to render the place a most delicious paradise' (Smith 1745).

Such one-sided views of paradise obscured the nearby human presence of the labour force. In the adjacent sugar plantations, enslaved Africans were overworked in the tropical heat, to cultivate sugar for Glasgow's sugar houses and to fund the development of the city.

In the Atlantic sugar triangle, the plantation workforce of the Glasgow planters remains the most elusive part. The origin of this workforce is even more obscure. The Glasgow sugar planters obtained their enslaved labour force from the West African coast, all the way from Sierra Leone down to Nigeria (Curtin 2002). Ironically, at the time of writing, Glasgow's Kelvingrove Museum displays various artefacts from Sierra Leone, the Republic of Congo and Benin in Nigeria. The overall theme of the display is 'masks which share a secret knowledge'. Despite this, Glasgow's slaving connections with these countries is still a secret.

Although West Africa may seem even further removed from Glasgow than the Caribbean, again, there was a deep and persisting physical link. One of the largest West African forts was owned by one of Glasgow's leading merchants, Richard Oswald, who transported tens of thousands of Africans across the Atlantic. His story has become well known in recent years (Hancock 2001), yet his physical presence is still obscure in Glasgow. Oswald's empire operated from just down the Stockwell from Glasgow's Shawfield Mansion. Built in 1742, this included 'a convenient square court' of houses, cellars and vaults for storing his imports (Glasgow Courant Jan 12-19 1756). However no trace remains as the site has been built over several times. Oswald's African slave fort crops up in the surviving papers of various Scottish sugar merchants, as it was a main source of slaves for the plantations of the Scots:

> 'I drew on you in favour of Messrs Richard Oswald & Co. £235 sterling for five negro men & four boys' ...... '£137 sterling in favour of Messrs Richard Oswald & Co. for two young Gold Coast men & three boys' .... '£396 sterling in favour of Messrs Richard Oswald & Co. for the twelve Gold Coast Negroes we put on your estate' (Thoms 1967).

Like the surviving Caribbean plantations of Glasgow's sugar merchants, Richard Oswald's slave fort still stands in Sierra Leone. In recent years it has become the subject of growing heritage interest, albeit via America, not Scotland (De Corse 2006). Built by the Portuguese it is an expression in stone of the control of the enslaved in a single place, in a prelude to much more widespread control, once on the sugar plantations. Ironically, this ruined African slave fort gives a much more physical impression of Oswald and his source of fortune than can be gleaned today in Glasgow. A Caribbean-born author described a similar African slave fort as 'probably the most beautiful building that I have ever seen' (Phillips, 2002, 304). At first, this seems a bizarre sentiment for a fort which is a symbol of the uprooting of his ancestors. However he explains how history is illuminated by such buildings:

> 'We have clues to our past, our present and even some idea of our future if we study buildings and their origins. I first visited the fort in the late eighties. As a man of African origin, I was coming face to face with a part of my Atlantic history. It was disturbing, but I wished neither to look the other way, nor to romanticise the encounter. I wished simply to understand' (Phillips 2002).

Conclusions

Within Glasgow's literature, and its later historical role as 'Second City' of the Empire, the city stakes a claim as a main player in the global system of British trade. This paper has suggested that failure to interact not just historically, but also physically with the full sugar cycle, has meant that Glasgow is gradually losing its identity as a leading eighteenth century colonial port among Britain's traditional Atlantic Port Cities, not least in the tourist market and in historical research.

We have seen how all six points of the sugar triangle are interdependent, yet vary greatly in their visibility in Glasgow. Demolition and rebuilding has obscured the development of Glasgow's early Merchant City, including the merchants' townhouses, orchards and sugar houses. Perhaps the only hope of a deeper understanding in Glasgow is through physical links with the wider sugar cycle. In this cycle, the physical remains gradually increase as we move outwards from Glasgow to the countryside, and across the Atlantic. It is to the country houses, estates, sugar plantations and slave forts that we need to look, to achieve a deeper connection with Glasgow's colonial sugar connections.

Glasgow's motto begins with the line 'This is the tree that never grew'. This tree lies at the heart of the city's municipal coat of arms. It is still prevalent in the townscape, indelibly carved on stone buildings and on cast ironwork throughout the city. Despite the fact that Glasgow's fortunes depended on connections with very distant places, the city's tree is still firmly rooted in home turf. It often takes the fresh perspective of incomers to challenge the old, entrenched, parochial views. Another writer, born in the Caribbean and raised in Britain, sees his origins through the analogy of just such a tree, floating on the Atlantic:

'Lord, I have been washed from shore to shore, as a tree in the ocean. The branches of my fingers, the roots of my feet, could grip nothing, but now they have found ground' (Walcott 1977).

The main drive to keep Glasgow's history up to date comes not from academics or residents, but from visitors, who require a basic honesty about the city's development. However a modern demand for inclusiveness drives Councils to somehow try to 'create' it through the appointment of consultants, festivals and promotional statements. Glasgow's paradox is that the multicultural city already exists, and doesn't need to be reinvented. The resident, tourist and novelist needs to be able to interact with the true multicultural Glasgow, based on a sound sense of heritage, involving people from many nations, not one which has been created through politically correct slogans. At the time of writing, the cultural spin is typified by a poster, ironically on the site of one wing of the Shawfield mansion:

'Welcome to the Merchant City, the historic heart of Glasgow, where the tobacco lairds (sic) and traders that once made Glasgow the Second City of the Empire came to do business, socialise and build their townhouses .... That same spirit of entrepreneurialism still characterises the area today and it is experiencing a remarkable rebirth as the city's foremost cultural, creative, design and artistic quarter' (Poster on site of east wing of Shawfield Mansion, 2012).

One of the best ways to revive a physical sense of Glasgow's early colonial history is through experiencing and questioning surviving physical remains of the sugar cycle. On the Caribbean side of the Atlantic sugar triangle, we can wander through numerous deserted sugar works, for example on Nevis and St Kitts, littered with steam engines, plant and ironwork stamped 'made in Glasgow'. We can also take on board the much earlier legacy of a landscape still dominated by windmills, boiling coppers, and massive stone sugar works.

On the Glasgow side of the Atlantic, we have seen in this paper how the remnants of the early colonial, or pre-tobacco period, are much harder to find. Yet Glasgow is no different from Liverpool, where slavery, 'though absent from official civic accounts, is nonetheless present in the city streets and architecture' (Dresser 2007). In Glasgow's fellow Atlantic Port Cities, this physical link has been taken much further to imply in their modern histories that:

'In Bristol, 'There is not a brick in the city but what is cemented with the blood of a slave'; and in Liverpool, every brick of their town was 'cemented with the blood of an African' (Nicholls 1881-2, 165; Longmore 2007).

Such statements are far too shocking to be made outright in Glasgow, at least initially, until more evidence is found and taken on board by the public. There is a more basic realisation that for Glasgow to come to terms with its origins simply means having the physical information available to allow questions to be asked about its involvement in the full scope of the sugar cycle. In particular, this would allow challenging the old parochial views of Glasgow's great and good merchants who were supposedly 'clean handed' (Mitchell 1870, 83).

Glasgow has a tough image, but is it brave enough to face up to the full responsibility of its multicultural roots? This is the big question. Like the African-Caribbean author who used the analogy of a tree, following Glasgow's sugar trail has meant embarking on a journey to find an elusive connection between Glasgow and the Caribbean sugar islands. Neither the Caribbean writer (above), nor the present author, are direct descendants of enslaved Africans. Yet the conclusion, after following the sugar trail across the Atlantic, is that the search is just as important to a sense of origin, and the true identity of our places of birth.

The further the global sugar trail was followed, it became not only a search for the global identity of Glasgow merchants, but equally a search for the writer's own personal identity as a Glaswegian.

Bibliography

Birmingham City Archives (BCA), *Boulton & Watt Collection, Papers of John Watt, Survey of Castle Semple Estate, Renfrewshire 1728*, Ms. 3219/2.

BCA, Boulton & Watt Collection, *Papers of John Watt, Survey of Milliken Estate (formerly Johnstone), Renfrewshire 1731* Ms. 3219/2.

Brown, A. 1795. *History of Glasgow*, Edinburgh: Dunlop & Wilson.

Burgess, M. 1998. *Imagine a City Glasgow in Fiction*, Glendaruel: Argyll Publishing.

Clow, A. and N.L. Clow 1952. *The Chemical Revolution*, London: Batchworth.

Curtin, P.D. 2002. *The Rise and Fall of the Plantation Complex*, Cambridge: Cambridge University Press.

De Corse 2006. *Survey of Bunce Island Fort, Report for Sierra Leone Government.*

Devine, T.M. 1975. *The Tobacco Lords of Glasgow*, Edinburgh: Edinburgh University Press.

Dresser, M. 2007. *Slavery Obscured,* Bristol: Redcliffe.

Dufill, M. 2004. *The African Trade from the Ports of Scotland, Slavery and Abolition* Vol. 25, No.3, 102-122.

Dunn, R.S. 1972. *Sugar and Slaves: The Rise of the Planter Class in the English West Indies, 1624-1713,* Chapel Hill: North Carolina.

Eltis, D., D. Richardson and D.B. Davis 1999. *The Transatlantic Slave Trade: A Database,* Cambridge: Cambridge University Press.

Eyre-Todd, G. 1934. *History of Glasgow*, Glasgow: Jackson, Wylie & Co.

Gibb, A. 1983. *Glasgow the Making of a City*, London: Croom Helm.

Gibson, J. 1770. *History of Glasgow*, Glasgow: R. Chapman and A. Duncan.

Glasgow Courant (Newspaper).

Glasgow Journal (Newspaper).

Gordon, G.F.S. 1872. *Glasgow Past & Present*, Glasgow: J. Tweed.

Hancock, D. 2001. Scots in the Slave Trade, in N. C. Landsman (ed.) *Nation and Province in the First British Empire*, 60-93. London: Bucknell University Press.

Hicks, D. 2007. *The Garden of the World Studies in Contemporary Archaeology, 4,* BAR International Series No.1632.

Hill, J. and N. Bastin 2007. *A Very Canny Scot – 'Great' Daniel Campbell of Shawfield and Islay 1670-1753 His Life and Times*, Barnham.

Longmore, J. 2007. The Impact of the Slave Trade on Eighteenth Century Liverpool, in D. Richardson, S. Schwartz and A. Tibbles (eds) *Cemented by the Blood of a Negro?* 225-249. Liverpool: Liverpool University Press.

McKean, C. 1990. Architecture and the Glasgows of the Imagination in K. McCarra and H. Whyte (eds) *A Glasgow Collection - Essays in Honour of Joe Fisher*. Glasgow: Glasgow City Libraries.

MacInnes, A.I. 2008 [1660-1707]. *Circumventing State Power-Scottish Mercantile Networks and the English Navigation Laws in Water and State in Europe and Asia*. Delhi: Manohar.

McUre, J. 1830 [1736]. *History of Glasgow*, Glasgow: Hutchison & Brookman.

Mitchell, J. O. and J. G. Smith 1870 *The Old Country Houses of the Old Glasgow Gentry*, Glasgow: James Maclehose.

National Archives of Scotland (NAS), Customs Accounts, Port Glasgow (from 1742), Ref. E504/28/1.

NAS, Letters of Capt. David McDowall 1728-33, Ref. GD 237/12/35.

NAS, Castle Semple Papers, *Action of molestation and declarator by feuars of Lochwinnoch against Col. Wm McDowall anent his draining and ditching at said loch in alleged contravention of their rights*, Ref. GD 124 /6/221.

National Library of Scotland (NLS), Letterbook of Col. Wm. McDowall, 1726-35, Ref. 301/107.

Nicholls, J. F. and Taylor J.I. 1881-2. *Bristol Past and Present (3 vols)* Bristol and London.

Nisbet, S. M. 1992. The Growth of Port Glasgow in the 18th Century, *Renfrewshire Local History Forum Journal*, Vol.3.

Nisbet, S. M. 2009. Early Glasgow Sugar Planters in the Caribbean, *Scottish Archaeological Journal* 31.1-2, 115-136.

Nisbet, S.M. and T.C. Welsh 1992. *Robert Allason and Greenbank*, Giffnock: Eastwood District Libraries.

Nisbet, S.M. 2012a. A Glasgow Slaving Tragedy - The Fair Parnelia, *Scottish Local History* 42 (Feb 2012).

Nisbet, S.M. 2012b. The Shawfield Mansion, *Scottish Local History* 44 (Sep 2012).

Oakley, C.A. 1937. *Scottish Industries Today*, Moray: Moray Press.

Phillips, C. 2002. *A New World Order*, New York: Vintage.

Semple, W. 1782. *History of the Shire of Renfrew*, Paisley: Alex Weir.

Sher, R.B. and A. Hook 1995. *Glasgow and the Enlightenment*. East Linton: Tuckwell Press.

Sheridan, R.B. 2001. Caribbean Plantation Society 1689-1748, in P.J. Marshall (ed.), *The Oxford History of the British Empire, The Eighteenth Century*. Oxford: Oxford University Press, 394-414

Smith, W. 1745. *A Natural History of Nevis*, Cambridge: J. Bentham.

Smout, T.C. 1963. *Scottish Trade on the Eve of the Union 1660-1707*, Edinburgh: Oliver & Boyd.

Smout, T.C. 1962. The Early Scottish Sugar Houses 1660-1720, *Economic History Review* 14 240

Thomas, H. 1997. *The Slave Trade: The History of the Atlantic Slave Trade 1440-1870* (Picador). London: Simon and Schuster.

Thoms, D.W. 1967. *Mills and Colhoun Letters*, Unpublished PhD Thesis, University of Canterbury.

Trouillot, M.R. 1992. The Caribbean Region: An open frontier in Anthropological Theory, *Annual Review of Anthropology* 21.

Walcott, D. 1970. *Dream on Monkey Mountain*, New York: Farrar.

Walker, F.A. 1999. Glasgow's New Town, in P. Reed (ed.) *Glasgow - The Forming of the City*, Edinburgh: Edinburgh University Press.

Wright, N. and A. 1991. Hamilton's Sugar Mill, Nevis, Leeward Islands, *Industrial Archaeology Review* XIII, 2, 114.

Records of the Burgh of Glasgow Vol. IV.

Whyte, I. 2006. *Scotland and the Abolition of Black Slavery 1756-1838*, Edinburgh: Edinburgh University Press.

Celebrating the end of Scottish history? National identity and the Scottish Historical Exhibition, Glasgow 1911

Neil G.W. Curtis

The 1911 Scottish Exhibition

In 1888, 1901 and 1911 Glasgow hosted three internationally significant Exhibitions, dominated by the twin themes of Industry and Empire that were first seen in the 1851 Great Exhibition in London, though they were civic affairs, mobilising the city's business and professional establishment in their organisation (Kinchin and Kinchin, 1988; Rembold, 1999). The 1911 Exhibition was billed as the 'Scottish Exhibition of National History, Art and Industry': the only one to have an explicit focus on a Scottish historical theme. Rather than having one large exhibition hall enclosing a variety of functions, smaller buildings for different purposes were constructed, including a machinery hall, Palaces of History, Fine Art, Decorative Art and Industries, a Concert Hall and the 'Auld Toon'. Alongside such educational elements, a substantial 'Entertainments Section' at the opposite end of the park included a 'Mountain Scenic Railway', aerial railway and, as a visitor described it afterwards,

> '...the joy wheel, the aquarium, with its immense octopus guarding the entrance, the joy house or hall of illusion, and the African village, with its straw huts and natives at work and play. From tropical Africa we stepped into the Polar regions and saw the Lapps and their reindeer...' (Bailie, 1935: 14)

Nearby was 'An Clachan', an evocation of a Highland village, while there were also commercial pavilions, such as those of the German Potash Syndicate, the Canadian Pacific Railway and the Royal Scottish Arboricultural Society, bandstands and restaurants. Although the most popular section was the 'Mountain Scenic Railway' with 1,285,000 patrons, it is striking that in second place was the 'West African Village' with some 900,000 visitors and in third place 'An Clachan' with 700,000 (Knight, 1911: 7). These were well ahead of other entertainments such as the Joy House, Aquarium and Aerial Railway. Officially not part of the Exhibition, but dominating its skyline to the west, were the buildings of the Art Gallery and Museum and the University of Glasgow. The Exhibition was open from May to November 1911 and attracted over 9 million visits, leading to profits of approximately £20,000 mainly resulting from the takings of the entertainments.

Purposes and participants

Although there had been previous attempts to establish the teaching of Scottish history in the University of Glasgow, it was not until after the 1908 Edinburgh Exhibition that this idea was reinvigorated by combining it with an exhibition in Glasgow with a Scottish historical character. The official guide to the Exhibition therefore stated that,

> 'The inception of this [Exhibition] had its origin in the belief, shared by many, that the time had fully arrived when Scottish History should be placed in a different plane than it had hitherto occupied in the education of the rising generations of Scottish children, and not less in the teaching of the subject in our schools and colleges. It was thought that to attain this object a movement should be initiated for the raising of such a sum of money as would adequately endow a Chair of Scottish History and cognate subjects in Glasgow University. At the outset of the movement it was thought that the objects might be best attained by instituting an Exhibition in which the National History, Art, and Industry of Scotland were expounded.' (Scottish Exhibition, 1911a: 10-11)

Approximately 1500 people are listed in the exhibition catalogue (Scottish Exhibition, 1911b) as contributing to the exhibition in the Palace of History. Among them was a small group of perhaps fewer than twenty who managed the historical aspects of the exhibition). George Eyre-Todd, a journalist, became secretary of the Historical Committee, while the Lord Provost's Secretary, John Samuel, who had suggested combining the fund-raising for the Chair of Scottish History with the proposal for the Exhibition, was a member of the Historical Executive Committee. As Convenor of the Historical Committee, they enlisted the Professor of Surgery in the University, John Glaister, while Andrew Pettigrew, Chairman of the department store Pettigrew and Stephens, former Town Councillor and recently appointed Justice of the Peace, became Convenor of the Exhibition's Executive Committee and was subsequently knighted for his services to the Exhibition. The Marquis of Tullibardine, who later became the 8th Duke of Atholl (Townend, 1970), was appointed as President of the Exhibition. A fuller analysis of those serving on the many committees would show how these

Figure 1. Main Gate to the 1911 Exhibition

people were embedded in the long-standing Glasgow business, professional and political establishment, such as the reappearance in 1924 of Tullibardine, Pettigrew, Eyre-Todd and Walker (the Exhibition architect) as Patron, President, Secretary and a Vice-President respectively of the newly founded Highlanders' Institute (*The Bailie*, 14/10/1925: 3).

The 1911 Exhibition was opened by the Duke of Connaught, Queen Victoria's only surviving son, with links to the land-owning aristocracy also fostered by the organisers, most notably Lord Tullibardine. A study of the exhibition catalogue shows that the list of donors to the Exhibition includes what is virtually a roll-call of the Scottish aristocracy: the Dukes of Argyll, Atholl, Buccleugh, Fife, Montrose and Sutherland, the Marquises of Ailsa, Breadalbane, Bute and Linlithgow, the Earls of Camperdown, Elgin, Galloway, Mar and Kellie, Moray, Rosebery, Stair and Wemyss, the Countess of Seafield, Cameron of Lochiel and MacLeod of MacLeod, while visitors during the Exhibition included foreign royalty such as the Crown Prince and Princess of Sweden (*Daily Record and Mail*, 08/07/1911).

While museums lent 17% of the items on display, most loans (58%) were from individuals and other institutions, such as libraries, churches, clubs and burgh councils (25%). The University of Glasgow's Hunterian Museum was the most significant public lender, perhaps encouraged by the Exhibition's aim of raising funds for University, but also benefitting in the longer term from donations by people who had lent material to the exhibition, such as A. Henderson Bishop. Of the public collections listed as lending material, the absence of material lent by the National Museum of Antiquities of Scotland in Edinburgh is most striking. This was because the management of the collection was in the hands of the Society of Antiquaries of Scotland, while the collection was owned by the nation, resulting in the Society believing that it could not lend items to the exhibition because it had 'no power to allow any objects added to the National Collection to pass out of their custody' (*Minutes of the Council of the Society of Antiquaries of Scotland*, 21/02/1911).

The Palace of History

The heart of the Exhibition was the Palace of History, the contents, organisation and layout of which were recorded in an illustrated catalogue (Scottish Exhibition, 1911b). This includes a list of the items on display, some with accompanying notes, recording the cases in which objects were displayed or the wall on which paintings were hung. While the stated main structuring principle of the displays was the juxtaposition of portraits of illustrious people with associated objects, notably Sir Walter Scott, Allan Ramsay and Robert Burns, the actual organisation of the displays was unclear and led to complaints. With more than 100 people taking less than two years, however, it is perhaps the quality and quantity of the material assembled that is more striking than the apparent disorganisation of the displays.

Figure 2. Palace of History and the 1911 Exhibition

The Palace of History was created from a pre-existing building, with a substantial extension that internally made it appear functional, almost industrial. Although there were two entrances and no clear routeway, the North Gallery is the first described in the Exhibition catalogue and was the ideal place to start a visit with its display of historical portraits sections 'from the beginnings of modern portraiture to the death of Sir Walter Scott' (Scottish Exhibition, 1911b: 10-11), offering a chronological narrative that was otherwise absent from the displays. The West Gallery was mainly devoted to weapons and militaria such as uniforms and medals, with other sections showing other numismatic items and displays of French, Dutch and Swedish material to emphasise the connections, often military, with Scotland. As the Official Guide put it,

> 'Firearms and weapons, swords, targes, and pistols, used during the times when history was making in Scotland, furnish their grim story to the mind and imagination. Here may be seen the weapons handled by the Covenanters when religious liberty was at stake, there the sword of Robert the Bruce, or the sword of Sir John de Graham, and of Bonnie Prince Charlie. Not less instructive is the large collection explicative of the military prowess of Scottish sailors and regiments.' (Scottish Exhibition, 1911a: 9)

The East Gallery displayed *'General Agricultural Implements'*, *'Punch and Toddy Ladles'*, *'Spectacles and Cutlery'*, *'Historic Costume'* and *'(Free)Masonry'*. There was also a section exemplifying the focus on great men by displaying portraits and relics of Scottish explorers such as James Bruce, David Livingstone and John Rae. The South Gallery

Figure 3. Palace of History - South Gallery

in the old part of the building was an alternative entrance to the Palace of History, displaying Norwegian items, heraldry, sports and pastimes, and ecclesiastical objects. The adjacent Prehistoric Gallery had a more explicit structure than any other part of the Exhibition, in which 'Sixteen Large Wall charts are placed in their sequence in time around this Room, beginning at the left on entering and finishing at the right. A like sequence has been attempted in the position of the relics' (Scottish Exhibition, 1911b: 808) with displays highlighting the 'evolution' of pottery and of axeheads from stone to iron. The display also emphasised that 'Man at those times was not a savage, but a skilled craftsman and artist' (*ibid*: 809) by the display of finely worked objects of glass, amber, gold and jet.

Urban progress and squalor

Nineteenth century Scotland had seen dramatic urbanisation, such that by 1911 50% of the population lived in towns of more than 20,000 inhabitants, with the country being the most urbanised in the world after England (Devine, 1999: 328). Pride in these accomplishments was one of the aims of the Exhibition, with the Palace of Industries comparing Scottish achievements with those of other countries. As the Marquis of Tullibardine said at the initial ceremony, 'they should be able to show so far as industry and art were concerned that Scotland was not simply a mere postscript to England but was able to stand on her own feet' (Glasgow Herald, 23/04/1910).. The industrial strength of 19th century Glasgow depended on the work of thousands of people who flocked to the city, many of whom lived in overcrowded, insanitary and decaying buildings. The establishment of the City Improvement Trust in 1866 (Worsdall, 1991:

7) was an attempt to deal with some of these problems, but 'not only were the slum properties removed but also the University buildings in the High Street, the picturesque castle an mansion house in the Gorbals and the seventeenth-century buildings in the Saltmarket and Bridgegate, including the last of the half-timbered houses.' (*ibid*: 8) It is perhaps not surprising, therefore, that the 'Auld Toon' was created with reconstructions of demolished buildings from various parts of Glasgow and 'typical' examples of a Scottish castle and town hall. Likewise, the Palace of History highlighted town life with 10% of the exhibits on this theme, not counting some 1000 coins. There was, however, little mention of the urban working class history of Scotland other than a display of beggars' badges that say more about the control of beggars by burgh and parish authorities than they do about the experience of poverty.

Figure 4. Palace of Industry

Urban life was therefore represented by an emphasis on small towns and the traditional role of the burgh in maintaining social cohesion as well as the importance of commerce – both themes close to the hearts of the organisers. By presenting this idealised image of urban life, the Exhibition was able to make a link between pre-industrial Scotland and a future based on commerce and industry, without having to tackle the portrayal of large-scale urban poverty and the harshness of industrial employment. Despite the historical emphasis of the Exhibition, some of the most popular attractions were therefore those that emphasised the importance of technology and industry to the present and future of Scotland, such as the electrical illuminations of the whole site and the displays of industry and engineering. As a visitor described it,

'Here we understand why Glasgow enjoys herself so well, for here is the record of her accomplishments in applied science. This is the secret of her wealth and power. Here rather than in her chequered past is Scotland's real interest for us, our country's great hope for the future. Surely a strange lesson to learn from an Historical Exhibition.' (EM Shearer, *Daily Record and Mail* 28/09/1911: 7).

History or nostalgia?

The Exhibition openly acknowledged its debt to Sir Walter Scott, with almost one hundred relics such as the original manuscripts of some of his novels, first editions, letters in his handwriting, furniture used by him while writing various novels and even items of clothing worn by him. Emphasising this dominance, the catalogue caption of his portraits states that it 'fitly occupies the place of honour in a Scottish "Palace of History."' (Scottish Exhibition, 1911b: 61) Pittock argues that 'In Waverly, the 'old' consists of north and Highland Scotland, the clans, Jacobitism and the Scoto-Latinist intellectual tradition; the 'new' is Britain, settled prosperity and empirical common sense.... Scotland is childhood, Britain adulthood: this is Scott's essential and repeated equation.' (Pittock, 1993: 147) This sense of a gulf between the present and the historical past about which he wrote was discussed by Scott through the mouth of the fictional narrator of the Chronicles of the Canongate:

'My own opinions are in favour of our own times in many respects, but not in so far as affords means for exercising the imagination, or exciting the interest which attaches to other times. I am glad to be a writer or a reader in 1826, but I would be most interested in reading or relating what happened from half a century before. We have the best of it. Scenes in which our ancestors thought deeply, acted fiercely, and died desperately are to us tales to divert the tedium of a winter's evening.' (quoted in Vakil, 1993: 409)

The gap between present and past is very clearly seen in the way that the series of historical portraits in the Palace of History ended with 'The Great Literary Period' of the late 18th and early 19th centuries, the near total absence of items dating to the latter half of the 19th-century and the creation by the same organisers of the 'Auld Toon' elsewhere in the Exhibition in which 'many shall wander..., thinking of the days that have gone forever in Scotland.'(Scottish Exhibition, 1911a: 11) As Cairns Craig (1996) has argued, this attitude placed Scottish history with little relevance to life in contemporary Scotland. Instead,

'Nostalgia for the past is a strongly-developed strain in Scottish fiction, as it is in the Scottish character. The past is important to small nations living close to powerful neighbours, for they must take pride in their history if they are to keep their identity. Scotland's past, thanks above all to Scott, is habitually viewed romantically or sentimentally, so that Mary Queen of Scots and Charles Edward Stuart are accorded the same veneration as Bruce and Wallace by people who in real life would certainly have fought against all they stood for.' (Anderson, 1979: 145)

The most popular Scottish authors at the turn of the 20th-century were probably James Barrie, Ian McLaren and SR Crockett, now known as the 'Kailyard' school (Anderson, 1979; Carter, 1976), which emphasised rural quaintness and decline, just as is seen in the displays in the Palace of History and the 'Auld Toon'. Ian Carter, commenting on the works of Ian Maclaren, one of the most prominent Kailyard novelists, said that

> 'He writes of the virtues of peasant life as if by writing about them he could preserve them. And the large number of people in England and Scotland, in Canada and America who suddenly discovered that Scottish peasant life was admirable at the moment when it was in its death throes bought his books and sighed with him over the extinction of "the last of the old Scots folk" ' (Carter, 1976: 9).

The overall picture of Scottish history therefore emphasised the stories of 'great men', the importance of the aristocracy and royalty, church and burgh life, while portraying a specifically Scottish history in the pre-Union past. Unsurprisingly, there are also geographical patterns, with 42% of the items on display in the Palace of History being lent by owners based in Glasgow and the West of Scotland, compared with 19% from Edinburgh and the South-East. The North-East was proportionately well-represented at 17%, though this was the result of the leading role of Professor James Cooper, who had previously been a minister in Aberdeen, in the Ecclesiastical sections, and the loan of prehistoric items from Aberdeenshire by Graham Callander, Director of the National Museum of Antiquities of Scotland and native of Aberdeenshire.

Religious identity

With the vast majority of people actively attending church, the role of religious history was an important aspect of Scottish identity in 1911. The Exhibition highlighted the importance of church history, with a number of sections displaying many objects, despite the comment that 'Scotland is in the unfortunate position of having less to show... than in any other Christian country. Nowhere else has the destruction of what is ancient been so complete, and nowhere else have circumstances produced so little...' (Scottish Exhibition, 1911b: 964). Nonetheless, it was possible for the catalogue to claim that the displays of ecclesiastical literature were especially representative and had 'bulked so largely in Scotland during the struggles for religious liberty' (Scottish Exhibition, 1911b: 7)

An important feature of the 1707 Union was the protection of the presbyterian church in Scotland, ensuring that it would not be subject to government control, unlike the episcopal Church of England.

By the end of the nineteenth century, arguments about secular interference had led to a number of divisions in the church, notably the Disruption of 1843. By 1911 there were therefore two main presbyterian churches in Scotland: the established Church of Scotland which was identified with Conservatism and the United Free Church of Scotland which, with its history of a desire for disestablishment, had close links with the Liberals. (Jackson, 2012) The Scottish Episcopal Church was much smaller, though important among the aristocracy in and the North-East.

Rev James Cooper, Professor of Ecclesiastical History at the University of Glasgow played a significant role in the organising committees and had a significant impact on the representation of church history. The selection of material emphasised the dangers of extremism, with the 1551 catechism of Archbishop Hamilton described as showing 'great moderation and judgment, and if it had been issued earlier might have done much to check the violence of the reformation movement in Scotland' (Scottish Exhibition, 1911b: 1057). Likewise, Episcopalian liturgy was 'not only considerable in itself, but of great and far-reaching importance' (*ibid*: 1069), whereas the later Covenanters were described as 'the extreme men in the S.W. of Scotland who took up arms in support of their position' (*ibid*: 987).

While Cooper was an important member of the Church of Scotland, of which he became Moderator in 1917, he preached a sermon in 1902 on the benefits of 'a United Church – a United Reformed Church – for the British Empire' (quoted in Kidd, 2008: 213). He was a founder of the 'high church' Scottish Ecclesiological Society and the Scottish Church Society, the latter accused by a critical minister of being 'proved a wicked Jesuitical conspiracy, hatched by traitors, to change the pure Church of Scotland again back into a devilish hierarchy of prelatic and Popish tyrants, and to blasphemous idolatries' (*The Bailie*, 25/01/1899: 2). Despite the Exhibition's emphasis on moderation and ecumenism, this did not extent to Roman Catholicism, despite the many Catholics in Glasgow, displaying only 'a few books published by or for Scottish Roman Catholics' and largely dismissing their contribution to Scottish history in the phrase 'for some time after the Revolution they were very active in Scotland.' (Scottish Exhibition, 1911b: 1090).

Patriotism and politics

The Exhibition has been seen as relating to a resurgence of Scottish national identity and moves towards home rule at the turn of the 20the century, such that 'with nearly a third of the cabinet Scots, or sitting for Scottish seats, independence seemed within reach' (Kinchin & Kinchin, 1986: 96). However, as will be discussed below, the emphasis on Scotland's heroic past with its battles against England could be read as being more concerned with establishing Scotland and England as equal within the Union rather than as an argument for independence. This was exemplified by the Scottish Patriotic Association , of which the Exhibition's instigator, George Eyre-Todd was chairman in 1911 (Eyre-Todd, 1934: 144). It had been formed in 1901 to campaign for the equality of Scotland and England in the present through, 'the proper presentation of Scottish history in Scottish schools and the proper quartering of the royal arms when used in Scotland, and it stood against the use of the terms "England" and "English" when "Britain" and "British" were meant. Also, with less popular appeal and less likelihood of a successful issue, it protested against an error in the royal title. King Edward, it pointed out, was neither the seventh of the name to sit on the British throne nor the seventh to rule Scotland.' (Eyre-Todd, 1934: 144)

The importance of the royal and aristocratic aspects of Scottish history was emphasised in the Exhibition by the Scots Baronial architecture and heraldry, notably the Palace of History which was modelled on Falkland Palace (Bailie, 1935: 10) and on which was 'hoisted the Banner of the King of Scots - the lion rampant and double tressure' (Scottish Exhibition, 1911b: 1108). As Ash (1980: 145) has noted, history in the later nineteenth century 'remained central to nationalist thinking and propaganda. For the romantic and generally Tory wing of the [nationalist] movement this appeared in an interest in heraldry, genealogy and the Jacobite cause', but for most people 'Scottish history had little to offer' (ibid: 146) to help them explain their position or prospects in the world.

The political background to the exhibition was therefore more complex than a superficial rewarding might suggest. Far from being part of a campaign for home rule, the Exhibition's leaders were committed Unionists. Andrew Pettigrew, chairman of the Executive Committee, was a former Conservative town councillor (*The Bailie* 14/10/1925: 4), Professor John Glaister, Vice-Chairman of the Executive Committee and Chairman of the Historical Committee, had been President of Conservative Association of the Glasgow St Rollox Division and 'of incalculable value to the cause of Unionism' (*The Bailie* 16/03/1898), while Eyre-Todd was listed as being a Conservative in *Who's Who*. The importance of this political association was emphasised by the appointment of the Marquess of Tullibardine as Honorary President of the Exhibition. Not only was he an important member of the aristocracy as heir to the Duke of Atholl, he was also a leading member of the Conservative Party, having been elected as MP for West Perthshire in the January 1910 general election. At the initial ceremony in April 1910, Pettigrew praised him saying that,

'personally he believed most fervently, from the last step which the Marquis had made in entering the House of Commons after a stiffly contested election, that it only wanted time and opportunity for him to become what Scotland had been looking for during many years - a real leader of the Scottish people.' ('Scottish History Exhibition: the initial ceremony', *Glasgow Herald* 23/04/1910)

The Conservatives were 'acutely aware of the sensitivities surrounding issues of nationalism and national identity, and of the depth of Scottish feeling and the potential resentments which might be aroused by attempts to absorb or marginalise it.' (Walker and Officer, 1998: 19) As one of the participants at the inaugural meeting of the campaign to found a Chair of Scottish History suggested, 'they could not commemorate the Union of 1707 in a better way than by establishing a Chair of Scottish History in the University.' ('Scottish History and Literature - Proposed Chair or Lectureship', *Glasgow Herald* 26/04/1907) In this they again followed the lead of Sir Walter Scott, who described the Union of 1707 as 'an event which had I lived in that day I would have resigned my life to have prevented but which being done before my day I am sensible was a wise turn.' (quoted in Vakil, 1993: 409)

However, Liberalism was still the dominant force in Glasgow politics in the early years of the 20th century, though it had been weakened by the split over Irish Home Rule in the 1880s that had led to the formation of the Liberal Unionists. At the same time, socialist ideas were being promoted in Glasgow (Devine, 1999) by a number of charismatic leaders, including Tom Johnston who edited the Independent Labour Party's newspaper *Forward*, which had been founded in 1906 (Knox, 1999: 169). While the main concerns of the ILP were economic and social, in an issue of *Forward* a fortnight before the official opening, Johnston made a forthright attack on the Exhibition,

> 'The history you're going to get is the history Lord Tullibardine thinks will suit your present state in culture development; it's the history the Duke of Connaught likes and the story of Kingly heroes and Queenly Saints, who gave their lives for their subjects; the Reformation history you'll get is the history that won't raise questions and murmurings about the Marquis of Ailsa's property; the Church history won't tell you how the discoverer of chloroform was treated for daring to impugn a test declaring that women must suffer pain at child-birth and you can rest assured that you'll hear nothing whatever about Muir or Mealmaker or Baird or Hardie or McKinley or any other political martyrs. Not one word either about the Chartists, or about Sandy Macdonald. Not a word!' (Johnstone, 1911: 4)

Partly inspired by moves towards Irish home rule, the Scottish Home Rule Association was established in 1886 and then the Young Scots Society in 1900 (Finlay, 1997). Both organisations had strong links with the Liberal Party who, with the support of a growing number of Labour MPs, introduced a series of Home Rule bills in Parliament before the outbreak of World War I (Pittock, 1991) as part of their campaigns for wider social reform. The Unionists' feared that Home Rule would rejuvenate pre-Union animosities with England. As the Marquis of Tullibardine claimed in a 1912 debate in the UK Parliament, 'I am quite certain the result would be to drift back on the whole stream of progress which has been flowing ever since the time of the Union, and to put us back into the small backwater of Scotland, if you put us back into the position of separation in which we were before the Union.' (Tullibardine, 1912: 1471) As a result, 'the Conservatives and Liberal Unionists closed ranks in defence of the union and empire and in 1912 finally merged as the Unionist Party' (Devine, 1999: 308).

Conclusion

With almost a quarter of the items in the Palace of History relating to vernacular life and the dramatic confections of 'An Clachan' and the 'Auld Toon', this quotation could almost refer to the nostalgic air of the Exhibition. As Lindsay Paterson said in his review of the Scotch Myths exhibition of 1981:

> 'By the beginning of this century – in the music hall, on picture postcards, in newspapers – what had developed was a grotesque amalgam of the romantic and the kailyard, attracting to it a whole array of mythic symbols, of dubious national character traits, of false social experience. But the falseness mattered little for its acceptance: like all myths, it operated as an ideology to help people adjust to their environment. Urban Scots wanted to believe that there was a Scotland that was like that: it embodied, if on a thoroughly inadequate way, their aspirations to escape from a squalid, inhuman reality.' (Paterson, quoted in Craig, 1996: 106)

Far from being merely of entertainment value, the Exhibition organisers thus intended that visitors would leave with a view of Scottish history that concluded with Scotland being an equal partner with England at the heart of the British Empire. The portrayal of Scotland in the Exhibition was therefore one that may have had little to do with the lived experience of most visitors, especially the many who had an Irish or Catholic background, instead managing to 'paper over the geographic, class and religious divisions in Scotland' (Finlay, 1997: 13) to demonstrate a Scottish identity explicitly allied to the Union, Protestantism, trade, self-improvement and the importance of the aristocracy. While this was a Conservative viewpoint, revealing the political beliefs of the organisers, it was also a mainstream one. For example, Peter Hume Brown, the first Professor of Scottish History in the University of Edinburgh and Historiographer Royal at the time of the 1911 Exhibition, published *A History of Scotland for Schools* in 1907, republished in 1910 and as *A Short History of Scotland* with editions in 1908, 1930 and 1951. In this he said 'since the Union of her Parliament with that of England, Scotland has not only grown rich and prosperous for her own good, but also for the good of the whole British Empire'(Brown, 1908: 578), while in a genealogical table he lists 'Edward I (VII of England)' (*ibid*: 590). Rather than Scottish history being portrayed as something deserving political debate, politics and historical debate were kept apart. Instead, the aim of the Exhibition organisers was to retrieve the type of history espoused by Walter Scott that could unify Scotland, but which had faded during the nineteenth century such that 'a general interest in Scottish history had ceased to be the mark of broadly educated Scotsmen and had come instead to be seen as the mark of a narrow parochialism most Scots wished to abandon.' (Ash, 1980: 10)

After World War I there was little public support for Home Rule in Scotland, with a couple of attempts to present private member's bills in Westminster by Labour MPs failing (Lynch, 1992). Further, the association of Home Rule with socialism, and the

Liberal support of the minority Labour government in 1924, meant that 'the Scottish establishment swung behind the Unionists' 'to halt the irresistible march of socialism' (Devine, 1999: 315). As a result, the Unionist Party became 'Scotland's pre-eminent political party' (Torrance, 2012: 4) from the 1920s to the 1950s, though this was largely forgotten by the 1970s. The inter-War years did see the establishment of a number of organisations committed to the establishment of a Scottish parliament, including the right-wing Scottish Party and the centre-left National Party of Scotland which merged in 1934 to form the Scottish National Party. Lynch (2002:4) has noted that 'the SNP is not driven by history, language, culture or tradition… Indeed, people associated with these visions of Scotland – such as the Celtic romantics – were swept out of the SNP and its organisational predecessors in the 1930s.' Faced with the dominance of the Labour Party in Scotland by the 1970s, internal debate in the SNP led to it positioning itself as an alternative centre-left party to avoid the charge of being 'Tartan Tories', with policies that spoke of the economic and social benefits of independence, rather than being 'a party of intellectuals, poets, writers or the like, primarily concerned about culture or language in the same way as other nationalist movements.' (Lynch, 2002: 4)

The study of Scottish history has changed significantly from the interests of the Exhibition organisers , and of the first Professor of Scottish History and Literature in the University of Glasgow, Robert Rait, who was an expert on the 1707 Union and Scottish politics of the period. In recent decades there has been significant work on the 19th and 20th centuries and the lives of the working class, Catholic and Irish people who were excluded from the history portrayed in the 1911 Exhibition (e.g. Devine, 1999). Scottish history has not been politically significant, however, beyond the banal use of disconnected icons like Wallace and Bruce, with little reference to the 700th anniversary of the battle of Bannockburn in the run-up to the 2014 independence Referendum. Lord Tullibardine's fears of separation continue to resonate among unionists, however, with his claims of patriotism having its descendants in the claims of 'proud Scots' campaigning against independence.

A generation of critical scholarship has resulted in a much richer view of Scottish history that cannot be reduced to a simple narrative or the stories of a few key individuals. In this, the hopes of the Exhibition organisers that Scottish history would regain academic credibility have now been fulfilled, but emphasising aspects that would have appealed much more to Tom Johnstone. There has been less success in improving popular understanding of Scottish history teaching of the subject in schools, with the Conservative version of history that uncritically focuses on romantic myths and famous men still powerful. Ironically, this had led Hassan (2012: 89) to say, 'Isn't it time to scotch one of the most enduring 'Scotch myths' that has grown up in modern Scotland, after kailyardism, tartanism and Clydesideism: the myth of anti-Tory Scotland?' Perhaps due to the trauma of World War I and the changed politics after the war, the Exhibition itself appears to have faded rapidly from the collective memory. Nonetheless, its approach continues to dominate the public perception of Scotland's history while simultaneously removing debate about history from Scottish politics. Perhaps the Exhibition can best be seen as a dramatically successful event in 1911, but one that both displayed Scottish history as having come to an end, and that contributed further to 'the strange death of Scottish history' (Ash, 1980) and so the marginalisation of historical discussion in 20th century Scottish political life.

Acknowledgments

This paper grew out of a presentation I was encouraged to give by Charles Hunt at the University Museums in Scotland 1998 conference 'The Role of Collections in the Scottish Intellectual Tradition'. Since then, I have been helped by many other people, notably Hayden Lorimer, John Morrison, the late Graham Ritchie, the staff of the Glasgow Room, Mitchell Library and Andrew Martin of the National Museums of Scotland Library. Main thanks, however, go to my family: to Elizabeth Curtis for invaluable encouragement and discussion and to Eric and Mary Curtis for their enthusiastic help in finding many valuable sources as well as leading me to an interest in Glasgow's history.

Bibliography

Anderson, A. 1979. The Kailyard Revisited, in I. Campbell (ed.) *Nineteenth-century Scottish Fiction: critical essays,* Manchester: Carcanet, pp. 130-147.

Annan, T & R 1911. *Souvenir of the Scottish Exhibition Glasgow 1911*, Glasgow : T & R Annan & Sons

Ash, M. 1980. *The Strange Death of Scottish History*, Edinburgh: Ramsay Head Press.

Bailie, J. 1935. The Scottish Exhibition of National History, Art, and Industry, Glasgow, 1911, in *Old Glasgow Club Transactions* 7:2 (1934-35), pp. 7-15.

Brown, P.H. 1908. *A Short History of Scotland*, Edinburgh: Oliver and Boyd.

Carter, I. 1976. Kailyard: the literature of decline in Nineteenth Century Scotland, *Scottish Journal of Sociology*, 1:1, pp. 1-13.

Craig, C. 1996. *Out of History: narrative paradigms in Scottish and British culture*, Edinburgh: Polygon.

Devine, T.M. 1999. *The Scottish Nation, 1700-2000*, London: Penguin Books.

Eyre-Todd, G. 1934. *Leaves from the Life of a Scottish Man of Letters*, Glasgow: Brown, Son & Ferguson.

Finlay, R. 1997. *A Partnership for Good? Scottish Politics and the Union since 1880*, Edinburgh: John Donald

Hassan, G. 2012. 'It's Only a Northern Song': The Constant Smirr of Anti-Thatcherism and Anti-Toryism, in Torrance, D (ed.) *Whatever Happened to Tory Scotland?*, Edinburgh: Edinburgh University Press pp76-92.

Jackson, A. 2012. Sociability, Status and Solidarity: Scottish unionism in the era of Irish Home Rule, 1886-1920, in Torrance, D (ed.) 2012. *Whatever Happened to Tory Scotland?*, Edinburgh: Edinburgh University Press, pp. 14-28.

Johnstone, T. 1911. *Forward* 22/04/1911.

Kidd, C. 2008. *Union and Unionism: Political Thought in Scotland, 1500-2000*, Cambridge: Cambridge University Press.

Kinchin, P. and Kinchin, J. 1988. *Glasgow's Great Exhibitions 1888, 1901, 1911, 1938, 1988*, Bicester: White Cockade Publishing.

Knight, W.H. 1911. *Manager's Report*, Glasgow: anon. publisher

Knox, W.W. 1999. *Industrial Nation: work, culture and society in Scotland, 1800*-present, Edinburgh: Edinburgh University Press.

Lynch, M. 1992. *Scotland: a new history*, London: Pimlico

Pittock, M.G.H. 1993. Scott as Historiographer: the case of *Waverly* in J.H. Alexander and D. Hewitt (eds) *Scott in Carnival: selected papers from the Fourth International Scott Conference, Edinburgh 1991*, Edinburgh: Edinburgh University Press, pp. 145-153.

Rembold, E. 1999. Negotiating Scottish Identity: the Glasgow History Exhibition 1911, *National Identities* 1:3, pp. 265-285.

Scottish Exhibition (Scottish Exhibition of National History, Art and Industry, Glasgow) 1911a. *Official Guide*, Glasgow: Dalross.

Scottish Exhibition (Scottish Exhibition of National History, Art, & Industry, Glasgow) 1911b. *Palace of History Catalogue of Exhibits*, Glasgow: Dalross.

Torrance, D. 2012. Centenary Blues: 100 years of Scottish Conservatism, in Torrance, D. (ed.) *Whatever Happened to Tory Scotland?*, Edinburgh: Edinburgh University Press, pp 1-13

Townend, P. (ed.) 1970. *Burke's Genealogical and Heraldic History of the Peerage, Baronetage and Knightage*, London: Burke's Peerage.

Tullibardine, Marquess of 1912. *House of Commons Debates 28 February 1912 vol 34 cc1446-91* [http://hansard.millbanksystems.com/commons/1912/feb/28/scotland-federal-government checked 24/01/2013]

Vakil, C. 1993. Scott and Scottish Enlightenment Philosophical History, in JH Alexander and D. Hewitt (eds*.) Scott in Carnival: selected papers from the Fourth International Scott Conference, Edinburgh 1991*, Edinburgh: Edinburgh University Press, pp 404-418.

Walker, G. and Officer, D. 1998. Scottish Unionism and the Ulster Question, in CMM Macdonald, *Unionist Scotland 1800-1997*, Edinburgh: John Donald Publishers, pp. 13-26.

Worsdall, F. 1991. *The Glasgow Tenement* Edinburgh: W & R Chambers.

Scotland Then for Scotland Now: Scottish political party uses of history, image and myth

Murray Stewart Leith

Introduction

The significance of national identity in contemporary socio-political terms cannot be emphasised enough. Although it suffered a decline as a focus of study during the middle to later part of the 20th century, the examination of nationalism never died away, and interest in the subject has only blossomed as political events during the last few decades of the 20th century highlighted the passion and importance of national identity in the contemporary world. The power of the 'imagined community' (Anderson 1983), where groups of individuals coalesce around a common sense of history, culture and belonging, has seen the rise of nationalism as a political movement in many sub-state areas – even in long established states such as the United Kingdom. Nationalism has never gone away as the 'story of nationalism mirrors history and modern history mirrors the story of nationalism (Harris 2009, 1).

In 1707, the Act of Union established the UK in 'perpetuity' as the English and Scottish parliaments voted themselves out of existence and one legislature was empowered in their place. This state of affairs lasted for almost 300 years, but in 1999 a new Scottish Parliament, albeit a devolved one came into being, and the unity of the UK was now open to question. It has been argued by Mitchell (1996) that the UK was never a unitary state, but better understood as a Union State. This argument challenges the historical understanding of the UK over the previous centuries. Furthermore, while the creation of a distinctive Scottish parliament may have led to questions about the nature of the political Union in certain quarters, truly momentous occurrences have taken place that certainly raises it in all. In 2007, the Scottish electorate returned a nationalist party, the SNP, as the largest political grouping in that parliament and the SNP formed a Scottish Government among whose primary political objectives while in government was the dissolution of the Union. The 2010 British General election saw the Scottish electorate turn once again to Labour, and return a strong majority of Union supporting MPs to Westminster. This may have seemed to illustrate that the SNP had risen as far as it could, but in 2011 it challenged all political preconceptions of Scottish politics. Despite the deliberate design of the electoral system so that no one party could (or rather should) capture a majority of seats, the SNP did just that, gaining 69 out of the 129 seats available

This somewhat meteoric rise of a party which seeks the creation of an independent Scottish state requires an examination of the importance of national identity, and the idea of the nation, within Scotland today; as political tools. As academics we must be aware of the importance of history, place and identity as not only concepts and ideas, the search for understanding, or areas of study, but also as weapons in the political battlefield for control of Scotland, and Scotland's future. It is a simple maxim of politics that parties seek power, they seek to control the organs of the state in order to remake, amend, or alter that state to bring about their objectives and policies. It is with this maxim in mind that we conduct this examination of the employment of history and place in the development/maintenance of national identity in contemporary Scotland.

It is important to consider the focus of each party as a whole – and seek an understanding of usages by the party as a group rather than just focus on specific individuals. This is possible through an examination of the political manifestos that each party issues at national elections. Since the early 1970s, all political parties have issued distinct manifestos for Scottish elections, even though the elections were for the Parliament of the United Kingdom. This has not been an historical standard practice for parties established at the British level. Manifestos came into general practice during the 20th century along with the other trappings of mass politics and the idea of issuing specific ones for separate nations within the UK would have seemed preposterous in the 1930s. However, within only a few years Labour led the way when they issued a manifesto entitled 'For A' That', at the 1950 British General Election. Clearly invoking a particularly Scottish sense of belonging from a particularly Scottish individual, Robert Burns, the party played the Scottish identity card willingly, although the actual contents of the manifesto reflected the same document issued in other parts of Great Britain. However, 1950 seemed to be a one off event, and Labour discontinued the practice. Yet they touched off a trend, and while Labour would, throughout the 1950s, continue to vie with the Conservative and Unionist Party for the vast majority of the Scottish vote, they did not see fit to issue different manifestos. While both the Conservatives and the Liberals would later do so, this would be from a declining party and a minor party in terms of distinctly Scottish support.

Focusing on national identity and the nation as a place, for much of the 20th century it would be fair to say that Scotland was absent from the political debate at elections times, in that the parties saw it as a firm and clear part of the United Kingdom, that required no particular or different consideration. However, after the 'unexpected' vote share achieved by the SNP in February 1974, Labour (re)joined the ongoing practice of the other major parties and began to issue Scottish manifestos at all General Elections – a practice all continue to this day. It is these political documents, the core documents of party, produced with 'immense care' (Cooke 2000) and the hymn sheet for all candidates to sing from on the campaign trail, the media to peruse and employ, and opposition parties to challenge and attack, (Kavanagh 2000) that we shall examine for examples of historical usages; as they stand for the party as a whole, creating part of the historical record that may be compared across time. Yet before turning to the specific documents themselves, let us consider the core issues that shall lead any analysis – the ideas of the nation, belonging to the nation, and of how elites engage with such ideas.

Nationalism, National Identity, the Mass and Elites

The SNP are a classic example of a political movement 'seeking or exercising state power and justifying such action with nationalist argument' (Breuilly, p2, 1993), and a central tenet of the nationalist ideology is a sense of national identity. The importance of national identity in this work lies in understanding it as the continual 'reproduction and reinterpretation' of myths, traditions and history of the nation in continuing a connection between the individual and the group (Smith 2001) and the role of political parties and elites in that process. However, among the various important caveats that must be highlighted here is that the SNP must not be considered as the only political party that engages in nationalistic behaviour. The reality is that all political parties in Scotland engage with the idea of the nation, and all proudly proclaim their Scottishness. When it comes to Scotland, all the major political parties are nationalists, but not all are Nationalist in their political goals (Leith and Soule 2011). All employ history to reproduce and reinterpret Scotland and Scotland's role in the UK, but only one of them seeks independence from the United Kingdom. Another significant caveat is that when terms such as myth or interpretation are employed this should not be taken to mean that they are falsehoods or creations of the elite rather it illustrates the idealised employment of history or territory. The concept of myth here is not to be taken as a somewhat amorphous, semi-historical, perhaps even untruthful, event, but will be considered as a belief or 'fact' held by the group in question to be true; although this point has been argued by a number of scholars (Ozkirimli 2010).

Let us now turn to a consideration of the strength of national identity in contemporary Scotland and the role of the elites in forming and shaping national identity in general. For if nationalism is an elite led movement, in this era of mass politics it gains strength through the numbers of individuals that support the idea that they themselves belong to the nation, and that the nation is simply something more than a territorial entity on a map. The existence of a strong sense of national identity in Scotland is almost a given within most academic studies – be they historical, sociological, political or otherwise (see, for example, Morton 1999, McCrone 2001, Henderson 2007, Leith and Soule 2011) – due to Scots long having held a strong sense of national identity (McCreadie 1991). Significant data has been, and continues to be, collected over time, gauging the strength of that feeling. The results are shown in Table 1.

Table 1. National Identity (forced choice %)

	1974	1979	1992	1997	1999	2003	2006	2014
Scottish	65	56	72	72	77	72	78	65
British	31	38	25	20	17	20	14	23
Other/None	4	6	3	8	6	8	8	12
Base N	588	658	957	882	1482	1508	1594	1339

Source – 1974-1997 Scottish Election Surveys, 1999-2014 Scottish Social Attitudes

While the strength of expressions of Scottishness within the population of Scotland have not changed significantly since devolution took place, this is only because a substantial percentage of Scots already felt distinctly Scottish, in addition to or rather than, British. Even at the lowest point for devolution/home rule supporters in 1979, after a failed attempt to establish a Scottish Assembly, over half of the population of Scotland declared themselves Scottish rather than British. At the highest point in that decade, at a time when the SNP had literally exploded onto the political scene, gaining a third of the vote in the October 1974 British General Election, the figure reported for Scotland had been 65%, but by the early 1990s it had risen to 72%. Yet, the post devolution figures show little dramatic difference, with the 1999 and 2006 figures being almost identical and 2014 levels being identical, on Scottish Identity, to 1974. Therefore, it may be safe to say that the movement towards devolution had some impact, but the majority of the change clearly took place prior to actual devolution itself. The figures today are almost pre-devolutionary. What has been highlighted is that while there has been a change over the past four decades, that change only strengthened an already existent and distinct sense of Scottishness within Scotland – which had increased prior to the establishment of a Scottish Parliament. Nonetheless, we should remember that many of the reports from such mass surveys tell us that while a majority of individuals within Scotland will choose Scottish over British if forced into a single identity, a majority are also happy to share these identities, being both Scottish and British. While a significant minority refuse to do so, preferring Scottish alone as their sole identity, they remain a minority within Scotland

Leaving the mass feeling to one side, we now turn to the political elites within Scotland. Elite groups within any society regularly employ the relationship between nationalism/national identity and history. Seeking specific political outcomes, they will influence the way in which the past is interpreted (Coakley 2004), using those interpretations to justify their vision of the future, a point well emphasised among the variety of nationalism schools of thought (Breuilly 1996, Calhoun 1997, Smith 1986 and for an overview see Ozkirimli 2010). Political elites have significant agency within any nationalist movement, as they consciously employ nationalism as a focus for political mobilisation – and this is very much the case in Scotland. As stated above, of the four major parties within Scotland all employ some sense of nationalism (to a greater or lesser extent) – partly as a result of the strong sense of Scottishness that exists within the electorate.

An important role for nationalism as a political movement is the ability to provide a sense of order to individuals within a rapidly changing social setting (Breuilly 1993); and this could well be the case in Scotland. The significant changes that have taken place in Scottish society since the 1960s have been clearly illustrated (Pittock 2008) and it is no coincidence that only during this period has the SNP emerged as a serious electoral force. Prior to the late 1960s, the party had spent years on the political fringes, although today it stands at the heart of power in Scotland. Miller (1981) was the first to highlight the changing nature of Scottish electoral behaviour in the 1970s, when compared to England, and since then the difference have only increased. It is clear that Scottish voters now operate in a distinct political manner within the UK, and the party system in Scotland is distinctly Scottish in tone and operation. This is, again, partly due to the existence of a sense of Scottishness within the electorate. Yet while such feelings exist within the electorate each party also enforces that feeling within the electorate as they hunt for votes from the group as a whole. Parties recognise, interact with and seek to inform the particularly Scottish identity of the masses as they seek support as this is the central precept to which the majority of votes will cleave.

In elections and political events in Scotland all parties must take the Scottish dimension into account; even those which operate within a British and Scottish context. The SNP has one distinct advantage over other major parties in this – they do not need to be both British and Scottish in their political presentation. The other major parties must balance these identities in their activities. They must present a distinctive Scottish face, yet they must ensure they reflect an identity that all members of their prospective electorate can recognise and be comfortable with. Even the Scottish Conservatives, who see Scotland as an integral part of the UK, act as an 'ethno-political elite' within the national political setting of Scotland. In some elections, such as the 1997 British General Election they have been the most overt in terms of using nationalism and national identity as a banner.

The Employment of History

The employment of historical imagery or rhetoric to justify political goals or objectives is not a new phenomenon. Since the birth of 'Scotland', political elites have created a sense of identity by appealing to historical myths in their documents or by creating clear links to the past, and also to the future (for it is the future 'Golden Age of Independence' that is as often employed as any past 'Golden Age'). The Declaration of Arbroath shows how such a tactic has a long pedigree. The Declaration is 'the first recorded statement of a mythical history of Scotland and the origins of the Scots' (Smith 2003, 124).

Smith discusses how this historical document made the claim that the Scots are descended from Scota, the daughter of the Pharaoh who drowned in the Red Sea chasing the Israelites. The declaration speaks of the 'nation', and places in that nation the ability to choose and support who rules them. King Robert was elected with 'the due consent and assent of us all'. In perhaps one of the most quoted sections of all, it states that the fight is 'not for glory, nor riches, nor honours, but for freedom alone, which no good man gives up except with his life'.

The document was clearly issued as part of the ongoing diplomatic efforts to gain independence for Scotland (Smith 2003) and while it may have had some impact then, and even centuries later when the Stewart dynasty was removed and forced into exile (Cowan 2003), it would not become a true 'classic' until the 20th century (Smith, 2003). Indeed, in many respects it had more impact centuries after it was written. Nonetheless, it represents a truly significant, sophisticated, political statement by a group of individuals – including the middle ranks of society – that draws upon a group identity as a nation and clearly forms that nation in a tribal, territorial and political manner. Simply put, it is one of the first, and perhaps the clearest, enunciations of Scottish nationhood that can be found in history.

More important though, is the manner in which that claim is made, and the specific rhetoric that supports it. In the Declaration, the political and social elite provide a mythological and historical foundation for the nation, a foundation that draws upon key figures and events of the past. They highlight the historical roots of the nation, into antiquity, they highlight the long sojourn of their people in Scotland, and the sovereignty they enjoyed there, and they highlight the resistance of those people to outside invaders (in this case, the Romans). The actual accuracy of these claims is not important, what is, is that these claims were made, and the manner in which they are made. Arbroath stands as a classic example of political employments of history and myth to create a sense of not only the Scottish polity, but a sense of Scottish national identity.

The Declaration of Arbroath is one of the documents which served to create a base upon which later political elites would build a specific sense of Scottishness (Webster 1997). This identity was forged around some basic and elemental principles – place, religion, and people. Furthermore, one of the constant themes within the national story it weaves was 'interfering Englishmen' (Brown 1998). Furthermore, the Declaration is one of the documents that serves as the basis for the emergence of other distinct myths in more recent Scottish rhetoric (Kearton 2005). These include such foci as territory, sovereignty, freedom, contractual government, and democracy. As we turn to contemporary documents we see many of these themes continued.

In many respects, the Declaration of Arbroath is a forerunner of the more mundane, and regular political manifestos that have become part of the political landscape in Scotland. Clear themes emerge from a general consideration of these manifestos over the past forty years, and the most obvious is the emphasis on Scotland as a territorial entity. Since the 1970s this has became a stronger aspect of the rhetoric of all the major parties, as has the issue of sovereignty (Leith 2008). Likewise, all parties, at different times but as a general constant, have emphasised the civic and inclusive nature of Scottish society and the need for democracy in Scotland, and this has especially become a core theme of the SNP. However, each party has employed different aspects at different times in their manifestos and to illustrate this let us now consider the content of the documents themselves. The analysis below is concerned with manifestos issued for Westminster elections, but the statements remain true for manifestos issues for Holyrood elections too. With only a limited number of elections to the Scottish parliament, the parties have tended to follow established patterns. Despite the differences in authority and power, the issues and statements contained within Scottish parliament manifestos reflect the patterns of British focused manifestos.

Labour and Conservatives

The two main parties of the United Kingdom, Labour and the Conservatives, began to recognise the need for specifically Scottish manifestos as early as 1950. It can be no coincidence that this period saw the culmination of the Scottish National Covenant Movement which had collected over two million signatories, who, while pledging themselves loyal to the Crown, also sought to secure a Scottish Parliament. The Covenant started with the words 'we, the people' (Brand 1978) three simple words that the Constitution of the United States begins with and which has allowed that State to form a sense of nationhood from an historical basis. Of course, 1950 was also the year that the Stone of Scone was appropriated from Westminster Abbey and returned to Scotland, before being handed back to the British authorities. Such an event shows the strength and importance of historical symbols and items. At a base level it may well be nothing more than stone, but the importance of such a symbol is much more difficult to measure.

The Labour Party manifestos for Scotland have gone through a clear cycle, moving from a very limited use of specifically Scottish images and statements in their earlier 1970s versions, to a heavier employment of Scottish motifs in the 1990s, and then back towards a more limited consideration in the early 21st[t] century. Although a specific sense of Scottishness is often portrayed as a group identity, the 'us' employed within the rhetoric is both British and Scottish, with the stress on the maintenance of the link between the two. What is not noticeably present, in general, are direct appeals to a specific and exclusive sense of Scottishness. The exception to this pattern of behaviour is in the 1990s, specifically the 1997 manifesto, a period of heightened awareness of all things Scottish.

In 1997, the rhetorical appeals to a sense of national identity were unequivocal and obvious. The existence of a firm and clear sense of Scottish national identity was openly acknowledged, and terms such 'our nation', and 'we, the people of Scotland' were employed. The 'us' was Scottish, and the UK was recognised as a state of distinct nations and regions. Wherever Britain was mentioned (and it was, a lot), it was alongside Scotland. Although there was little use of specific historical references within the document, they did occur, although used as a means by which to view the future. Visual identifiers that created a specifically Scottish feel were also limited – the most obvious was the tartanised cover. Although in many respects a universally employed material and style, tartan remains a distinctly Scottish motif – and its use (or the avoidance of use) has been one of the ongoing dances within Scottish politics in general and Scottish nationalism in particular.

However, 1997 represented a distinctly different pattern from the norm for the Labour Party in Scotland, and after devolution it has generally shied away from focusing on Scotland so distinctly. While two of the last three British Prime Ministers have been born in Scotland, the most recent was Scottish in both birth and upbringing, Gordon brown shied away from his national identity. When he spoke of identity he spoke of Britishness. His speeches were littered with the term, and he rarely identified himself as a Scot. It is clear that Labour will employ a sense of Scottishness and Scotland when they feel it necessary, but prefer to avoid such a focus. When the SNP challenge failed to materialise at the British level after the 1997 election and in the early years of the Scottish Parliament, Labour manifestos shifted back to a previous pattern and reduced the Scottish aspects. Even the Scottish Parliament manifestos, unsurprisingly sprinkled full of the terms, Scotland and Scottish, employ very limited appeals to identity and even less visual national motifs. Even after 2007, and the rise of the SNP as a minority Government, in 2010 and 2011 Labour in Scotland did not wrap itself in the Saltire of in any stronger sense of Scottishness – a move it may regret not making.

The Conservatives reflect a somewhat similar outline to Labour in that they represent a pattern of change, moving from a limited, almost absent sense of Scottishness and Scotland, to a strong usage of identity and historical motifs and imagery and then back again. During the 1970s and 1980s, the Scottish manifestos differed little from the 'British' ones. The early 1970s were the more pronounced in terms of Scottish identity and a focus on Scotland as a distinct territorial unit, but the appeals to a sense of 'us' were firmly British. Unionism was the inherent underpinning within the document, and any appeals to a distinct sense of Scottish identity had disappeared by the end of the decade. For the Conservatives, the nation was the United Kingdom. Throughout the 1980s, Conservative manifestos were little different in Scotland, being the British document with a few 'Scottish' additions, but identity was British and any sense of Scottishness as a distinct identity was almost completely absent – as was any use of a particular Scottish historical motif or image.

This pattern changed during the 1990s and by 1992 the terms Scotland and Scottish became more prominent and the difference between Scotland and the United Kingdom distinct. For the Scottish Conservatives, the acceptance of Scotland as a nation, albeit within a Unionist framework had arrived. By 1997, this shift towards a more Scottish focus, and the employment of particularly Scottish images and motifs had emerged into a full fledged nationalistic display. Gone was the Union logo of the past, and a clearly Scottish Lion now roared for the Tories. This was just the most obvious of all the changes. In their attempt to head off devolution, the Scottish Conservative Party adopted a firmly Scottish sense of identity in their message, their imagery, and their use of history. The party appealed to voters to maintain the historic Union that had lasted for 290 years, declaring themselves the 'Scottish Party', consistently evoking Scotland as a nation in their rhetoric. They also invoked a clear sense of Scottish martial history through a photographic motif, although clearly linking it to British images at the same time. The employment of the distinct Scottish landscape, always a strong set of images for any party, were quite significant at this point in time.

Yet this strong employment of historical motifs, imagery, land and identity, disappeared fairly quickly. The Lion logo remained during the next decade, but other images tended to invoke Britain rather than Scotland and any appeals to Scottish identity were very limited. In 2005, the sense of Scottish identity was present, but when the issue of sovereignty was raised, it was done to support that of the United Kingdom. The idea of contractual democracy was also raised, and this was a contract between the Scottish people and the party – but within the devolution and Union framework. There can be no doubt that the Scottish Conservatives were aware that their electoral appeal remained limited in Scotland and they seem to have chosen to focus on their core electorate of Union supporters. History for them was/is from 1707 onwards.

Scottish Liberal Democrats

The creation of a specific sense of Scottish identity has never been a priority for the Liberal Democrats. Throughout the past four decades all the manifestos of the Scottish Liberal Democrats (and the party has been distinctly separate and Scottish since 1949) hardly focused upon Scotland as a territorial entity or employed any specific historical evidence to support their electoral stance. In fact, the party has never employed any of the major historical themes that occur in other parties documents. There are few appeals to a sense of territorial belonging, a specifically Scottish sovereignty, freedom or democracy. This is not to say that these issues do not crop up in terms of policy discussion during the past few decades. As the only party committed to a federal UK, they have long focused on a more democratic and semi-sovereign nature for Scottish politics. However, the party has never employed any historical themes or specifically Scottish myths to support these or other policies. At later points during the 1990s, the party did provide a more firm territorial focus, and Scotland the place was an evident theme in their manifestos during that decade, but again not as a support for the policy of devolution, simply as a result of their support for that policy. As with their major opponents, the location of politics within Scotland since devolution has meant Scotland becoming a core component of the rhetoric but for the Scottish Liberal Democrats, this is as a given, rather than an emotive driver.

The Scottish National Party

Perhaps not unsurprisingly, the SNP are the party that has most regularly employed and adopted openly nationalist imagery and historical themes of motifs of the nation within their manifestos. Nonetheless, they have not always done so, nor do they take the most obvious and nationalistic of stances – like their political opponents there have been, over the last forty years, distinct changes in the manner and tone of SNP images, rhetoric and use of history. One significant and noticeable change over time has been the nature of Scottishness and Scotland that can be found in SNP documents. In the 1970s a distinctly anti-English tone could be found with many negative comments on the Anglicisation of Scotland, or the need to limit English incomers ability to own land could be found; echoes of Scotland's resistance to outside invasions since early history it appears. But these have disappeared, or rather transmuted. What has replaced this ethnically focused set of complaints has been the idea of the other major parties (mainly Labour and Conservatives) as being 'London' controlled or run (Leith 2008). Thus the theme of 'interfering Englishmen' is still prevalent, albeit now in a purely political, rather than an ethnic manner. While it is now fair to say that the modern SNP seems to lack a distinct ethnic character (Hamilton 1999), this has not always been the case in the contemporary period.

Another significant change has been the shift to an inclusive sense of Scottish identity. While earlier documents always presented a generally inclusive sense of Scottishness, some clear boundaries around membership of the nation were present; again this is no longer the case. No 'out' groups are identified today, the 'other' is never highlighted and Scottishness is very much an open, welcoming, and inclusive identity. The modern SNP represents the challenges to the creation of an independent Scotland as constitutional or political arguments against greater democracy or the unwillingness of political opponents to accept the sovereignty of the Scottish people, not as an ethnic issue.

What is always present in SNP manifestos is a strong sense of Scotland as a place – Alba, Caledonia, whatever the territory is named (and sometimes in political speeches such terms are openly employed); it is a theme that is a constant throughout, and very much becoming a stronger aspect of the discussion over time. As the shift in identity has been to one more inclusive in nature, the emphasis on Scotland the land, rather than Scotland the tribe, has become the norm, and although this trend can be identified among most political parties, it is perhaps somewhat stronger among the SNP. This was most obvious in the SNP party election broadcasts, (or PEBs) of the 2010 and 2011 elections. In one of the 2010 PEBs, the imagery was of Scotland's landscape, from modern streets, to small rustic villages, and from farmlands, to an open mountain top, from which the individual (supposedly representing a Scottish voter) yelled '*Freedom*' and which echoed back from the mountains.

Therefore, we can see that what is also present – although not always prevalent – is a willingness to use significant levels of historically based rhetoric and imagery to support various SNP political positions and policies. Unlike the other parties, this is not limited to the 1990s, and is not a very contemporary usage either. The 1983 manifesto alone had over 5% of the discussion focused on identity rather than policy, and a wide use of history throughout. It is interesting to note that it is not the Declaration of Arbroath that the SNP cited in 1983, but the US Declaration of Independence.

The strong presence of history continued throughout the 1980s and 1990s, with the party regularly employing the ideas of Scotland with a distinct culture, a distinct history and a distinct territory. However, it is interesting to note that even when direct historical references were given, they were done with the future in mind. The past was not an age to be hankered back to, but an example of how great Scotland could become (again?). For instance, in 1997, when the SNP (like other major parties) employed significant levels of Scottish identifiers in their manifesto, they spoke of being 'A nation once again' with links made to the pre 1707 Scotland. But even this section quickly gave way to a discussion on what a future independent Scotland would look like.

The SNP have also followed the same route as other parties, and during the early part of the 21st century, the blatant employment of history in their manifesto was lessened. What remained was the presence of, and emphasis on specific motifs that echoed history; clear links that allowed historical themes to echo through – claims about territory, sovereignty, the importance of Scottish democracy and the need for freedom.

Conclusions

Manifesto statements are the presentation of the party as a whole, and widely employed and disseminated through various channels at election times. But they are not the only means by which political parties and elites seek to employ history to aid a particular cause. All political leaders make regular speeches to their parties and to the public, and take these opportunities to employ historical references as rhetorical support. The most obvious historical reference to be employed in Scotland over past decades has been William Wallace. Interestingly, this individual transcends the political divide and has been used to support both Unionist and Nationalist objectives – although in more recent times it has perhaps been the Nationalists that favour such an historical symbol. In 1995, Alex Salmond stated that the SNP stood 'with Wallace, head and heart...freedom, freedom, freedom' and he has often allied himself or the party with figures from Scotland's past (Gallagher 2009) such as Mary, Queen of Scots. While Gordon Brown may have only made one passing reference to Scotland in his 2009 speech as Labour

Party Leader, in a 2008 speech in Scotland he was happy to invoke historical references to the Highland Clearances and individuals who fought against them. Nor do the Conservatives miss the opportunity to employ history for their own ends. In 1996, the Stone of Scone, removed centuries ago by Edward I of England and incorporated into a chair used for the coronation of English Kings and Queens, was returned to Scotland with much pomp and circumstance. This seemed to have little impact upon Conservative fortunes at the next election though. As more than one paper leader or letter to the editor stated, it would take more than a ceremonial returning of the Stone and a kilted Conservative Scottish Secretary to make the party of Thatcher appealing to the people of Scotland.

The employment of such romantic figures and ceremonial episodes, whether in speeches, manifestos or dress, serve a key purpose. They allow contemporary political accounts to engage in long standing motifs in Scottish history – motifs such as freedom, independence, and democracy (Edensor 1997). As we have seen above, these motifs are clearly linkages throughout the political history of Scotland as these themes crop up in both historical and contemporary political documents. History serves a significant political purpose, and all parties in Scotland will seek to employ it for political gain *when the time is right*. The height of the devolution debate in the late 1990s saw all the major parties engage with history in an attempt to gain political advantage, yet at the same time we have seen that the use of history has declined in recent years, and the emphasis on/ nature of identity and nationhood has changed somewhat.

As Scotland has developed and matured as a devolved political system the focus of political debate has become more firmly Scottish. It is perhaps as a result of this that the parties no longer feel the need to blatantly employ the trappings of Scottishness. Or rather that Scottishness has become such a firm part of the political landscape that it is a banality that is omni-present and thus requires no further emphasis (see Billig 1995 for a discussion on the banality of everyday nationalism). Scotland *is*, and being Scottish *is*, with Scottishness a wide and inclusive identity. Thus, the sense of Scottishness is no longer reliant upon history or rather some specific interpretation of an historical event or character. If it was fair to say that Scotland was absent from the core UK political debate during much of the 20th century that is clearly no longer the case in the 21st. Now it is fair to say that in some regards, history is now absent from the core Scottish political debate, or rather aspects of history are absent - it is the motifs of history that are important – those threads that connect the past with the future and none stand forth more so than the land in this. This is because in contemporary politics the issue is no longer about Scotland's past, but about Scotland's future nationhood, but that nationhood requires roots and the land, and historical places, events and other motifs can provide those roots.

Addendum

Since this chapter was first written, political change within Scotland has continued to march apace. First, with the election of the SNP as a minority in 2007 and then with its overwhelming re-election in 2011 as the first single party majority Scottish government, devolution and constitutional change came firmly back on the agenda (Kenealy 2016). After reaching an agreement in Edinburgh with the coalition government at Westminster (HM Government 2012) the SNP controlled Scottish Government began to undertake steps for a referendum on whether Scotland should be an independent country, which was subsequently held on September 18th, 2014. It has been argued that, while the polls were open on that day, the Scottish people were Sovereign (Sillars 2014). Nonetheless, the Scottish electorate ultimately chose to leave that Sovereignty at Westminster, with 55% voting No, and 45% voting yes, on a turnout of 85% -a figure not witness in any electoral event since women were granted entry into the franchise in 1918. But this No vote has not meant that Scotland has remained unchanged. As Rosie notes 'It seems remarkable just how far Scotland has changed over this last tumultuous year' (2015, 383). Scotland has changed, yet it has not, at least not in terms of identity and belonging being key parts of the questions so often asked and answered throughout society. Scotland has become even more firmly the focus of events, with Holyrood replacing Westminster as the place that should make ALL decisions for Scotland in the minds of a majority of Scottish residents for the first time since devolution occurred (Scotcen 2015).

Yet this road to potential independence, or continued membership of the United Kingdom, was fought on a variety of fronts and a variety of issues, from the economic to the social, from the political to the personal. On one side was the Yes campaign, predominantly driven by the SNP, but including a variety of groups, from the Scottish Greens and Women for Independence, to others such as the Radical Independence Campaign, or the National Collective, a group of artistic and creative individuals who supported independence. The No side, initially known as Better Together and later as No Thanks, was a coalition group formed by the Unionist supporting political parties of Scottish Labour, the Scottish Liberal Democrats and the Scottish Conservatives. Both sides, with different ideas of Scotland's future, and perhaps even its past, fought their battles with a firm sense of Scottishness inherent in their very presentation.

The Yes campaign was early in its use of positive national symbols by employing the saltire on a wide ranging basis – often with a large YES adorning the flag itself. While it never became any sort of official emblem, it was carried by crowds at rallies, affixed to cars and jackets, draped across windows and fluttered from buildings. The Yes symbol clearly evoked a sense of Scottishness and Scotland, with its colours being a white yes within a blue circle. It became the eponymous symbol of the debate, appearing on lapels, hats, coats, and as s tick on badge on lamp posts, doors, walls and pavements throughout Scotland.

The visual battle was one sided in this respect as the NO thanks (the reworked Better Together campaign group) symbol was far less evident, even though it was the resultant majority opinion. The NO thanks badge did evoke the Saltire somewhat as well, with a stylized X cross through the (N)O, although this symbol did not seem to capture the public imagination as did the Yes. What is interesting is that the NO thanks badges did not seek to employ any sense of Britishness as this was a battle in Scotland, for the future of Scotland. The Saltire was employed, albeit to a lesser extent than the Yes campaign, in another clear battle for control of this national symbol. Lion Rampant flags often waved at Yes rallies, but never at those of No. When the Union Jack was waved it was at rallies outside Scotland (although it was also employed by the politically un-supportable Orange Order in Scotland) that sought to show fraternity between Scotland and other parts of the UK, and seek to keep Scotland in the Union.

With the symbolic battle quite literally held daily in the streets, and a rhetorical battle lasting over two years, what was quickly evident that among all the colour and noise, was the absence of history in many regards. The 2014 debate was about looking forward, not looking back. When arguments were raised, in support or defence of the status quo, it was the economic that so often took the fore, with arguments about whether people would be better off independent or in union, and often by specifically how much. When Scottishness was discussed, it was the civic modern Scottishness of a cosmopolitan nation, where birth, colour and creed did not matter, only a belief in Scotland and residence in the nation itself mattered. Although 2014 was also the 700th anniversary of the Battle of Bannockburn, this was not an issue or a focus. 'People who will be voting [for independence] in September are doing so for economic and political reasons, not for Robert the Bruce. Bannockburn is wisely not mentioned by Scottish politicians today' (Dr Fiona Watson, cited by Merrill 2014). When history was employed it was often a negative portrayal or dismissal of the British Empire, one in which Scotland was wrongly conceived of as a colonial entity (Kidd and McClymont 2014).

Yet this absence of history or absence of its proper use should not be construed as it being unimportant. Like identity, history was unchallenged in many respects. The battle for the future was fought under the auspices of the ideas of the future. Few meaningful attempts were made by the political elites to redraw a sense of Scottishness or recreate a sense of Scotland's historic role or place within the Union. The Scottish sense of identity, the connection to the land, the places and historical events are an accepted part of being Scottish. It is the idea of a future Scotland that forms the ongoing argument. And the fight is not over.

In the aftermath of the referendum itself, membership of the SNP skyrocketed to over 100,000 people, it almost swept the board at the Westminster elections of May 2015, winning 56 of 59 seats, and it again became the Scottish Government (albeit as a large minority) after the Scottish Parliament elections of May 2016. The newly 're-elected' First Minister and SNP Leader, Nicola Sturgeon, has made it clear that the fight for independence will continue (Green 2016). It will be interesting to see what role history, identity, land and belonging will play in the next battle for the future Scotland.

Bibliography

Anderson, B. 1983. *Imagined Communities: Reflections on the Origin and Spread of Nationalism.* London: Verso

Billig, M. 1995. *Banal Nationalism.* London: Sage

Breuilly, J. 1993. *Nationalism and the State.* Manchester: Manchester University Press

Broun, D. 1998. Defining Scotland and the Scots before the wars of independence, in D. Broun, R. J. Findlay and M. Lynch (eds) *Image and Identity: The Making and Re-Making of Scotland through the ages.* Edinburgh: Edinburgh University Press

Calhoun, C. 1997. *Nationalism.* Buckingham: Open University Press

Coakley, J. 2004. Mobilizing the past: nationalist images of history *Nationalism and Ethnic Politics*, 10, 531-60

Cooke, A.B. 2000. The Conservative Party and its Manifestos: A personal view, in I. Dale (ed.) *Conservative Party General Election Manifestos 1900-1997.* London: Routledge.

Cowan, E. 2003. *For Freedom Alone: The Declaration of Arbroath*, East Linton: Tuckwell Press

Edensor, T. 1997. Reading Braveheart: Representing and Contesting Scottish Identity, in *Scottish Affairs* 21, 135-158.

Gallagher, T. 2009. *The Illusion of Freedom: Scotland under Nationalism.* London: C. Hurst and Co.

Green, C. 2016. SNP to launch a new drive for independence, says Nicola Sturgeon, *The Independent*, 12th March 2016

Hamilton, P. 1999. The Scottish National Paradox: The Scottish National Party's lack of Ethnic Character, *Canadian Review of Studies in Nationalism* 36(1), 17-36.

Harris, E. 2009. *Nationalism: Theories and Cases.* Edinburgh: Edinburgh University Press

Henderson, A. 2007. *Hierarchies of Belonging: National Identity and Political Culture in Scotland and Quebec*, Montreal and Kingston: McGill-Queen's University Press.

HM Government and Scottish Government, 2012. *Agreement between the United Kingdom Government and the Scottish Government on a referendum on independence for Scotland* Edinburgh, 15 October 2012

Kavanagh, D. 2000. *British Politics: Continuities and Change.* Oxford: Oxford University Press.

Kenealy, D. 2016. The Economy and the Constitution under the SNP, 2007-2016, *Scottish Affairs* 25(1); 8-27

Kearton, A. 2005. Imagining the Mongrel Nation, *National Identities* 7(1), 23-50.

Kidd, C. and McClymont, G. 2014. Scottish independence essay: Say No to colony myth, *The Scotsman*, 6th August 2014.

Leith, M. 2008. Scottish National Party Representations of Scottishness and Scotland, *Politics* 28(2), 83-92.

Leith, M. and D. Soule 2011. *Political Discourse and National Identity in Scotland*, Edinburgh: Edinburgh University Press

McCrone, D. 2001. *Understanding Scotland: the sociology of a nation*, 2nd ed. London: Routledge.

McCreadie, R. 1991. Scottish Identity and the Constitutions, in B. Crick (ed.) *National Identities: The Constitution of the United Kingdom*, Oxford: Blackwell.

Merrill, J. 2014. 'Bannockburn anniversary: Scottish freedom … and not a hint of Mel Gibson', *The Independent*, 21st June 2014

Miller, W.L. 1981. *The end of British politics? Scots and English political behaviour in the seventies.* Oxford: Clarendon Press.

Mitchell, J. 1996. *Strategies for self-government: the campaigns for a Scottish Parliament.* Edinburgh: Polygon.

Morton, G. 1999. *Unionist-Nationalism: Governing Urban Scotland.* East Linton: Tuckwell.

Özkirimli, U. 2010. *Theories of Nationalism: A Critical Introduction* (2nd Ed.) Basingstoke: Palgrave Macmillan.

Pittock, M. 2008. *The Road To Independence? Scotland Since the Sixties.* London: Reaktion.

Rosie, M. 2015. Scotland: All Change? *Scottish Affairs*, 24: 383–388

ScotCen's Scottish Social Attitudes survey, 2015, available at http://www.natcen.ac.uk/media/1123194/ssa15-tables-for-web.pdf

Sillars, J. 2014. *In Place of Fear.* Glasgow: Vagabond Voices.

Smith, A.D. 1986. *The ethnic origins of nations.* Oxford: Basil Blackwell.

Smith, A.D. 2001. *Nationalism, Theory, Ideology, History.* Cambridge: Polity.

Smith, A.D. 2003. The poverty of anti-nationalist modernism, *Nations and Nationalism*, 9, 357-370.

Webster, B. 1997. *Medieval Scotland, The Making of an Identity*, London: Macmillan.